GRAND PRIX GREATS

A personal appreciation of 25 famous Formula 1 drivers

GRAND PRIX GREATS

A personal appreciation of 25 famous Formula 1 drivers

Nigel Roebuck
Foreword by Murray Walker

PSL
Patrick Stephens Limited

Cover pictures (top to bottom) **Front**: Alain Prost, Gilles Villeneuve, Ayrton Senna, Mario Andretti; Prost — Silverstone, 1988. **Back**: Niki Lauda, Nelson Piquet, Keke Rosberg, Alan Jones. (*Photos: John Townsend*)

Title page Gilles Villeneuve winning the 1981 Spanish Grand Prix.

First published in May 1986
New paperback edition 1989

British Library Cataloguing in Publication Data

Roebuck, Nigel
Grand Prix greats: a personal appreciation of 25 famous Formula 1 drivers.
1. Grand Prix racing — History
I. Title
769.7'2'0922 GV1029.15

ISBN 1-85260-031-4

Patrick Stephens Limited is part of the Thorsons Publishing Group, Wellingborough, Northamptonshire, NN8 2RQ, England

Photoset in 10 on 11 Souvenir Light by Harper Phototypesetters Limited, Northampton and Printed in Great Britain by Butler and Tanner Limited, Frome, Somerset

CONTENTS

FOREWORD
by Murray Walker

Motor racing is very well documented. If you want to know the piston area of the 1937 Mercedes-Benz W125 (it was 86 sq in!), who has had the greatest number of successive GP pole positions (Niki Lauda: six in 1974), the story of the one and only Austrian Grand Prix at Zeltweg in 1964 — or any other obscure fact — there are books that will tell you. I know because I collect them!

But in a sport that's just as much about men as machinery all too few of them *really* tell us about that vital ingredient — the drivers. And by that I mean really tell us about them as people — their backgrounds, their personalities and lifestyles, their beliefs, their quirks, their foibles, their likes and, even better, their dislikes!

Nigel Roebuck's superb book which you now hold in your hands does just that and I promise you that once you've started reading his warmly penetrating and revealing pen-pictures of some of the greatest drivers the world has known you'll find it very difficult to put it down. For Nigel is uniquely qualified as a biographer of the men he describes so well, being not only one of the world's leading historians and writers on Grand Prix racing but also truly a friend of the drivers. A friend that they're happy to confide in by telling him about their real thoughts and feelings. I know from personal experience that that is a very difficult state to achieve!

I write this foreword in grateful appreciation of Nigel's friendship and help to me over many years, and full of admiration at his ability so clearly and entertainingly to have recorded the essence of so many of Grand Prix racing's greats. My one regret is that, having whetted my appetite, he hasn't dealt with more of them. So, in commending you to what I hope is Part One, I now look forward to its successors!

Murray Walker
Fordingbridge, Hampshire.

ACKNOWLEDGEMENTS

The author is grateful to the following individuals and organisations for the photographs in this book: *Autosport,* Jeff Bloxham, Michael Brown, Paul-Henri Cahier, Jim Chini, Bob Constanduros, DPPI, Edita Lausanne, Geoff Goddard, Jeff Hutchinson, Nick Loudon, David Phipps, Cyril Posthumus, Jad Sherif, Alan Smith, Keith Sutton, Claude Vialard, Emmanuel Zurini.

INTRODUCTION

On the question of a title for this book, I have to tell you, my publisher won the day. Originally I was thinking in terms of something much more esoteric and arty, but frequently I was reminded that the purpose of a title is to attract, rather than confuse. In the end, therefore, I acquiesced . . .

Principally I used the argument that *Grand Prix Greats* was not entirely accurate. I have written about 25 drivers, and by no means can *every* one of them be described as 'great'. Ayrton Senna, for example, will justify the adjective in time, I have no doubt, but as I write this he has completed only two Grand Prix seasons.

As characters, however, I believe all are worthy of inclusion, and it was on that basis that they were selected. Jean Behra, for example, is here because he was my childhood hero, a racing driver who captured my imagination as no other ever did. Even I would be hard-pressed to argue a case that he be bracketed with Fangio, Moss or Brooks, but on his day he could be very great indeed.

The idea for the book came from 'Fifth Column', which I have written for *Autosport* these many years. I started doing those pieces as a means of fleshing out a Grand Prix weekend, writing of conversations and incidents which had no real place in a 'grocery list' race report.

Once in a while, though, there comes a weekend of no real note, and the 1984 German Grand Prix at Hockenheim was one such. I wrote the report as soon as I was back, but on the Thursday — column day — there seemed to be nothing worthy of expansion.

Hockenheim was invariably like that. In 1981 I was saved by a long and achingly funny chat with a visiting Frank Gardner, and that time forgot all about the Formula 1 race, instead recounted the wonderfully dry Australian's reminiscences: 'That first Porsche 917 . . . the computer said it needed only nine-inch rims. But the computer wasn't strapped in the driving seat . . .'

This time, however, I had no Gardner on whom to fall back. Was there anything else about the weekend? Where had I been? I was beginning to get desperate when I suddenly thought of Rosemeyer. Of course! I always paused briefly at his memorial on the *autobahn* down to Heidelberg. That would justify a piece about him.

There was not a mention of modern Grand Prix racing in that column — and it attracted more interest than I could believe. 'Is there a book about him?' asked Derek Warwick at the next race, Zandvoort. 'Someone should write one,' he said, and not long afterwards I had a call from PSL about that very thing. Again, it seems, the Rosemeyer piece had sparked their interest.

Since childhood I have been obsessed with Grand Prix racing, but my interest in it has always lain chiefly with the human aspect, the drivers rather than the cars. I love to *watch* racing cars, but primarily I see them as a means of allowing a driver to express his own particular personality — in some cases, art. Not all those in this book I have liked, but *every* one I have admired for what he has brought to the greatest sport known to man. I hope that comes across.

Nigel Roebuck
Dorking, Surrey.

CHRIS AMON
In search of luck

'The curse of commercialism is the ruin of sport, and the degeneracy of motor racing as a sport is due to the financial issues now involved. The charm disappears, and I can see in the near future the sporting element obliterated altogether by the all-devouring monster of commercialism — the curse of the twentieth century . . .'

I quote this to show that nothing changes. The words were actually spoken by Charles Jarrott in 1905. Seventy years on, the likes of Mike Hailwood and Chris Amon were saying the same thing. On the wall of my study hangs a picture of Christopher's Ferrari in an elegant power slide at Oulton Park in 1968. Above his signature are the words, 'In memory of pre-Mafia Formula 1'.

Amon was the first Grand Prix driver I came to know well, and one of comparatively few I would have wanted as a friend even if he had been unconnected with racing. To those outside their circle, many Grand Prix drivers are not especially interesting or attractive people. Their conversation, as with showbiz folk, tends to be dominated by 'The Business', and can be wearisome.

Perhaps it is unrealistic to expect anything else. Fifty or sixty thousand bucks a week, after all, can concentrate the mind wonderfully. A lot of history's great drivers have been self-centred, greedy and oblivious of any world beyond their own. In normal society such character defects might mean a lonely life. In Formula 1 they are extolled as virtues. They say of Laffite, for example, that he is 'too nice a guy'. Where's the killer instinct? Jacques, happily, is far too well-balanced a man to care. For him, motor racing is merely one of the good things of life, which is as it should be.

'There are people in this business', Amon would say, 'who worry me. At GPDA safety meetings they'd shout about cutting trees down, flattening banks and erecting guardrail all over the place. I'm surprised some of them didn't ask for guardrail in their hotel rooms. After all, most people die in bed . . .

'Okay, fine, then you'd get into a race with some of these crusaders, and find they'd happily put you *over* their precious guardrails without giving it a thought! This was something I never could understand. I wasn't anti-safety — no one wants to get killed or maimed — but I thought it was a double-edged sword, because more safety also meant more indiscipline. Stewart I take my hat off to, because his attitude was never ambivalent. He worked hard for circuit changes, and he drove hard. But absolutely fairly.

'So long as I was in a car I trusted, I never worried too much about the track. It was up to me to keep out of the trees. And if a guy screwed up trying to pass me I'd give him room rather than put him over the fence. God strewth, of course I would! What kind of a man would do otherwise?

'When I started, going off the road meant hitting a telegraph pole or a house or something. And it meant that for the other guy, too. So respect for each other — commonsense, really — was essential, and it stayed with me. Some of these people screaming for run-off areas and catch fencing and stuff gave the impression they intended to use it before the weekend was through . . .'

A willingness to admit fear is surely the act of a brave man, and this Chris was always prepared to do. For one thing, he loathed Indianapolis, but even he never truly knew why, beyond the fact that at Brickyard speeds someone else's accident tends to be yours in a blink. Amon disliked the feeling of being hemmed in — 'Bruce McLaren used to say that the only way to get me competitive there would be to paint trees on the walls . . .'

He loved the traditional 'dangerous' road circuits,

Oulton Park 1968. Amon and his beloved Ferrari V12 exuberantly chase Stewart's Matra in the Gold Cup. Downforce and slicks were not yet into the Formula 1 vocabulary — a slow time for technology, but great for spectators . . .

with Spa being his particular favourite. And one of the greatest drives of his life — pushing Rodriguez's much faster BRM all the way in 1970 — came only days after abandoning a final attempt to come to terms with Indy.

'I came back very worried,' he says, 'because, there's no doubt at all, I was frightened of the place. It had never happened to me before, and I couldn't understand it. But I was pleased with the way I went at Spa — I reckon if you were going to get scared anywhere, it would be there. We averaged about 150, with all the barbed wire and trees and stuff — and I hadn't gone much quicker than that turning left all the time at Indy!

'On the last lap I made myself go through the Masta Kink without lifting, and you have to remember this was the March 701, which was a pretty horrible motor car. That was left-right between houses at over 180 mph . . . so why the hell did Indy worry me? Don't ask me . . .'

As history tends to remember Moss for *not* winning the World Championship, so it stamps Amon as 'the man who never won a Grand Prix'. Inescapably, by being disorganized (often on a heroic scale), insufficiently disciplined in much of his off-track life and always, apparently, with the wrong team at the wrong time, he ran a good part of the way to meet ill luck. It seemed his cards always came from the bottom of the pack. Even when he was dealing himself.

Jochen Rindt would say that Stewart and Amon were the only drivers he considered true rivals. JYS is a little more circumspect: 'I rated Chris's raw talent in the very top bracket. It was easy for him, flowing and natural. His car control was lovely to watch. The sad thing was, I think a lot of his ability he squandered . . .'

So, too, he did. For one thing, he had never the ego on which real success must feed. He procrastinated more than anyone I have ever known. *Mañana* was the way he lived — the way he liked to live.

I had a call from him one Wednesday in August of 1975. 'Mo Nunn's asked me to drive the Ensign in Austria this weekend. Want a lift?' I put aside my abhorrence of light aircraft, and duly presented myself the following morning. For reasons clouded by the passing years, we left late. By the time we reached Austria, the military airfield at Zeltweg was shut for the night, which meant going into Graz. It took time there to organize a hire car.

'Right,' Chris said, 'now, where are we staying?' No one knew. 'Didn't I mention it?' 'No.' 'Oh . . .'

'There aren't that many hotels in Zeltweg,' I said. 'I don't think it's in Zeltweg', came the reply.

'Well, what's the name of the place?' I asked. Silence. Finally, he said he remembered something about 'knickers'. 'Niklasdorf?' I ventured. It had to be, so we called all the hotels until one said, yes, Ensign were booked in. As we arrived, they were finishing dinner.

That weekend was Chris's first with the team, and Nunn and his people found it a revolutionary experience. 'He's incredible,' Mo said. 'We move the wing by a notch — and he can tell. We're not used to that.'

Race day was awful. During the morning warm-up Mark Donohue crashed at the flat out Hella-Lichtkurve, and by early afternoon was known to have no chance of survival. The race was run in Wagnerian conditions, rain and black skies and occasional lightning. Everyone was glad to have it over.

In the evening Amon's emotions were mixed. Upset about Donohue, he was nevertheless happy to be back in Formula 1 — and relieved to be in one piece. 'Schnapps!' he commanded at the end of the meal. 'For everyone!'

'Is he always like this?' Nunn whispered. 'I mean, we've never had a driver who even *smoked* before, let alone . . .'

Chris, for better or worse, would never accept that a racing driver's life had to be monastic. If that were the case, he often said, the game wasn't worth playing. 'I think that was probably shaped by my time at Ferrari', he smiles. 'We used to test at Modena all morning, then have lunch with the Old Man. And there was always wine with the pasta. Once, in my early days there, I realized we'd each had a bottle of Lambrusco — you know how easily that stuff goes down. And Ferrari said, "Good — you'll go faster this afternoon!" I did, too, believe it or not . . . But, whatever people might have said, I never went near booze for days before a race. When it was over, okay, I'd have a drink or two.'

Three years Amon worked for Maranello, and they were far and away the happiest of his racing life. It has become the dreary norm for racing drivers to have little knowledge of — or, for that matter, interest in — the heritage of the sport (ie, anything that occurred within it before they became involved). But Chris was

Last race for Ferrari. Chris talks with Mauro Forghieri and Pedro Rodriguez during practice for the British Grand Prix of 1969.

What might have been. Amon takes out the flat-12 Ferrari 312B for its first test at Modena in September 1969. Within weeks he left for fresh pastures at March . . .

obsessed with racing in childhood, and he accepts that possibly this worked against him during his own career.

'I suppose I arrived in Europe with a bit of an inferiority complex. Here I was, nineteen years old, racing against Clark, Gurney and so on. And it was some time before I started to believe I really could be competitive with them. Before I left New Zealand I even raced against Stirling — or, rather, I was in the same race as Stirling! I didn't see an awful lot of him, actually. He was in a Cooper-Climax and I had my old Maserati 250F, slithering around in the rain. At one point I got into a huge slide, and a second later he comes past, with a wave of thanks! He thought I'd moved over for him . . .'

The 250F fitted in perfectly with the young Amon's romantic notion of Grand Prix racing. The archetypal car of the mid-fifties, and here he was, racing one at seventeen and acquiring a taste for oversteer which never left him. Going on from there, the logical dream was to drive one day for Ferrari. And in 1968, given even a light dash of luck, he should have been World Champion. Eight times out of eleven he qualified on the front row, and there should — *should* — have been at least three victories. At Spa he was on the pole by four clear seconds. At St Jovite he led, clutchless,

by more than a minute when the gearbox broke. In Spain a fuel pump fuse gave out.

No race better summed up Chris's career, though, than the British Grand Prix of that year. For most of it he trailed Jo Siffert's Rob Walker Lotus 49. 'You know, Seppi and that car hardly ever finished a race — but the one time they won it had to be me behind. It was the same with Pedro at Spa two years later. I knew that BRM couldn't last, but that day it did . . .

'We got the Ferrari handling probably better than anything else, but that old V12 just had no power at all. It sounded fruity, and Ferrari engines were always supposed to have loads of steam, so I don't think people believed it — certainly Ferrari didn't! But in a straight line we got blown off. I think I drove some of my best races that year.'

Mauro Forghieri is rather less inhibited in his appreciation of Amon's skills: 'As a test driver he was the best I have known, and it's a fact that we never gave him a car worthy of him. As far as I'm concerned, he was as good as Clark . . .' The fact remains, though, that Jimmy won 25 Grands Prix, and Chris left the sport with only a couple of non-championship wins against his name. Ironically, he won Le Mans, which puts a premium on luck. He won other sports car races, too, and beat Rindt fair and square in the Tasman Championship.

His biggest tragedy was leaving Ferrari at precisely the wrong moment, when the new flat-12 engine was being introduced, when Fiat takeover money would enable the Commendatore to spend on racing as he had never been able to before. After three years of low power and poor reliability, though, Amon decided he had to have a Cosworth, and signed for the infant March team.

'I will win a Grand Prix, Chris,' said Ferrari, on the occasion of their parting, 'before you do . . .'

After March came two years with Matra, and it was the Ferrari saga once again; excellent chassis, lovely noise, no horsepower. Here, too, there should have been victories, most notably at Clermont Ferrand in 1972, where he held sway at the front, then punctured a tyre. His comeback drive to third that day ranks with any I have ever seen. 'Amon — Seigneur!' went the headline in *L'Equipe* the following morning. Chris' response was slightly indignant. 'It was one of my better drives, maybe, but the main thing was the car was on the pace for once . . .'

He was downbeat, too, about the 24-hour test in the Matra sports car at Ricard — when the lights went out in the middle of the night! It happened as the car wailed past the pits, immediately before the flat out left-right swerves.

'Obviously', he says, in that slow and laconic drawl, 'it was a bit of a shock when it happened. I just went on to auto pilot, quite literally, let my instincts take the car through and then stopped.' The Matra did not so much as clout a kerb.

Like many of routinely gentle and polite manner, Amon's temper — though rarely lost — was the kind to make you seek cover. He tended to be too easy-going, that was the problem. Dissatisfaction was kept fermenting and bottled up too long, and when the cork popped it did so with some vim.

Most of the time, though, he was excellent company, a splendid raconteur with wit as dry as Gordon's. Perhaps his personality was simply too human to be altogether compatible with a Grand Prix career. Often he reckoned he had been born into the wrong era: 'I don't see much in the way of ethics in racing now,' he said, shortly before his retirement. 'It seems quite wrong to me that people should be able to buy their way into Formula 1. In any sport money should be secondary, as it always was for a guy like Jimmy Clark.' By the mid-seventies such sentiments were hardly mainstream.

Deeply cynical about racing towards the end of his career, Chris nevertheless remained too trusting. In 1972 a publisher commissioned me to write the Amon biography, and over the following winter I spent many days at Chris's house with a tape recorder, marvelling at his uncanny recall, enjoying the flood of anecdote.

Sample: 'I did this Indy car race at Fuji in '66, with Hill and Stewart. It was us against the USAC regulars, and the whole thing was done on a pretty tight budget — I mean, we were supposed to go up to the circuit by train and then bus! Happily, though, Graham knew the Rolls-Royce agent in Tokyo, and he laid on a Silver Wraith or something for us, complete with chauffeur. That was great, sweeping past the USAC brigade in their bus, giving them a Royal wave! They didn't like

---

A Formula 1 victory at last. Chris's March 701 soundly defeated the similar car of Jackie Stewart in the International Trophy at Silverstone in 1970.

us at all . . .

'There was a hairpin at Fuji, and I don't think most of the Americans had ever had to deal with one before. At least, it didn't seem that way. Qualifying was in their style, one at a time, and the first six or seven just never made it round at all. Graham, Jackie and I sat in the pits, awaiting our turn and getting more and more hysterical. Every time we'd hear an Offenhauser screaming down to the hairpin absolutely flat, then a violent screeching of locked wheels, then a brief silence — as they ploughed over the grass — then finally "boof" as they clobbered the bank! A couple of minutes would then elapse before some red-faced American would walk in, scowling at us . . .

'I had an old Vollstedt for that race, a bit unusual in that the pedals were arranged brake-throttle-clutch . . . But it got going quite well in the race, and I had a good old dice with Andretti for third place, which ended with me on top of a bank.

'I was lapping a guy called Chuck Hulse, who was in one of the old Indy roadsters — most of which didn't have mirrors! Not that mirrors would have made a lot of difference to this guy, actually, since it turned out that he was blind in the right eye, and also deaf in the right ear! Yes, you've got it, I went to overtake him on the right . . .

'For reasons I never quite understood, he suddenly elected to turn sharp right, and that was the end of my race. He had absolutely no depth of vision whatever — apparently, they said, because he'd been on his head so many times. I wondered which had come first — the chicken or the egg . . .'

We seemed to have the basis of an entertaining book — and then the publisher did an overnight bunk. Unwittingly, I was the latest in a long line of people who had let Amon down. 'Doesn't matter,' he shrugged. 'Actually, it was quite therapeutic just to talk it all through.' There had been no contract, nothing. I know better now. I wonder if he does.

Primarily, though, it was his own integrity which let him down. After a desultory year with Tecno in 1973, he decided to build his own car, in partnership with John Dalton. An unproven designer came up with an over-sophisticated car, and from the start the project was a disaster. Very early in the unhappy machine's life, Chris knew it would never work.

That autumn of 1973, he had a firm offer to go back to Ferrari — something of which he had dreamed almost from the day he had left. But no. He was committed, had given his word to Dalton. A few weeks later Teddy Mayer offered him the Yardley McLaren M23 for 1974, and got the same response. Halfway

---

For the first half of the 1972 French Grand Prix Amon and the Matra MS120D convincingly led Hulme and Stewart — until delayed by a puncture. Chris's comeback drive to third at Clermont Ferrand was quite sensational.

In the grossly under-financed Ensign, Amon drove some amazing races during 1976, his final year of Formula 1. Here he pressures Hunt's McLaren at Zolder.

through that season, when the Amon F1 project was in tatters, Rikki von Opel left Brabham. Bernie Ecclestone rang Chris, who again said no. At the next race, Brands Hatch, Carlos Pace was in the Brabham, Amon's car not even entered. 'I'd like to put a match to it . . .' he said.

Thereafter Chris was in a state of limbo for some time, dabbling with Formula 5000, but without much enthusiasm. But there was one splendid day in the early summer of 1975, when he was reunited with the actual Ferrari P4 with which he and Lorenzo Bandini had won at Daytona and Monza eight years earlier. He drove it now at Oulton Park, and at one stage took me round for a few exhilarating laps. I watched him at work, sideways through Old Hall, and wondered again how all that skill had gone to waste. 'Wonderful', he said afterwards. 'Like being back with an old girlfriend for a few hours . . .'

Most onlookers thought him crazy to accept the Ensign drive a few weeks later, but soon they had to acknowledge that his talent and class remained. The following year Amon startled the rich teams many times, actually contriving to qualify the budget car third in Sweden. But twice it broke, putting him upside down at Zolder, head on into a barrier at Anderstorp.

Edgy that such a thing might happen again, he withdrew from the German Grand Prix after Lauda's accident. 'The 'Ring is harder on cars than anywhere else', he said. 'If I'm going to have a shunt, I want to be rescued — and from what I've just seen with Niki, it takes too long here.'

Afterwards came the campaign to 'ban the 'Ring'. Chris was not too concerned. 'I don't see what all the fuss is about', he said. 'As far as I'm concerned, they ruined the Nurburgring in 1970 when they opened up the corners and knocked all the trees down. That took most of the challenge away.'

Since the end of 1977 he has been back in New Zealand, farming and prospering, settled at last, with his English wife and three children. He is still going to give up smoking 'sometime soon', and I suspect he misses Europe more than he might admit. For him, the original generous host, an ideal Sunday was spent having a few friends in for lunch, maybe watching some cricket on television in the afternoon, walking his beloved dogs. But there were other Sundays, too, days at Clermont and Monza and Spa, when crowds revelled in his artistry, groaned as he headed for the pits. It truly was a lost career.

MARIO ANDRETTI
The man from Nazareth

I remember talking to Mario one time about a leading figure of the Racing Establishment, a man whose motives for involvement seemed other than selfless. 'What', I wondered, 'makes him tick?'

'God knows' Andretti replied. 'A bomb, let's hope . . .'

He is fond of saying that he was put on this earth to drive race cars, that he never entertained any other career. But he could, I feel sure, have made a fair living from his laconic one-liners. When Mario is in the mood to talk, which is most of the time, he is a delight.

Once we were chatting about another driver, a man years past his best but refusing to face it, accepting third-rate drives as and when they were offered. 'What's the matter with the guy?' Mario murmured. 'He's like some kind of professional blind date . . .'

In the days when he and Lotus were on top, writing a Grand Prix report seemed to take no time at all. His quotes took care of half the story for me. The only problem was getting them down in the notebook while listening for the next. Andretti's repartee soon persuaded me always to carry a tape recorder.

For the journalist, then, he was gold, and undoubtedly some of his colleagues resented that. 'Why are you guys always writing about Andretti?' Jody Scheckter once asked me. 'Always it's Mario this, Andretti that . . .'

In his later years Scheckter mellowed quite a lot, but at that time responded to the sight of a reporter as one who had recently trodden in something unpleasant. On a good day you got a monosyllabic grunt, difficult to translate into great prose.

My abiding fascination for American oval racing of all types has in some ways been a curse, for it has taken me to places like Indianapolis and Daytona. And when you know how Cale Yarborough or Al Unser can behave after 500 miles balls to the wall, you're inclined to bristle at, say, Patrese's petulance after an untimed practice session.

Andretti, of course, grew up with the American way of doing things, and was smart enough to realize early in his career the importance of the star system. Childhood years in an Italian displaced persons' camp shaped his philosophy for life. When he sailed with his family for New York in 1955, it was without a backward glance.

He had been born in Montona, near Trieste, an area of Italy which became Yugoslavian soon after the war. Life, he remembers, was pretty good in the late forties.

'Then Communism arrives. Everyone's supposed to be equal, right? Well, that much was true. Everyone *was* equal — we all had nothing! That's how we wound up in the camp, and that's why we moved to the States. You don't forget those things, that your mother was always crying and you didn't know why. So I don't need anyone talking to me about Communism, thanks very much. I'm not just blowing smoke. I've been there.

'The proudest day of my life was when I became an American citizen. The Italians can't believe I mean that, but it's true. A passport will never change the fact that the blood in my veins is Italian blood, and I have certain feelings for Italy, but that's as far as it goes. It sure as hell didn't offer me anything when I was a kid.'

In all things — the occasional passing manoeuvre apart — Mario is therefore conservative, a trait he shares with pretty well every driver I have known. And this, he reckons, is easily explained: 'The kind of guy who goes racing is obviously a man who likes to take care of himself, not have the state do it. In the cockpit you're pretty much alone . . .'

This is not to say, however, that Andretti is an uncompassionate man. Late in 1978 I was at work on a book with him, and shortly before Christmas went to Brazil (where he was Goodyear testing) for some taping sessions. One evening in Sâo Paulo we had been out for dinner and were walking back to the hotel. In a side street, crouched in a shop doorway, was one of the city's countless crippled beggars.

'Jesus,' Mario mumbled, 'this place is full of sprint car drivers . . .' But the black humour — which necessarily abounds in a business like racing — was swiftly followed by the handing over of a sizeable note. 'I have no time', he went on, as if embarrassed by the gesture, 'for people who won't help themselves, but that's not the same as people who can't . . .'

Getting to know drivers well is not easy when you encounter them only at the races. The pressure is on all weekend, and reasonably enough there is little time for talk of anything but understeer and throttle lag. During that week in Brazil, though, we were gathering material for the book, giving Mario the opportunity to reminisce about his life and me scope for insight into his real personality. Who would have suspected, for example, that the new World Champion enjoyed visits to Carnegie Hall for performances of *Rigoletto* or *I Pagliacci*? 'The blood in my veins is Italian blood . . .' Yes, I remembered that.

What impressed me most about him was his ability to deal with people, be they engineers, track workers, waiters, fellow drivers or fans. Each wanted different things of him, and he was comfortable with all of them. We'd walk into a restaurant, and before so much as a drink had been ordered there was a mumbled buzz of people speaking his name, cocking their heads towards him, not wanting to turn round, stare. And, inevitably, they would start to drift over, wanting to impress a girlfriend, shake his hand, have him sign a page torn from a diary.

The following summer, a couple of days before Silverstone, the book was launched at a reception in London, and afterwards a few of us repaired to an Italian restaurant for lunch. 'Hey, Mario!' shouted an American voice as we walked across Trafalgar Square. Handshakes all round, more autographs. And when we arrived at the restaurant the head waiter performed one of the great double-takes of all time. The great Andretti . . . here!

Proof positive of Mario's charisma, though, came from an unexpected source. My wife's interest in motor racing is about the same as mine in juggling, but Andretti's presence and charm left her very impressed. 'There', she remarked, after meeting him for the first time, 'is a star. Even if you didn't know who or what

The man who has done it all. Andretti's championship dirt car smokes the tyres at Sacramento in 1969.

Early Ferrari outing. After problems on the opening day, Mario tried desperately to qualify his 312B for the 1971 Monaco Grand Prix, but a damp afternoon thwarted him.

he was, you'd know that much about him.'

True enough, he *is* a star. 'As far as the Indy crowds are concerned,' A. J. Foyt was once moved to say, 'only Mario and I matter a damn . . .' This is the only occasion in recorded history on which Anthony Joseph has been heard to bracket another driver with himself! The thing is, he was probably right . . .

By 1982 it seemed that Andretti's days in Formula 1 were over. He had decided not to stay with Alfa Romeo — 'Not even if it would save the space programme!' — and committed himself once more to CART or, as he still instinctively says, 'championship racing'. A one-off drive for Williams at Long Beach was disappointing, but later in the year came 'The Call'. With Pironi injured, Enzo Ferrari needed someone to partner Tambay at Monza.

From America came word of Andretti's acceptance. 'Did I agree?' he said when I called him. 'Hey, this is Ferrari! At *Monza,* man! How does a guy say no to that?'

His arrival at Malpensa was a *tour de force.* The cavalry was on its way, coming to the rescue. Television cameras picked up the Alitalia jet before it landed, and stayed on the aeroplane as it taxied to a halt. Reporters gathered at the foot of the steps.

The door opened, and Mario came out alone, smiling broadly and holding up both arms. On his head — blessed touch of showmanship — was a Ferrari cap. It was pure theatre, a matter of giving people what they want, and so easily achieved. That piece of television film probably put another 10,000 on the Monza gate.

By the same token, when he arrived at the circuit on Friday morning, Andretti was in new overalls, bearing all the usual Ferrari patches, just as he had worn 'Williams' gear at Long Beach. Not for him a regular driver's suit with a temporary Prancing Horse stitched on slightly askew.

'Ferrari had hired me for the weekend, and I had to do the best possible job for him, in all ways. I can't stand anything slipshod, in racing or in anything else. To me there's no virtue in scruffiness — particularly when it's contrived. I don't think it's clever for a guy like Hunt to show up for a formal dinner or something in sneakers and jeans. I just think it's ignorant. Okay, when you're World Champion they have to stand for that because they need to have you there, but afterwards . . .'

Andretti put his Ferrari on the pole at Monza that weekend, and finished third in the race. Two weeks later suspension failure put him out at Las Vegas, and that was almost certainly his final appearance in a Formula 1 car. He rather likes the fact that it was in a Ferrari, although in Grand Prix racing his name will be for ever synonymous with Lotus.

'There's no question that the two most important figures in my career have been Clint Brawner, who gave me my first championship ride, and Colin Chapman. Brawner was kind of maddening in some ways, always a little sorry for himself. Ask him the time, and he'd tell you how the goddam watch was built! But he ran a good operation, and we did well together.

'In the same way, working with Colin was no trip to Paris, either, but you're always going to have problems with a genius, right? When I look back on our association, it seems like we got together at exactly the right time. In the mid-seventies our careers were at a low point, and there was a lot of energy from both of us to get up and out of it. We sparked each other.

'You know, the only thing people ever remember about Japan in '76 is that Hunt took the championship, and Niki quit the race. That's

understandable, I guess, but my win there may have been the most important of my life. It was the last race of the year, the first Lotus victory in a long time, and Colin really got fired up. Through that winter he thought about nothing but the next season, and came up with the 78.

'That car was so far ahead of the rest — except that on the straightaways it couldn't get out of its own way. We won more races than anyone else, but not the championship, and so there was still this competitive fire going inside of him. And he produces the 79, which finally did the job for us . . .'

It was at Monza in 1978 that Mario achieved his life's ambition, winning the World Championship. And it was also there that he lost his team mate, a man who had become one of his closest friends. Ronnie Peterson died in hospital twelve hours or so after the race.

'I have to say I was in some kind of turmoil for a while. Like, my emotions were jumbled around, highs and lows. I'd gotten what I most wanted, and at the same time lost another close friend. We knew that night Ronnie had broken bones, but no one thought he might die. That was the real shock of it. Racing has beautiful moments, but unhappily it is also this.

'Sometimes it bothers me that I don't get fazed when

World Championship team. Mario Andretti and Colin Chapman joined forces at a low point in their careers, but their partnership sparked a period of Lotus domination.

In the Lotus 78 Mario ran away with the 1977 Italian Grand Prix at Monza. There, 23 years before, he had watched Ascari, and decided on the course of his life.

friends die. I grieve, sure, but I never start to think about quitting or anything like that. There's a force there that prevails. I can't tell you what it is, but it's sure as hell stronger than common sense. It has to be. I doubt there's a guy on earth who loves life more than I do, but I also love what I'm doing, and sometimes it has its dues, unfortunately.

'It's no secret I go for top dollar, but if I'd gotten into racing just for the money I'd have quit a long time ago, like some of those other guys. I hate to see people quit prematurely. If guys like Jackie Stewart really loved this sport, they never could have left it. They would still be in it for the fun. I can't believe anyone who would put his life on the line simply for dollars . . .

'Stewart, I guess, has the strength of character to be comfortable with what he did, but I worry about people who come back because I worry about their motives. Most likely they got bored and frustrated — which is the worst thing in this business. Frustration takes you to the grave.'

In the mid-eighties Andretti has established himself once more as the leading Indy car driver of the day, a position indisputably his going on twenty years ago. Retirement, he insists, is not in his mind.

'I'm beginning to think that a man's peak years are in his forties, even as a race driver. I get less tired now than when I was younger. I don't keep to any kind of fitness programme and it seems like I don't need one. I'm always driving race cars — and I'm always race car fit.'

He learned his trade, of course, in the hardest school, running sprint cars on dirt ovals, and never disputes suggestions — allegations, sometimes — that his undeniably aggressive style has its roots here. The driver criticized by Hunt for trying to pass on the outside at Zandvoort is the man who fought countless battles with Foyt on the bullrings of Indiana and Pennsylvania.

'Sure,' he agrees, 'that's where I got my education. Half the trick in racing is knowing how to mess up the other guy. You have to know the safe ways of doing it, but basically you have to intimidate him, harass him. I learned that from guys like Don Branson on the ovals. He could do it to the point of artistry.

'I can't pretend that my personality doesn't change when I'm in a race car. And it's not a romantic thing, either. I get very mean. I want it *all,* and it comes from those dog-eat-dog days in the sprints. You had to drive them very desperately to succeed . . .'

Mario left full-time Grand Prix racing at the same time as Alan Jones, each man ascribing his decision, in part, to dissatisfaction with the cars of the time.

Ground effect was coming to its lunatic peak.

'By 1981 the cars were getting absurd, really crude, with no suspension movement whatever. It was toggle-switch driving, with no need for any kind of delicacy. Stab and steer was the way you drove. Experience? Forget it. It counted for nothing, and that really upset me. If your skirts were working, you were in good shape. It was that simple, and it made leaving Formula 1 a lot easier than it would have been. I've always done this because I absolutely love to drive race cars, but there was no pleasure in those things at all.'

One morning, during that week in Brazil, we arrived at the track early. By now I was fully at ease with Mario's freestyle approach to São Paulo rush hour traffic, appreciating for the first time that a line of trucks was nothing more than a moving chicane, their tailboards a series of clipping points.

Chiefly remarkable was the fact that Andretti never seemed to use the brakes, simply weaving from lane to lane as gaps opened and closed. It was all done with effortless fluency, without a break in the conversation. 'Ever been round Interlagos?' Mario said, as we drove in.

We did four or five laps before the red flag was waved, and Andretti obviously enjoyed redefining the limits of a VW Passat: 'Here I'm in fourth in the Lotus . . . let's try going in a little deeper this time . . .'

It is in this conscious pleasure of simply controlling a car that Mario stands apart from so many of his colleagues. For him it will never be work. Around him is every trapping of wealth and success, but mention, say, sprint cars and the Wall Street stockbroking partner becomes a raw racer again, recalling almost lyrically his early days.

'To me there's no finer sight in the world than an evening sprint car show . . . the stands and infield in darkness, with just the track floodlit . . . and you get a big field of those babies down there, waiting to go. Just beautiful. And when they get moving! The alcohol fumes from the exhausts and that deep, muscular noise . . . There's a magic about it, and for me nothing in racing gives you quite the buzz of pitching one of those things sideways into a turn at 120 mph. I haven't driven one for years, but just thinking about it gives me goosebumps . . .'

Andretti owns a glorious 640-acre Pennsylvania estate, which I visited a few years ago. 'Racing', I suggested, 'has given you an awful lot . . .' It was the wrong way to put it.

'Racing', he retorted, '*gives* you nothing but fun. Anything else you have to take. A lot of people have a talent for it, but most never realize their full potential. It's easier to leave that last bit untapped. But I was never a weekend racer. Right from the start being one of the boys was never enough — and I gave up a lot because of it. Sure, I'm a rich man now, and I'm not one of

---

Image of 1978: Andretti and the Lotus 79. Six Grand Prix victories brought Mario the World Championship, his life's ambition.

After quitting Formula 1 at the end of 1982, Andretti resumed a full-time Indycar career with the Newman/Haas Lolas. Now nearing 50, he remains one of the front runners.

those people cursed by false humility, either. I'm proud of what I've achieved. But I'm not impressed by money in itself — not unless people have done something to earn a life in first class.

'What I really hate are these rich, snobbish nothings, who never did a thing in their lives. My wife and I were invited to Reagan's Inaugural Ball, I guess because I'd contributed to the campaign. And there were plenty of people like that there. I never saw anything so chaotic in my life! We get there, and there's a line of mink coats standing in the rain, waiting for them to open the goddam doors. Here's American high society getting soaked through and pretending it's just killing time. Screw this, I thought, and I told security that I needed to see the guy in charge. They let us in finally,

which really upset the mink coats . . .'

I miss Andretti's presence in Formula 1, the laid-back manner and the easy smile and, yes, the one-liners. Through the eighties he continued to do his thing in Indycar racing, always there, always a front runner. There was never any wilting of the spirit, as anyone will attest who has seen him qualifying for the 500 or disputing a piece of asphalt with son Michael.

In his later years, all trace of competitiveness gone, Graham Hill would say he'd carry on so long as he enjoyed it, and why not? But that line of thought is anathema to Mario: for him, running at the front is intrinsic to the pleasure, the reason he's always been in this thing. Right from the start, as he says, being one of the boys was never enough . . .

ALBERTO ASCARI
Milan dynasty

You love Monza, or you hate it. More than any other circuit, the venerable *Autodromo* conjures fierce emotions. It is a place of anarchy, a Rio Carnival with racing cars. But while I detest the Brazilian resort — with or without carnival — to the point that I refuse to go there any more, Monza I adore. Legend has marinated there these sixty-odd years. True, they have taken away much of its original character with chicanes, but its essential nature remains. Ghosts ooze from every building.

There is, in the paddock, a restaurant. Not a rip-off snack bar of the kind found — and wisely passed up — at most circuits of the world, but a *restaurant*. This is Italy, where they do more than eat to live. Over the weekend of the Grand Prix you must queue endlessly, run the gauntlet of pickpockets, to get in here, but once inside there is refuge from the bedlam. And the pasta is wonderful.

I have also eaten there in times of quiet, when one or two people are testing, no more. *Tortellini alla panna* and a few glasses of Barolo, warm sun, engines shut down for a while. Everything comes together to remind you it's a fine thing to be alive.

But Monza, too, triggers unhappy thoughts. Peterson died here, and Rindt. And so, one afternoon in late May of 1955, did Alberto Ascari. The stop press in our local evening paper baldly presented the facts: 'Milan: Ascari, racing driver, killed in crash'. It seemed scarcely credible they could be talking about *the* Ascari. A handful of words to dismiss a man of such gift?

I remember at the time vainly hoping that it could have been another of the same name. Perhaps it was merely the optimism of childhood, but there did seem grounds for doubt. Testing was not then a round-the-clock activity, and this was a Thursday. Why would the great Ascari have been at Monza that day? And, even more to the point, how could he have been in

a racing car only days after hurting himself in the Monaco Grand Prix? The papers on Monday had all carried pictures of the Lancia's spectacular flight into the harbour, given details of Alberto's unique rescue by frogmen.

On Friday morning they confirmed the news of his death. It was *the* Ascari.

He had broken his nose in the Monaco accident, and been advised to rest completely for a few days, but the following weekend was the Super-cortemaggiore Grand Prix, a 1,000 kilometre sports car race at Monza. Lancia, not taking part, had given permission for Ascari to share a factory Ferrari with his young protégé, Eugenio Castellotti.

At mid-morning that Thursday, Castellotti called Ascari's apartment in Milan. He was at the track, testing the new car, and suggested that Alberto should come up to watch. There was no thought in anyone's mind at this point that he should drive — indeed Ascari left Corso Sempione in suit and tie.

In the paddock restaurant he lunched with Eugenio, engineers and mechanics from the Ferrari team and also his closest friend, Luigi Villoresi. There was some pain in his back, he said, and the broken nose was a little tender, but otherwise his unscheduled dip in the Mediterranean had left no mark.

Back in the pits Castellotti was amazed when Alberto suddenly expressed a wish to run a few laps in the Ferrari. If you leave it too long, he said, you can become inhibited.

Ascari was an intensely superstitious man, one of many preoccupations being his light blue crash helmet, which he regarded as a lucky charm. For that reason, Villoresi was astonished to see him buckling on Castellotti's white helmet. Not intending to drive, he had left his own at home. Before taking to the track he slipped off his jacket, but the tie remained in place,

The Ferrari team at Silverstone in 1951: Villoresi, Ascari, Gonzales. A victory against Alfa Romeo was imminent, and in the British Grand Prix it finally came to be — but Gonzales was the winning driver.

fluttering in the breeze as the Ferrari accelerated out of the pits.

His first lap was leisurely, the next one much quicker — within a few seconds of Castellotti's best in the morning. On the third he crashed, completely and inexplicably.

The Ferrari was running alone, its muscular six-cylinder note all round the circuit clearly audible in the pits. They heard Ascari accelerate from the Lesmos, flat out through Serraglio and on down to Vialone, ever louder now towards the end of the lap.

Suddenly the engine cut. There followed the sounds of destruction, then silence. Vialone is not far from the pits, and they ran there. Ascari, fearfully injured, had been thrown out. Within a very few minutes he died.

A little while later Mike Hawthorn arrived, also to test for Sunday. He found the paddock deserted, the bar like an echo chamber. Meazza, Ferrari's chief mechanic, was trying to submerge his grief. 'Ascari e

morto', he murmured, and Hawthorn, too, went into shock. 'He was', Mike would say later, 'the fastest driver I ever saw — faster even than Fangio.'

The bustle of Milan was stilled the day they buried him. Through the streets of the city the cortege made its ponderous way, and in their tens of thousands his silent people stood and threw their flowers in last remembrance. He was buried next to his father, Antonio, who had lost his life in the French Grand Prix thirty years before.

In the days following, as newspapermen sought explanation for the accident, much was made of the eerie coincidences which linked the deaths of father and son. There were frequent references to *cabela*, an Italian superstition based on numbers and dates, and one of which Alberto had been well aware. That being the case, articles claimed, was it not astonishing that he had taken the wheel of the Ferrari that day? Had he not broken many of his own rules?

As the notion took hold, more parallels came to

Right Monza 1951. Where it mattered most — before an Italian crowd — Ascari and Ferrari put it across the Alfa Romeos. Here Fangio, World Champion elect, gives vain chase.

There was no challenge to Ascari at Silverstone in 1952, the Italian leading all the way from pole position, finishing a lap clear of team mate Taruffi.

light. The elder Ascari had died at Montlhéry on 26 July 1925, his son on 26 May 1955. Each was 36 years old. For both the final accident came four days after a miraculous escape, and occurred at the exit of a fast left-hand turn. In neither case was there any obvious cause, any firm explanation.

'We checked the car thoroughly afterwards', Enzo Ferrari said, 'and were satisfied that, at the critical moment, it had been in perfect condition.'

Some suggested that perhaps Alberto's tie had blown in his face, distracting him for an instant, others that his perennial hay fever had made him sneeze. Or perhaps it was a black-out, a legacy of the Monaco misadventure? And there was even a story that Ascari had swerved to avoid one of the park workers who was crossing the track. This tale quickly gathered layers of embellishment. The man had confessed to a priest, claimed one paper. Now, said another, he was in an asylum, demented with guilt and anguish. And finally the word went out that there he had committed suicide . . .

Hawthorn, predictably more down to earth, offered logic, a racer's explanation for the disaster. In his mind the cause was a combination of unsuitable tyres and track surface. At that time, he contended, Englebert was unable to offer precisely the width of tyre required by Ferrari for the 750 Monza sports cars. They were too wide, Mike reckoned, for the rims and had a tendency to tuck under — particularly over the ripples at Vialone. He had experienced it himself, he said, during earlier testing.

Whatever else, Ascari had not simply made a mistake. That much was agreed by all. It was inconceivable that a driver of his class could have got himself into serious trouble at that corner, as was also said of Clark at Hockenheim thirteen years later. For all their differences in background, these two great World Champions had much in common, each dominant for much of his era. But in one particular aspect they were exactly similar: both were at their absolute best when running at the front.

'Ascari had a precise and distinctive driving style,' remembers Ferrari, 'but he was a man who had to lead from the start. In that position he was hard to overtake, almost impossible to beat, in my estimation. And that was not usual, for a driver in the lead can be preoccupied with staying there, unsure of how hard to push. Alberto was secure when playing the hare. That was when his style was at its most superb. In second place, or further back, he was less sure . . .'

The same was true of Clark, and certainly the most public mistake of Jimmy's career occurred when he was under great pressure from Gurney in the Race of Champions in 1965. I can still see the Lotus starting to run wide out of Brands Hatch's Bottom Bend, then going on to an almighty accident. At the time I doubted my own senses.

Clark was generally without rival at that time, and so it was with Ascari in his greatest years of 1952-53. Rarely was Alberto strained, but at Monza in 1953 he warred all the way with Fangio and Farina, Marimon also playing a role. Two Italians in Ferraris versus two Argentines in Maseratis. For the spectators it was a mesmeric afternoon.

Alberto led into the last lap, well knowing that he could expect no help from the ruthless Farina. Down to the final corner at Vedano (now Parabolica) a couple of tail-enders were ahead, and Ascari could only hope they had seen him. If he lifted, the day was lost. But he went in a little too quickly, and the Ferrari spun.

Perhaps these things happened to Ascari and Clark because their very superiority freed them from scrapping day to day. For each a Grand Prix weekend was invariably straightforward, a matter of taking pole position, leading all the way and collecting another trophy. All they had to do was show up.

As was often the way of it, Ascari began his racing career with motor cycles, then drifted into cars. In 1940, shortly before his 22nd birthday, he took part in the Mille Miglia in the very first Ferrari, the Tipo 815. Within a couple of weeks Mussolini, leading his country by the nose, took Italy into the war. Alberto, like many of his compatriots, was strongly opposed to the support of Hitler, and contrived to spend the ensuing years in building up a transport business with friend Villoresi.

It was so successful, indeed, that he did not automatically pick up his racing career again when hostilities ceased. By now he had a wife and two children, and their security was always paramount. But the pull of racing was strong. Villoresi had seen in Ascari a natural talent which far exceeded his own, and eventually Alberto was wooed back. By now he was 28.

After a couple of years with private Maseratis, he joined Ferrari for 1949, at Berne winning for the Commendatore his first Grande Epreuve. And through the following seasons it became clear that he and Fangio were on their own, a class above the rest. Wonderful battles — Ferrari against Alfa Romeo —

Ascari takes the flag at the end of the Italian Grand Prix of 1952. It was his sixth Grande Epreuve of the year — and his sixth victory.

On the grid at Silverstone in 1953. Ascari's performance was not quite perfect this time, for he failed to take pole position. As usual, however, he led the race from first to last . . .

were fought all over Europe.

For Ascari the great years were 1952 and 1953, when all the World Championship races were run for Formula 2. For all the rest these were demoralizing times, for Alberto won eleven of fifteen Grands Prix, one of which he missed to run at Indianapolis.

On 22 June 1952 he won at Spa, and on 21 June 1953 he did it again. In the course of those twelve months nobody but Ascari scored a single Grand Prix victory. That second one in Belgium was his *ninth* on the trot. Yes, the Ferrari was indubitably the best car, but these are dazzling statistics unapproached before or since. And it should be remembered that, between the Grandes Eprueves, Ascari was also winning pretty well every non-championship race!

Enough of the record book. What matters to my mind at least as much as the fact of victory is the manner of it. Not for me the pragmatist who hangs back and calculates, waiting for others to wilt, although it must be conceded that these are usually the men with the best tally sheet — and the men who reach

old age. But I have always liked leaders, those who try to stamp their authority on a race from the start. And Ascari, like Clark, always looked to grasp the initiative. People will say, of course, that only winning matters. But these two saw every lap as a race in itself. They won by imperious command.

Alberto's style was flamboyant only when it had to be, and generally there was no need. He was naturally relaxed at the wheel, inch-perfect of line, and this reflected an ordered and logical approach to life which was scarcely Latin. He took his pleasures simply, a calm and serene fellow who drove carefully on the road, liked to pass his evenings watching television and drinking the odd glass of wine. His voice was soft and deep. As Villoresi said, though, 'When he put his goggles on, those warm and friendly eyes suddenly became like steel, intense and concentrated.'

Revered in Italy he may have been, but Ascari did not become wealthy from motor racing. He lived in a pleasant apartment, and had a modest villa in the country, but thirty years ago racing drivers, like footballers, were hardly in the business to get rich. After his death, indeed, a fund was organized to help Alberto's family — this for one whose funeral had brought a city to a standstill. It raised a remarkable sum. 'Knowing what Grand Prix drivers earn today', Villoresi has commented, 'I would be embarrassed to say how little we were paid in those times . . .'

Ascari used to bring back precious stones, usually bought with winnings, from his trips abroad. They were, he reckoned, a good investment, and the thought that one day his family might have to get by without him was never far from his mind. He adored his kids, but was sometimes stern with them. Enzo Ferrari once took him to task over it. 'Every time I come home from a race', Alberto replied, 'I give them everything I can to make them happy. Usually I try to satisfy all their needs, even their whims. But, for my part, I would rather treat them harshly — I don't want them to love me too much. One of these days I might be gone. They'll suffer less if I don't let them get too close to me.'

It was largely for financial reasons that Ascari, at the end of his second World Championship year, announced that he was leaving Ferrari for 1954. He had signed for Lancia, and would drive the new and revolutionary D50 Grand Prix car. Italy was rocked.

In the event Ascari's decision was calamitous for him. The D50 project was way behind schedule, and through much of the year he was hardly seen. Occasionally he turned up to drive a factory Maserati. At Monza, the Lancia still not ready, he appeared in a Ferrari, and led until retirement. But at season's end the reigning World Champion had scored not a single point.

There were but two bright spots in 1954, and one was most unexpected. Alberto had no real taste for sports car racing, and loathed the Mille Miglia so much that the race was specifically excluded from his Lancia contract. But when Villoresi hurt himself in practice for the event, his old friend agreed to stand in — and in appalling conditions won by more than half an hour.

The other glimpse of light came in Barcelona, right at the end of the year, when the D50 finally made its debut. The dark red, side-tanked car was tiny by

Ascari's last race. The Lancia D50 thunders along the harbour-front at Monaco in 1955, close to the spot where it later went into the Mediterranean. Alberto survived with minor injuries, but was killed at Monza four days later.

contemporary standards, and skittish by any. If its power-to-weight ratio was impressive, it required an Ascari to master its wayward handling.

A season's frustration was uncorked in the Italian when he took the new Lancia out in practice. At his absolute best, Alberto stunned everyone by beating Fangio's Mercedes to pole position by a clear second. And for nine laps on race day he left the rest for dead — until the clutch began to go away. It was a brief demonstration, but no less electrifying for that.

The opposite-lock slides were no matter of self-indulgent crowd pleasing, for this was not the man's way. Nor had he suddenly changed the technique of a racing lifetime. It was possible to drive the Lancia smoothly so long as, like Villoresi, you were not driving it very quickly. But that was not Ascari's way, either. At the limit this car had to be fought, and so he fought it.

Alberto saw good things ahead for 1955, for the Lancia alone seemed capable of taking on Mercedes.

Over the winter the team worked away to calm their excitable new car, but they did not take away its teeth. Early in the new season Ascari won non-championship races at Naples and Turin. Failing brakes pitched him into the harbour at Monte Carlo, but it was late in the race and the car had otherwise been running perfectly. All the Mercedes were out, and Ascari momentarily held the lead in this, his last race.

Four days later came news of his death. 'I have lost my greatest opponent', said Fangio. 'Ascari was a driver of supreme skill, and I felt my title last year lost some of its value because he was not there to fight me for it. A great man, and a loyal and generous friend.'

Why, Ferrari once asked of his driver, if you worry for your children so, do you not stop this? And Ascari put his hands on the Commendatore's shoulders and looked him straight in the face. 'Without racing', he said, 'I would not know how to live.'

JEAN BEHRA
The chequered helmet

I had plenty to write about at Zandvoort in 1978. The World Championship was into its last stages, and it was clear that one of the Lotus drivers was heading for the title — but which? Would Peterson keep his word, and help Andretti? Those who knew Ronnie never doubted his integrity, but still Mario was untypically fretful in Holland.

After practice I sat and drank a glass of wine, bringing my notes up to date, and soon Denis Jenkinson joined me. 'Know who that is?' he asked, pointing at a swarthy, leather-jacketed figure nearby.

Certainly there seemed something familiar about the man, his grin, the way he held a cigarette and talked with his hands. But eventually I said no, I couldn't place him.

'Well', DSJ replied, 'you, of all people, should. That is Jean Behra's son . . .'

After Jenks had introduced us I did my best to stammer out to Jean-Paul what his father had meant to me those many years ago, and for the rest of the day Mario, Ronnie and all things recent were gone from my mind.

There have been many greater drivers than Jean Behra, but none who so completely captured my imagination. He was never World Champion, never even won a championship Grand Prix. But on his day he was capable of greatness, and you never knew whether this might be one of them.

Behra came to cars in 1951, after years of great success with a red 500 cc Moto Guzzi. Amedée Gordini offered a few drives with his impoverished Formula 2 team, and there he stayed until the end of 1954.

There were few successes in this era of Ascari and Ferrari, but 'Jeannot' savoured the odd moment of triumph. French motor racing was looking for an idol, and in Behra it found one. His only contemporary rival at home was the correct and phlegmatic Maurice Trintignant, a dapper little man whose driving mirrored his appearance. There was no passion there, no hint of derring-do.

Behra, in contrast, left no doubts of his willingness to risk everything for France, and he put himself firmly into legend one afternoon at Reims in June of 1952.

A fortnight earlier Pierre Levegh's foolish gallantry at Le Mans had left the fans feeling cheated. With but minutes of the race remaining Levegh, almost comatose after more than 23 hours at the wheel, muffed a gearchange to the engine's irreparable sorrow. The Talbot coasted to an oily halt, leaving a pair of factory Mercedes to sweep on to the flag. Wartime memories had not yet dulled, and for many this German triumph was intolerable. There was no compassion for Levegh as he was brought back to the pits. It was as if he had broken under torture. Which, in effect, he had.

Behra, too, had been at Le Mans, but his race ended in typical Gordini fashion, long before the fall of the chequered flag. For ten hours the blue car led, but by dawn Jean and co-driver Robert Manzon were out. Only once, in fact, did Behra make it through to the end of Les Vingt-Quatre Heures.

At the Reims Grand Prix, though, he dug into the soil of French racing folklore. The race was expected to be nothing more than another Sunday in an Ascari summer, but Behra drew cheers at the end of the first lap by leading all the Ferraris over the line. It seemed like the sort of defiant, futile, gesture the French so much enjoy, a man waving two fingers at his firing squad. Perhaps Alain Prost is right when he says his countrymen relish, more than anything, a glorious, emotional loser . . .

This day, however, Behra was anything but that. In the Champagne heat it was Ascari's car which wilted. Behra took a comfortable victory, and France took him to its heart.

Gordini days. Behra takes the little French car through Stowe on the way to second place — behind the Ferrari of Gonzales — in the International Trophy at Silverstone in 1954.

There are those who say, smilingly and without malice, that the unexpected pace and reliability of the Gordini at Reims stemmed from an engine rather larger than the rules allowed. No matter. There was probably little to choose between Enzo's 2-litre and Amedée's 2.5. David had beaten Goliath on home ground, and no one was too concerned about the sling.

It was a glory day, then, one of few for the little blue cars. Jean had another such, at Pau in 1954, when he beat Trintignant's Ferrari after a long and absorbing battle, but usually it was a matter of clinging on until the engine went away. He gave a perfect demonstration of this in the Berlin Grand Prix of 1954, run at Avus, the track which would ultimately claim his life.

This was a non-championship race, organized solely to allow the all-conquering Mercedes W196 streamliners to show their feathers to a German crowd. Karl Kling was allowed to win. The only memorable aspect of a droning afternoon was that Behra — running who-knows-what revs — kept the tiny Gordini in the silver slipstream for as long as his engine allowed.

Heroic futility again, perhaps, but it greatly impressed Alfred Neubauer, and when he came to consider his team for 1955 he thought of Behra as a team mate for Fangio and Kling. It has never seemed to me that Jeannot's free spirit would have long survived the Neubauer regime, but in any case the situation never arose. He had already signed a contract with Maserati, beginning the happiest association of his racing life.

Inevitably there was heavy criticism in the French press. Behra, they said, was deserting his people. The suggestion was in itself fatuous, for Jeannot, if anything, was patriotic to a fault. The move to Maserati — as team leader — was logical from every point of view. Better, he argued vigorously, to win in a red car than lose in a blue. And he had his own career to consider. At 34 he was recognized as one of the world's top drivers. He had spent four years at Gordini, he pointed out. He had paid his dues.

Moreover, Behra discovered at Maserati a way of life which sat perfectly on his shoulders. For him a day without some time in a racing car was a day lost, and he relished the chance to test as often as possible. Living at the Albergo Reale in Modena he would

Pau was one of Behra's favourite circuits, and he won the Grand Prix there three times. Here, in 1955, the Frenchman's Maserati 250F holds off Ascari's Lancia.

pound around the nearby autodromo, then pass the evening playing cards and drinking wine and telling jokes and talking racing. It was an existence he found completely fulfilling.

Raymond Mays (for whose BRM team Behra later drove) once told me a story very revealing of Jeannot's obsession with his job.

'Basically, he could never quite believe his luck — that people would actually pay him to drive racing cars. He sometimes got a bit demoralized if things weren't going too well, but he was never down for long, and I asked him how he kept his spirits up.

'He grinned a bit sheepishly, then said that he would glance at his passport when times were bad. "I look at all the stamps in there, places that racing has taken me to, and then I look at the first page. Name: Jean Behra. Profession: Racing Driver. And it reminds me again how lucky I am to have this life."

'I must say I found that rather moving — and rather different from most drivers I've known.'

In 1955 Behra may well have sought the solace of his passport quite often, for Mercedes reduced the Grand Prix season to a series of regal processions,

Fangio and Moss leaving the rest a little breathless in their wake. But there were consolations for Jean, non-championship wins at Pau and Bordeaux and several sports car victories.

At Aintree the Mercedes quartet qualified 1-2-4-5, with Behra's 250F splitting them. In the race the car lasted only ten laps, but the point had been well made. It was necessary, as Gilles Villeneuve would later say, 'to make a gesture, to keep your self-respect as a racing driver when the car is off the pace'.

The season, though, finished disastrously with a huge accident in the Tourist Trophy at Dundrod. Behra was many weeks in hospital, but the only permanent legacy was a plastic ear to replace the one severed in the crash. And this, with smiling black humour, he would use to advantage in packed restaurants. Sidling quietly over to an occupied table, he would beam and remove it!

'There are always places then', he would murmur. 'Usually several . . .'

Jeannot stayed with Maserati for 1956, demoted to number two in favour of Stirling Moss, for whom he had the profoundest respect. But it was an untypical season, consistent rather than dashing. He placed fourth in the World Championship and took many sports car wins, but somehow *sotto voce* and that chequered helmet never belonged together, and I rejoiced in 1957 when Behra allowed his natural racing personality — chancy but exhilarating — to come through once more.

This was his best season. Again he was denied the Maserati leadership, for Fangio arrived in Moss's place, but there were occasions when Jean was unquestionably the team's pacesetter. He won the inaugural Moroccan Grand Prix (not, alas, a Grande Epreuve that year), and also took a 250F to victory at Pau and Modena. With Fangio he completely dominated the Sebring 12 Hours with the fearsome new 450S sports car, which he also used to win the Swedish Grand Prix, partnered by Moss.

At Monza he chose to run the immensely temperamental Maserati V12, to my eye perhaps the most stirringly beautiful of all Grand Prix cars, and there gave an unforgettable display of throttle control as he fought Moss's Vanwall for the lead in the early laps.

By the end of the year, however, the Maserati story was over. There was not the money to continue, and in some sorrow Behra moved from the Reale to the freezing winter wastes of Lincolnshire.

He had raced for BRM twice in 1957, at Caen and Silverstone, events in which Maserati did not run. And, against admittedly token opposition, he had cantered away. But the 1958 season, albeit one in which he and the dark green car were usually well on the pace, brought no further wins.

Mays remembered this of him: 'A magnificent racing driver, and a charming man — but devastatingly temperamental. Everyone in the team thought the world of him, but he would go through phases of deep depression, for which we could hardly blame him.

'He and his wife had this puppy, to which they were completely devoted — I always think this story tells a lot about his character. They took it everywhere with them, and at Monza they left it in the car, complete with food and water and windows open, during practice. When Jean got back to the car the puppy was gone . . .

'And he became *demented*. Messages went out on

Days of the drift. Through Rouen's downhill swerves Behra's Maserati leads the Ferrari of Collins during the 1957 French Grand Prix.

The Maserati V12 had a sadly brief competition life, but Behra raced it in the Italian Grand Prix of 1957, and got into the lead several times during the first thirty laps — until it blew up.

the loudspeakers, all cars leaving the circuit were searched. Nothing. So he had an SOS put out on radio and TV, and miraculously the dog was handed in to the police that night. Only then did Jean become coherent again. If the dog hadn't been returned, I seriously doubt he would have been in any fit state to race the next day! A delightful fellow, but terribly emotional in a French sort of way . . .'

The 1959 season was Behra *in extremis*. He joined Ferrari, and this was like coming home: back to Modena, the Reale, the ceaseless testing. The new association began well. In the Dino 246 he won the Aintree 200 from team mate Tony Brooks, and in the Testa Rossa sports cars he was clearly faster than any of his colleagues.

But there was a strange and new desperation in his driving through the last months of his life. Here was a man who *knew* about cars, had a mechanical

understanding of them most untypical of the day, yet it seemed that the fall of a flag would drive any such thoughts from his mind. He would scald through the opening laps, apparently oblivious of a rev limit.

By now, of course, the revolution had started. Henceforth the driver's place was in front of the engine, and by that torpid summer of 1959 Ferrari was surviving on horsepower alone. Away from the really fast circuits the front-engined cars were cumbersome, off the pace, and perhaps this led to Behra's abuse of the single high card in his hand.

Not entirely, though. In sports car racing Ferrari was still supreme, yet Jean drove the Testa Rossas, too, with impassioned ferocity. In the Targa Florio his car came to rest upside down in a ditch.

End of the race you might have thought: for Behra, no. Local peasants helped him right the Ferrari, whereupon he kicked crumpled bodywork free of tyres and got back in. By some trick of the light, the V12 fired first press. But Jeannot was very disappointed with Brooks's reluctance to take over the wreckage.

At Le Mans he was fastest in practice — and almost last away, the car refusing to fire. And this was France, always worth a second a lap. After an hour or so Behra had that Ferrari into the lead, and as a piece of sheer driving brilliance it rivals anything ever seen at the Sarthe, ruthless and perilous and chilling. In the heavy traffic of the early laps he ran consistently under his pole position time, and never did his friends fear more for him.

Had the race been over 1,000 km rather than 24 hours, Jean would have won an immortal victory. As it was, he and co-driver Dan Gurney led for seven hours before retirement, Behra's parting shot a sequence of 'daylight' lap times at one in the morning. With only a single headlight working . . .

Once the mist had cleared from the oratory, however, there were undeniably signs of an increasing loss of perspective by the proud Gallic champion. I

prefer, he seemed to be saying, to shine before my people — even if briefly — than to coast and collect a distant place. Even as he flailed through the field at Le Mans he was killing all hope of victory, and he must have known that. The people, though, would go home loving him. And they would talk about Jean Behra for as long as cars were raced.

Two weeks later he was at Reims, where the adulation had begun, and again he was left at the start, this the consequence of a charitable decision not to run down 'Toto' Roche, the fat old man who used to drop the flag from somewhere in the middle of the road.

Jeannot finally got started, last by a long way. More lap records, more over-revving. It was again a display of awesome race driving, and took him up to third by half-distance. Even with smoke billowing from the engine he refused to lift off, and soon his last Grand Prix was over.

In the pits team manager Romulo Tavoni glanced at the tell-tale needle and began to shout. It was a mistake. Behra felled him with a single punch, and

Behra's last great exhibition of driving was at Le Mans in 1959, just a few weeks before he was killed. Here he talks with crew-cut team mate Dan Gurney during the night, while mechanics work vainly on the Ferrari.

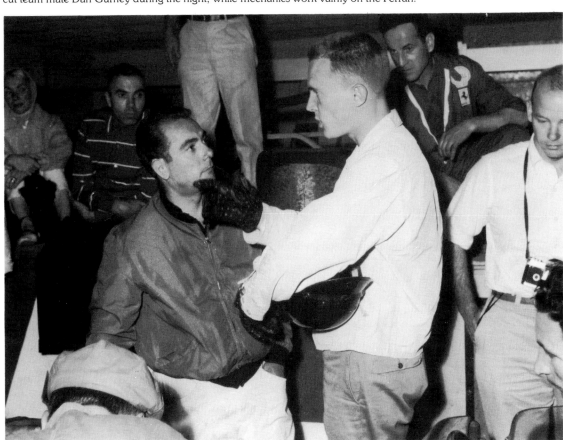

In the Aintree 200 of 1959 Behra raced a Formula 1 Ferrari for the first time — and scored an easy victory, heading the sister car of Tony Brooks.

when Tavoni came to he instantly sacked him. Jean sought an audience with Enzo Ferrari, but the Commendatore declined to see him.

At the Avus he arrived with a pair of Porsches, his own F2 creation for the German Grand Prix and an RSK sports car for Saturday's Berlin Grand Prix, which he had won a year earlier.

'It was an awful place,' Raymond Mays recalled. 'The track itself was ridiculous, just two long straights, a hairpin and that absurd banking. Jean was in the next pit to us, and I remember feeling very sorry for him. Everything had gone wrong for him, and he seemed very much alone that weekend. It was very upsetting to see this great racing driver having to race his own Formula 2 car in a Grand Prix — even working on it himself.

'He was always very fond of BRM, and we talked to him about coming back to the team — in fact, he asked us for a car for Avus, but unfortunately there wasn't enough time to get it organized. Maybe it is hindsight to some extent, but there seemed an air of tragedy around him in those last few hours of his life. And then, of course, came that ghastly accident . . .'

It was raining when the sports car race began, and the steep banking was lethally slippery. Jeannot was into a battle with the factory RSKs of Bonnier and von Trips, and on the fourth lap went on to the banking too high, too fast.

The little silver car spun out of control, hitting a concrete block at the lip of the banking. Behra was hurled out. A picture in a lurid German magazine of the time showed him like Icarus, silhouetted against the grey sky. Thrown against a flag pole, his body then fell behind the banking and into the paddock.

At home I saw the famous crash helmet on the television screen, then listened to what followed. Jean Behra — this man who, sleepless, would thrash his Porsche around country roads all night, going nowhere for the joy of it — was the first and last hero of my life.

Often I go to Silverstone, and even now I cannot pass the near corner of the paddock without thinking of that stocky figure in red sweatshirt and pale blue overall trousers, hopping into the BRM, buckling his helmet, flicking away a last cigarette . . .

TONY BROOKS
Hiding his light

'Brooks was a tremendous driver, the greatest — if he'll forgive my saying this — "unknown" racing driver there's ever been', says Stirling Moss. 'He was far better than several people who won the World Championship'.

News took its time arriving back in the fifties, or perhaps it was that Fleet Street paid little heed to Grand Prix racing. Whichever, I clearly recall a brief item on the BBC's old *Sportsview* programme one Wednesday evening in October 1955. It told of a Grand Prix victory by a British car, the first since 1923. And it was not by Vanwall or BRM, by Moss or Hawthorn. Tony Brooks had won the Syracuse Grand Prix in a Connaught. For a nine-year-old who thought he knew it all, this took some believing.

Brooks himself was perhaps less shaken by the events in Sicily than anyone else. Winning the race had been straightforward, and there were on his mind things of more pressing importance. He was 23, a student at Manchester University, and looming up were his 'Finals'. Racing — even at Grand Prix level — was a pleasing recreation.

If that sounds incredible in the commercialized times of today, it is less so when one has talked to Brooks. His talent was unforced and flowing. He was at ease lapping a place like Spa at over 130 in a front-engined car on narrow tyres. It brought no sweat to his brow.

'Syracuse was something right out of the blue', he says now. 'I'd been racing for about three years, mainly at club level, but it was mainly for fun, a nice break from my studies. I was going to be a dentist like my father, and I never had any thought of racing professionally. Even when I joined the Aston Martin factory team in 1955 I had no problems. There were no objections to my racing so long as I worked twice as hard to make up for the time I was away.

'When Connaught decided to do the Syracuse race, they asked me because they couldn't find anyone else!

I was swotting when they rang me, a few days before the race. Quite literally, I had never so much as sat in a Formula 1 car before, but I rather absent-mindedly said yes and put the phone down.'

Thirty years on we live in a world where young drivers pass every waking minute putting together deals and talking to potential sponsors — trying to *buy* a Formula 1 drive. Yet here was this young fellow boning up on gums and molars, agreeing that, yes, okay, he'd spare a couple of days for a Grand Prix drive . . .

Brooks laughed. 'Believe me, that's *exactly* how it was. I didn't get keyed up because I was so preoccupied with my Finals. On the aeroplane I worked on my books and never really gave much thought to the race.

'We missed the first day of practice, I remember, because the transporter hadn't arrived, so I hired a scooter that evening to learn the circuit. And the next morning I had my first experience of Formula 1. Connaught had an awful reliability record, and they ordered me not to do too much practice. I think they were terrified of not getting the starting money. Quite understandable, but it didn't really help me! When the race started I'd done no more than a dozen laps or so.'

Expected to dominate were the factory Maseratis, and Musso and Villoresi duly led the early laps while Brooks played himself in, learning a little more about car and circuit. The Connaught, he found, handled beautifully but was short on power. After ten laps the green car was in front, and Tony thereafter concentrated on driving hard through the corners, sparing the venerable Alta engine on the straights. At the finish Musso was nearly a minute behind.

'Obviously', Brooks smiles, 'I was very pleased at the time, but it didn't really sink in. I remember swotting all the way back, too . . .'

He passed his exams without problem, but the

Historic moment. In the gathering gloom of Syracuse in October 1955 Brooks' Connaught takes the flag to score the first victory by a British car in Grand Prix racing for more than thirty years.

Syracuse win did incline him a little more towards racing professionally. There would be plenty of time later for peering into people's mouths.

'I went to BRM for 1956, as number two to Mike Hawthorn. Their unreliability was almost legendary, but on paper the car was a flier. What it needed — and what BRM didn't have — was a good development team. That car was *lethal!* You had to corner it geometrically. If you tried to drift it, you just flew off the road. Mike had a long-chassis car, and in that you had at least some control.' Brooks judges the pause perfectly before adding, 'I had a short-chassis one . . .'

What the cars did have, however, was impressive horsepower and torque. At Silverstone that summer Mike and Tony led the early laps of the British Grand Prix. But all too soon Hawthorn was out, and Brooks came in for repairs to a broken throttle cable.

'I went out again, albeit laps behind, because I wanted all the experience I could get. BRM raced very seldom that year. The throttle was still sticking a bit, but I was very naive. Before the stop I'd been taking Abbey flat — believe me, I don't know how! — so I

thought I could carry on doing that, while being wary of the throttle at other corners. The problem was that during my long stop a lot of oil had been put down at Abbey.

'The car began to run wide, and I lifted off momentarily to get the nose to tuck back in. It made no difference, and I came off the corner three or four feet on the grass. Being that car, it just went completely out of control, spun into the bank, somersaulted and threw me out. Finally it landed upside down on the track again and set itself on fire, which was the only thing it could reasonably do . . .'

Happily, Tony was thrown on to grass and somehow suffered nothing more than a chipped ankle, but he had had his fill of BRM and accepted an offer to join Moss at Vanwall for 1957.

This was the beginning of a momentous time in British motor racing, but at first nothing seemed to go right. Then Brooks took a magnificent, if eventful, second to Fangio at Monte Carlo.

'From the start Stirling led Collins, Fangio, me and Hawthorn, but on the third lap he missed his braking point at the chicane and hit the barrier, which in those

In the early laps of the 1956 British Grand Prix Brooks's BRM ran second to team mate Hawthorn's car. After a pit stop, though, Tony hit oil at Abbey, and was thrown out of the somersaulting car.

days was a lot of sandbags with telegraph poles lying between them! Suddenly these poles were all over the road, and Collins got involved, finishing up on the harbourside. Fangio and I managed to slow down, but Hawthorn — perhaps unsighted — came rushing up behind me, hit my back wheel and flew into the air.

'Well,' Tony said, 'it's a bit distracting, that sort of thing. And by the time he'd joined Collins and I'd driven over the poles, Fangio was gone . . .

'A lap later I lost my clutch. Even with a clutch, the Vanwall's gearchange was horrible, but without one it was a nightmare — and the race was 105 laps that year. I can clearly remember that I had to change gear 23 times each lap, and by the end of the race my hand was like a piece of steak. I was well satisfied with myself that day.'

Two months later Vanwall triumphed in the British Grand Prix, the winning car shared by Moss and Brooks. But the win did not come easily. Tony had crashed badly at Le Mans, and was by no means fit when Aintree came around.

'I'd just taken over the Aston Martin at about three

in the morning. We were running second, but the gearbox was stuck in fourth, a fairly frequent occurrence. In the past I'd always managed to free it. I couldn't face cruising round for another thirteen hours, dropping down the field, so on my first lap I was wrenching away at the lever — and looking at it! That's about the first thing a learner driver is told not to do, and when I looked up I'd missed my braking point for Tertre Rouge. I almost made it round, but the car hit the sandbank and flipped.

'The car fell on me, and I couldn't move. I remember lying there, waiting for it either to catch fire or to be hit by the next car round. Sure enough the first guy through — Umberto Maglioli — hit the Aston, and knocked it off me! It was a piece of amazingly good luck, and I was sorry to have put Maglioli out of the race. It was poor return for his courtesy . . .'

Brooks did not break any bones, but had very severe abrasions and was in hospital quite a while, coming out only the day before practice began at Aintree. Astonishingly he qualified third, behind Stirling and Behra's Maserati. There was no problem in going quickly, only in sustaining it. He was weak after the spell in hospital, and readily agreed that he would hand over to Moss if necessary.

In the event, Stirling retired his own leading car, took over Tony's and put in one of history's greatest drives to come through the field.

'Moss', says Brooks, 'was phenomenal that day. Perhaps, if Behra hadn't retired, we wouldn't have won, but he did and the race had a fairy-tale ending. Tony Vandervell was thrilled, of course, and only surprised that it had taken so long. I truly believe he thought his cars were much better than they were. He had Stirling, Stuart Lewis-Evans and me, and frankly I reckon that must be one of the strongest driving teams of all time.

'Don't get me wrong, the Vanwall *was* a great car, but it was never an easy one to drive. You couldn't chuck it into a corner like, say, a Maserati 250F, and steer it on the throttle. You had to be very precise with it. And, as I said before, that gearbox was *terrible!'*

Although, in physical terms, Tony recovered swiftly enough from his Le Mans accident, the implications of the shunt had a profound effect on his mental approach to race driving. Always a devout Roman Catholic, he thought deeply as he lay in the hospital bed, reaching a conclusion he thought in keeping with his faith. Perhaps it later kept him from dying in a racing car. Almost certainly it cost him a World Championship.

'My philosophy changed somewhat after the Silverstone shunt with the BRM, and completely after the one at Le Mans. Each of those accidents came about through trying to compensate for a car's mechanical deficiencies, and I made a firm mental decision never to do that again. If something wasn't working properly, too bad.

'I always felt it was morally wrong to take unnecessary risks with one's life because I believe that life is a gift from God, and that suicide is morally unacceptable. I suppose there are those who would say that driving racing cars at all is an unnecessary risk, but I wouldn't agree with that. However, driving one which may be unsound or damaged, while not exactly suicide, is verging towards it. I don't want to sound

On the front row at Aintree in 1957, along with Behra and Moss. Still far from recovered from his injuries at Le Mans, Tony was only too happy to hand number 20 over to Stirling, who took it to a memorable victory.

Brooks shared the Aintree victory with Moss in 1957, but the following year needed no help from anyone in winning the Belgian Grand Prix for Vanwall at Spa, his favourite circuit.

theological about this, and I know thousands will disagree, but that's my view. I felt I had a moral responsibility to take reasonable care of my life.'

You might expect a man with such a philosophy also to have been a crusader for safety in motor racing, but to Brooks the two subjects are unrelated. His favourite circuits, after all, were Spa and the Nurburgring.

'Safety was never discussed in my time. Nobody gave any thought to it. Obviously we took the precautions we could, like wearing the best available helmet, but we hadn't even got round to flame-proof clothing. The attitude in those days was that the spectators had to be protected at all costs, and that was it. Towards the end of my career, in the early sixties, people began to talk about it — but only in terms of making the cars as safe as possible. The circuits stayed the same, and there was never any question of making them into "Scalextric" tracks.

'We accepted that Grand Prix racing was a challenge to the designer and driver to get a car round a road circuit faster than any other kind of car. We used to get resentful when we had to drive on artificial aerodrome-type circuits. The big attraction was driving a racing car on closed roads, and we accepted that the name of the game was keeping the car on the road. If you went off, you were in the lap of the gods. You

might get away with it, you might not. A good analogy is that of mountainneering: if you provide a safety net, no challenge remains.'

Brooks really warms to this theme, and there will be those who claim it flies in the face of his resolution never to take 'unnecessary risks'. Tony disagrees: if the car is sound, it is the driver's responsibility to keep it from an accident.

'Obviously no one wanted to get killed or hurt, but the challenge was to drive as fast as you could — at the same time realizing the consequences of a mistake. Nobody will persuade me that there isn't more of a challenge to a driver if he knows he might hurt himself if he goes off the road. *Of course* you can afford to have a go if you know that a mistake might mean going into a run-off area and losing a few seconds or, at worst, dropping out of the race. But when you were going into a corner faster than the next man — yet not so fast you were going to hurt yourself — that was a completely different game.

'I think there's a lack of discipline among some drivers today, but I don't altogether blame them. I think it's inevitable if you create an environment where they can make mistakes and get away with it. Brick walls and trees and ditches instil a discipline, believe me. I can remember drivers who were very quick on aerodrome circuits, but no threat at all on true road

An apprehensive Brooks in the Ferrari Dino 246 before the start at Avus in 1959. He liked the ludicrous German track no more than anyone else, but drove perfectly to head a 1-2-3 for the team.

After Jean Behra's death on the Avus banking the day before, none of the drivers relished the 1959 German Grand Prix. Here Brooks leads the Coopers of Moss and Gregory en route to his last Grand Prix win.

circuits. And the only explanation is that a totally different attitude of mind was needed at a circuit where you couldn't spin off with impunity . . .'

Brooks's opinions scarcely mirror contemporary thinking, but they come from an intelligent and rational man who thought about the dangers, weighed and accepted them. In his remarks there is no hint of buccaneering hindsight, no suggestion that 'racing drivers were real men in my day'. His manner is polite and mild, laced with dry humour. He is, above all, a man of logic. There is a discretion there, a modesty, yet like all great drivers he knows just how good he was.

In 1958 Vanwall won six of the nine Grandes Epreuves, Moss and Brooks taking three apiece, and Tony's victories came at the three classic circuits, Spa, the Nurburgring and Monza. He remembers Belgium with particular relish.

'I adored Spa, to me the essence of a true Grand Prix circuit, and never seemed to have any trouble going quickly there. Stirling tore away at the start, and I've always believed he was out to beat me that day as much as the Ferraris.

'In these days I suppose it sounds terribly dated and naive to say this, but I'd been to public school where one learned that "the team was the thing", and there was no way I was going to try and pass Stirling — even if I might hustle him a bit . . . But I'm not sure he believed that. He absolutely flew away on the first lap, got as far as Stavelot and missed a gear! In tennis terms it was definitely what you'd call a "forced error", and after that I had no real problems.'

Brooks and Moss always got along well, and still do, but odd remarks from Tony make it clear that he found irksome some of Stirling's demands as Vanwall number one. 'I think,' he smiles, 'that he always made very sure he had the best car — and if he thought he hadn't, he'd fix it so he did! That might mean my engine in his car, or vice-versa . . .'

At the Nurburgring Brooks scored what he

considers his greatest victory. In many respects it duplicated Fangio's drive a year earlier. In both cases a driver from another team caught the Ferraris of Hawthorn and Collins, caught them, beat them. In 1958, though, there was eventual tragedy: 'In trying to stay with me, Peter overdid it and had his fatal accident. Obviously I felt pretty bad about it at the time, although I certainly didn't feel *responsible* for it. He knew the rules of the game as well as anyone — and he knew that the game was dangerous.'

At the end of 1958 Tony Vandervell, sick at heart after the death of Stuart Lewis-Evans at Casablanca, disbanded his team. Moss went to drive for Rob Walker, and Brooks signed for Ferrari. It was a difficult season in many ways, for Cooper's revolution was under way, and Ferrari, still front-engined, were hard-pressed to keep up on all but the quick circuits. Tony nevertheless looks back on 1959 with pleasure.

'It was a gorgeous car to drive, that Dino 246, and its gearbox, after the Vanwall's, was a revelation. I won fairly easily at Reims and Avus, but I think we were unlucky that year. The Belgian Grand Prix, for example, was cancelled, and I would happily have taken anyone on in that car at Spa. We missed Aintree because of a strike in Italy, and then at Monza they changed the clutch for the race without telling me! It wasn't bedded in, so when I let it out at the start it slipped and burnt itself out. My race lasted 100 yards . . .'

For all that, Brooks went to Sebring for the last round of the World Championship still in with a chance of winning. And amazingly he and the other contenders, Moss and Brabham, qualified for the front row. But on the opening lap the rear wheel of Tony's car was hit by team mate von Trips — 'which is why I always say my change of philosophy may have cost me the championship. My natural inclination was to carry on. Believe me, that would have been the easiest thing to do, but I made myself come in to have the car checked over. I lost half a lap doing that, and still finished third. Stirling retired, and Jack ran out of petrol near the end! Still, in my own mind I think I did the right thing.'

Enzo Ferrari was immensely disappointed when Brooks left at the end of the year, and for Tony himself it was a sorrowful decision. But he was starting to think about a future beyond motor racing and had bought a garage, which he wanted to build up. That, he decided, would be impossible if he were spending half his life in Italy.

There was a plan, in 1960, for Brooks to renew his ties with Vandervell, to drive a new Lotus 18 with a Vanwall engine in the back. That sounded like the perfect compromise, Tony reckoned, but it never reached fruition: 'I think Vandervell wanted me to retire before I hurt myself. He was always trying to get me to go and see a dental surgeon friend of his in Harley Street!'

The season was therefore spent with the uncompetitive Yeoman Credit team, running 'last year's Coopers'. Brooks frequently showed his class, for example qualifying second at Spa, but his talent was squandered. For 1961 he returned, surprisingly, to BRM for what was to be his final year as a driver.

'It was pathetic. The new V8 engine was months late, and Graham Hill and I spent a hopeless year with heavy cars and very poor Climax engines. I got fastest lap at Aintree, but only because it was wet that day. And I finished third at Watkins Glen — our best result of the year. That was my last race.

'Graham always had much the better of the two cars, and I think I put up with more than I should have done. With a rather more commercial background and education I probably wouldn't have done, but I wasn't prepared to argue and stayed out of the politics, as I always did. And, to be honest, I really didn't like the 1½-litre go-karts very much. I've never changed my opinion that, to be worth driving or watching, a racing car should always have a bit more power than its chassis can cope with . . .'

At the age of 29 Brooks retired. He is the kind of meticulous man who would make a success of anything, and his garages thrive. In his small, neat, office are a few trophies and a lot of racing books, as well as photographs of his family. He met his Italian wife at the Rouen Grand Prix in 1956.

'I'm very happy with my life', he says. 'The business is doing well, and I get along with all my children. For six or seven years I went motor racing and thoroughly enjoyed it. But I never had the dedication of, say, Stirling. It was never going to be my life. Just a part of it.'

JIMMY CLARK
Leader lost

It was going to be a Porsche walkover, we decided. For the first couple of hours Bruce McLaren in the new Ford F3L had waged spirited battle with the Germans, but a driveshaft had failed. Ickx and Redman might become a factor later in the day with their GT40, but for now there was stalemate, a lull in the 1968 BOAC 500.

I wandered off to the Brands Hatch book shop, and was there numbed by appalling news; Jimmy Clark had been killed at Hockenheim a couple of hours earlier. Nothing had been announced over the PA and I found myself scarcely able to take it in. Impossible, surely, that the greatest driver could have died in a mere Formula 2 race at a circuit so bland? An hour later, driving back to London, I found a French station on the radio: 'Un grand champion est mort aujourd'hui,' intoned a sombre voice, and only then did it become reality.

For the drivers, however hardened, however accustomed to tragedy in their business, the fact of Jimmy's death was almost beyond comprehension. 'As well as the grief, there was another dimension altogether', remembers Chris Amon. 'If it could happen to him, what chance did the rest of us have? I think we all felt that. It seemed that we'd lost our leader . . .'

These days most Grand Prix drivers would chew on a razor blade before conceding the superiority of one of their number. Perhaps we don't have anyone head and shoulders proud of the rest just now; or perhaps those were simply more civilized times. They knew Clark's talent was on a plateau beyond their reach, just as Moss's contemporaries had acknowledged a few years before. How could they do else? For five seasons and more Jimmy had quite dominated Grand Prix racing, and done it with grace and ease.

Take 1965. Ten races in the World Championship, your half dozen best results to count. At the

Nurburgring Clark won his sixth of the year, putting a lock on the title by early August. The German was actually the seventh Grand Prix in the series, but Jimmy had missed Monaco due to a clashing commitment. He was at Indianapolis that weekend, winning the 500.

Let me take a little more time with the sheer statistics of the man's career: 72 Grands Prix, 25 wins, 33 pole positions, 27 fastest laps. Niki Lauda drew level with Clark on victories at Zandvoort in 1985 — his 168th start. You may argue that Formula 1 in Jimmy's era was less competitive than now, and certainly it is undeniable that usually he had the best car. But beyond doubt, too, is that he was by a league the greatest of his generation.

During childhood my 'local' circuit was Oulton Park, and — as school terms permitted — I always attended the big meetings there. At the British Empire Trophy of 1959 I was enraptured by the elegant drifting through Cascades of one of the Lotus Elites. Glance at the programme. Thus did I become aware of 'J. Clark'.

Rather more significantly, Colin Chapman was also becoming aware of him. By the end of the year the two had signed a contract, and in motion was perhaps the finest partnership Grand Prix racing has known. Initially Clark's agreement was only for Formula Junior and Formula 2, but Chapman had him running a third car in the Dutch Grand Prix of 1960 and the pattern was set. Never in Formula 1 did Jimmy race anything but a Lotus.

I spoke only once with Chapman on the subject of Jimmy. More than ten years after the tragedy at Hockenheim, Colin said, it was still difficult to accept the fact of his death. 'For me Jimmy will always be the best driver the world has ever known,' he began. 'In time, probably, someone else will come along, and everyone will hail him as the greatest ever. But not

The beginning of the Clark era. Jimmy and the Lotus 25 head for their first Grand Prix victory, at Spa in 1962.

me. As far as I'm concerned, there will never be another in his class.

'These days, of course, Grand Prix drivers are just that. They hardly ever race anything else — that's the way the sport has become, perhaps inevitably. But what you have to remember about Jimmy is that he excelled at everything. I think only Dan Gurney was a serious rival in Formula 1 — but think of Indy, of that sports car race at the Nurburgring with the little Lotus 23, of the saloon car races with the Lotus Cortina, Formula 2 . . .

'Jimmy came close to retiring a couple of times, you know, and I had mixed feelings about that. On the one hand, the idea of going racing without him was almost unthinkable. On the other, I loved him as a human being, and desperately didn't want him to get hurt.

'He had more effect on me than anyone else I've ever known. Forget his ability as a racing driver and his association with Lotus, forget everything he did for me in that sense. Jimmy was genuinely a good man. Intelligent, totally honest, and in many ways rather humble. It took him a long time to grow up, in the sense of who he was and what he'd done.

'I wasn't at Hockenheim that day. And for some time afterwards I was in a trance, really. I've never lost my love of motor racing, but . . . at the same time, I can't say I've ever felt quite the same about it since '68 . . .'

This was a side of Chapman I had never seen before. We were sitting in his office at Ketteringham Hall, and at one point he almost broke down. When his secretary brought in some tea he turned away, pretending to look for something while composing himself. That same day Colin also talked of Rindt, Peterson, Andretti and others who had driven for him. For all he had some affection, but there was not a shard of the emotion he felt at the loss of Clark. Clearly this quiet fellow from the Border country occupied a place alone in his thoughts.

I came into racing journalism a couple of years or so after Jimmy's reign ended, and 'met' him only once. This was Oulton again, in April of 1964. Here we had the reigning World Champion competing at a humble national meeting. And, what's more, in three races.

That day he drove an ageing Lotus 19 in the sports car event, an Elan in the GT race, a Lotus Cortina in the saloon car race — and he won the lot. It was bitingly cold, and I remember that he wore a stretched, rather tatty, sweater over his driving suit throughout the day. Only in later years did he become something of a snappy dresser.

Talking to him was a happy surprise. I approached

in trepidation with my autograph book, which he signed and handed back with a smile. Thus encouraged, I asked him about the new and fearsome Lotus 30 which, had it been ready, he would have been driving that day. 'Are you coming to Aintree next week?' I said I was. 'Well, we should have it there. It looks like quite a beast, actually. I'd like to have done a bit of testing with it before its first race, but that won't be possible. Still, I'm looking forward to it — it's a bit like the Indy car with two seats! So much more power than Formula 1, should be much more fun to drive . . .'

He had a light voice, unmistakably a Scot but with the lilting drawl of the Border country, and used it to great effect, amplifying a dry sense of humour. At Monza once Stewart was telling a horror story in practice, describing in graphic terms how his throttle had jammed before Curva Grande, how he had somehow — and he didn't know how — made it through the corner. From the assembled entourage there was a chorus of appreciation.

'Are you saying, Jackie,' interjected his countryman quietly, 'that you normally lift off there?'

Those present insist that even JYS was momentarily lost for a suitable rejoinder.

Stewart has always cited his comeback drive at Monza in 1973 as perhaps the best of his life, and actually it was almost a duplicate of Clark's six years before. On that occasion Jimmy lost more than a lap to the leaders when he pitted for an early puncture. He came out, caught them, unlapped himself — then made up that whole lap and passed them again eight laps from the finish! Like all the best heroic tales, however, this one did not end in triumph. As he took the Lotus 49 into its final lap, Jimmy felt the engine begin to cough, running out of fuel. Like that, Surtees and Brabham were quickly past again, and he stammered over the line third. His fastest lap precisely equalled his pole position time.

When I think of Jimmy Clark now, and the life which late he led, he is always in a 49, during that unforgettable season of 1967. I find it inappropriate that history tends to shackle his memory to the 1½-litre era of 1961-65. With around 200 horsepower, these were hardly Grand Prix cars for the Gods, but it was in them that Clark scored all but half a dozen of his 25 victories.

The truth is that, whatever the rules of his time, Jimmy would have dominated. I watched many of his races in the 25 and 33, and frankly tedious he made them, usually leading all the way, ticking off the laps. Spa he won four times on the trot, despite the fact that he loathed the place. In the Belgian Grand Prix of 1960, only the second Formula 1 race of his life, Clark very nearly ran over the body of Chris

Only the Monaco Grand Prix eluded Clark — in six starts he never crossed the finish line. In the ageing Lotus 33, with only a 2-litre Climax engine, he nevertheless set fastest lap in 1967.

On the limit in the Lotus 43 during practice for the Oulton Park Gold Cup in 1966. This car was never a great success, but Jimmy went on to win the American Grand Prix with it — the BRM H16 engine's only victory.

Bristow at Burnenville. Later team mate Alan Stacey was killed at Malmédy. Stirling Moss had been badly hurt in practice. These were images of Francorchamps which remained with Jimmy, and it was a mark of the man that he never allowed them to affect his performances there.

Similarly, if truth be told, he hated Indianapolis. At first, in 1963, it was an adventure, something new, an opportunity to drive a single-seater of real power and substance. He finished second that year, beaten only by Parnelli Jones, a certain ignorance of the Brickyard rulebook and a dose of good ol' Hoosier Establishment prejudice. Still, he won more than $56,000 'for turning left 800 times,' as he put it, and gained everyone's respect — not least because he didn't make a fuss. Parnelli's roadster had been dropping so much oil that Jimmy's lightweight Lotus, clearly the fastest car in the race, fell back on the slick surface. Jones should have had the black flag, and had their roles been reversed, Clark would have had! But while Eddie Sachs, who crashed on the oil in the last few laps, got into fisticuffs with PJ afterwards, Jimmy kept his peace. Two years later he ran away with the 500 — and Parnelli was second. That, in the minds of Clark and Chapman, was the right response.

Undoubtedly it was pride which took Jimmy back to Indy year after year. Quiet and unassuming may have been his character, his public persona, but those early experiences always rankled. He had not been impressed with the razzmatazz and red tape, the need for a man of his reputation to take a Rookie Test on his first visit to the Brickyard. That he found humiliating, an insult. And, just as Foyt took delight in winning Le Mans, plundering Europe, so Clark simply loved to whisk dollars away.

A colleague told me he once had a call from Jimmy: 'I'm at the airport. Can you come out here to meet me?' And when he got there he found a Clark he didn't know, morose and drinking brandy. 'I'm supposed to get a plane to bloody Indianapolis,' Jimmy told him, 'and I *really* don't want to go. All that fuss and pandemonium — I can't face it . . .'

He had simply wanted to talk. My friend heard him out and said he should follow his instincts. Clark, amateur in spirit but a pro who kept his word, gave him a rueful smile, picked up his bag, and went for his flight.

When, years later, I went to Indianapolis, my British accent seemed to spark off memories of Jimmy. They didn't speak of Hulme, Rindt, Hill, even Stewart. Everyone recalled Clark the gentleman, Clark the ace. It breaks Foyt's heart to speak well of a rival's ability — particularly one from outside God's Own Country — but of Jimmy he was unhesitating in his praise: 'He was just a fantastic race driver. I've never seen a better one.'

Chapman and Clark. Through the entire history of Grand Prix racing, this designer-driver relationship is perhaps the most fabled of all.

At the 500 I also met a man whose father had been a USAC Steward at the 1966 race. On that occasion Clark's ill-handling car twice got away from him and spun — and each time Jimmy kept it somehow from hitting the wall. Nothing like it had ever been seen at the Speedway, the guy told me. Why, the car had come off turn four backwards, engine dead, Clark then flicking the wheel to point the Lotus forwards again, finding low gear and popping the clutch out . . .

It was a disputed finish, both Jimmy and Graham Hill driving to Victory Lane, where the race was awarded to the Englishman — mistakenly, according to my informant. 'The lap scorers missed one of Clark's laps — gave it to his team mate Al Unser by mistake. Everyone knew it . . .' Why was the result allowed to stand? 'Oh, come on! USAC — admit a mistake? You can't be serious.'

I've dwelt on Jimmy and Indianapolis because it always seemed to me proof of his real greatness. Plenty of first quality Formula 1 drivers have failed at the Brickyard over the years. For Clark, it was simply another race — and, to him, somewhat of an overrated one. It was far more difficult, he would say, to get around Clermont-Ferrand or the Nurburgring properly.

In the same way he adapted without problem to the Lotus 49 and its new Cosworth DFV engine, which he drove for the first time in practice for the Dutch Grand Prix of 1967. True enough, the DFV had a lot more power than rival engines, but in the early days it didn't arrive very nicely, coming in with a belt at around 6,500 revs. Add to that the wilful nature of the original 49 chassis. Then recall that, after finding his feet, Jimmy ran away with the race.

He lived abroad that last summer, mainly in a Paris apartment, invariably driving to the Grands Prix in his yellow Elan. That was the point about Jimmy — he truly adored driving for the sake of it. He never could resist hopping into any car which interested him, and in this was very different from the head-over-heart Stewart.

'Oh, Jimmy would get into things I wouldn't look at', Jackie says. 'There was a race for Historic Cars at Rouen one year — and there he is, driving Pat Lindsay's ERA faster than Pat himself! When we'd do the Tasman Series, you'd find him in all sorts of weird and wonderful local specials — I mean, things I wouldn't even sit in. On the spur of the moment he went off and did a NASCAR race at Rockingham. It used to amaze me that Colin let him do these things . . .

'The truth of it was that, in a car, Jimmy liked to show off a bit. And that was in complete contrast to his normal character. He'd run a mile from making a speech, and you had virtually to push him into the VIP lounge at an airport. "Don't you understand," I used to say to him, "that these things make travelling that bit easier to take?" and he'd agree. But he'd never do it if he was on his own.'

Clark had gone into Grand Prix racing with the intention of retiring after three or four years, then returning for good to the farm at Chirnside. Most of his friends thought he would quit at the end of 1965, the season of his second World Championship and the Indy victory, expecting him to marry Sally Stokes, his longtime girlfriend, and depart the scene. In the event, it was that relationship which came to an end, and afterwards Jimmy seemed more than ever committed to racing.

'A lot of people have claimed he was thinking seriously about stopping,' Stewart says, 'but I know that wasn't the case. I also know he was never going back to farming again — not full time, anyway. That time of living in Paris changed him quite a bit. Out of a car he was still nervous in some ways — did you ever see his fingernails? — but he'd got used to quite a sophisticated way of life, and he liked it.'

Perhaps he never would have settled permanently in Berwickshire again, but there is no doubt that, in that year of tax exile, he missed the opportunity once in a while to go back to his roots. Through that summer he was able to visit Britain only once, for Silverstone and another memorable win. Pictures of the car that day — acutely understeering here, in an opposite lock power slide there — serve to remind us of the early 49's wayward character, but Jimmy was always its master. At the Nurburgring a fortnight later he was on pole position with it, more than *nine seconds* faster than anyone else.

On 7 April 1968 Clark should have been at Brands, driving one of the new Fords, but the cars were ready late, and by then he had committed himself to Hockenheim, in those days a place devoid of chicanes, almost devoid of guardrails.

'It was misty, wet and miserable that morning', recalls Chris Amon. 'I was next to Jimmy on the grid, and we spoke briefly before the start. But I remember he was very uptight that whole weekend. I was very close

Kyalami 1968. Jimmy's last Grand Prix brought the 25th victory of his career. This was also the final race in which Lotus wore green and yellow.

Shortly before his death in April of 1968. Amon said of Clark: 'I think we all felt we'd lost our leader . . .'

to him, but it was difficult to communicate with him at Hockenheim.

'I'm not suggesting that he had any sort of premonition of disaster — such as Bandini, I'm sure, did — just that he was a bit preoccupied. We'd both done the Tasman Series, and I think, like me, he was very tired and really didn't want to do that race. He was due to go back to Scotland for a holiday right afterwards, and he couldn't wait. He hadn't been home in a long time because of the tax thing.

'Anyway, we got started, and the Firestones were useless in the wet. Jimmy was about the same distance in front of me every lap, but he was only about eighth and not making any ground. That's how I knew the tyres were bad!

'Then one lap I noticed some dirt at the side of the road, and next time saw a stretcher coming over the fence. It was flat out there, no barriers, just trees, and it was fairly obvious if you went off at that point there was no way of getting out of it. But it never entered my head it could be Jimmy, because that Lotus was still in the same place, ahead of me. Turns out that on the lap Jimmy crashed, Graham Hill made a pit

stop and rejoined in the same place, relative to me. At the end of the race I complained to Forghieri about the tyres, pointing out that even Clark hadn't been able to get anywhere. And Mauro said, "Oh, Jimmy didn't finish . . ." I saw the look on his face, and then remembered the dirt at the roadside.

'The following morning was sunny and beautiful, and I went off to Pontresina for a holiday — just to get away from motor racing for a while. There were stories at the time that I was thinking of quitting. I wasn't, but it was never the same for me after that.'

Amon, like most drivers who knew Clark, loves to talk about him. 'I've often wondered', he says, 'what Jimmy would have made of modern Formula 1, with sponsorship and PR and no driving anything else. I think he would probably have hated it . . .'

At Jarama, the first Grand Prix following Clark's death, the sole Lotus entry was in the red, white and gold colours of the new sponsor. I rather like the fact that Jimmy's last Grand Prix win, at Kyalami on New Year's Day, came at the wheel of a 49 in green with yellow stripe. In more ways than one, an era had come to a close.

PATRICK DEPAILLER
No one for tennis

Once in a while the Wimbledon tennis finals clash with a Grand Prix weekend, and when that happens many of the drivers and their coterie disappear into motorhomes, curtains closed, to drool over McEnroe and other graduates of the Alcatraz Charm School.

They tend to do this as soon as the final session has finished. Sorry, no time for questions — and within ten minutes you think there's been a bomb warning. Mechanics and journalists apart, the paddock is almost deserted. Race? What race?

'Incroyable, hein?' Patrick Depailler grinned on one such afternoon. 'Wimbledon — and the whole world stop! Today I am the big star . . .'

The shame of the man. Here he was, sitting outside in the sun, openly flaunting convention. You couldn't be surprised, for Patrick was like that. He never comfortably fitted the mould for Grand Prix drivers. He looked the part, right enough, but his image was way out of the mainstream.

For one thing, he neglected the uniform. In an airport terminal you would never have taken him for a race driver. Where were the designer track suit and shoes, the wafer-like leather briefcase — and, above all, the racquet under the arm? By their logos shall ye know them . . .

I liked Patrick Depailler very much, and not only because he passed up all the camp accoutrements of the contemporary superstar. In a Chris Amon sort of way, his attitude to his life and job was refreshingly haphazard, comforting to those of us who recoil from the dour automatons who increasingly people professional sport.

I recall a dinner with the Tyrrell team in Austria one year.

'Where are you going from here, Patrick?' enquired Ken.

'Not sure,' came the mumbled reply.

'How d'you mean, you're not sure?' Tyrrell retorted.

'Well,' Patrick said, haltingly, 'I drove to Lyon to fly here, and my car is at the airport . . .'

'So what's the problem?' asked Ken, increasingly bemused.

'There is no seat on the flight back to Lyon,' answered his driver, 'so I think I have to go to Paris and then back home to Clermont Ferrand somehow. Then I have to find someone to take me to Lyon to pick up the car . . .'

Tyrrell shook his head in disbelief. Depailler, you see, had booked his ticket too late, the kind of mistake you or I might make.

This is not to suggest that there is great merit in being disorganized. People like that are often maddening to work with — as also can be those who live from one punctual appointment to the next. But as a rule of thumb it is the muddlers who inspire affection. Sad for the efficient, granted, but generally the case. Ken Tyrrell has employed greater drivers than Depailler, but I would bet there are few he has liked as much.

'In a lot of ways', Ken comments, 'Patrick was a little boy all his life. He was always wanting to go skiing or motorcycling or hang-gliding, things like that. And he had this trusting belief that everything would be all right in the end. He lived for the present.

'I gave him his first F1 drive, at Clermont in 1972, and then offered him a third car for the North American races in 1973. This was a big chance for him — and ten days before he goes and breaks his leg falling off a motorbike! Later, when he was driving full time for me, I had it written into his contract that he had to keep away from dangerous toys . . .'

Depailler, I always felt, made himself the driver he was, but that is not to dismiss him as a journeyman. He readily faced the fact that his ability to go quickly was not effortless and flowing in the manner of a Stewart.

'There are not many like him, you know! But it's true

I run all the time at the limit. I *like* to run at the limit, to push things as far as I can. I am the same at everything. If I decide to do something, I give it everything. All the time.'

It was always apparent that Patrick shone in circumstances calling more than usually for raw courage. In bad weather he excelled. And think of the Nurburgring in 1975. This was the height of Lauda's reign with Ferrari, a time when the Austrian was generally beyond reach. Whenever the name of Depailler is mentioned, for some reason I immediately recall the end of the first 14-mile lap: Niki in front, Patrick's Tyrrell close behind, the rest on the horizon.

A circuit like that brought out his great strengths, and another such was Mosport. In 1976 he fought a race-long battle with Hunt's McLaren there, and looked set to move ahead in the closing laps. Right at the end, though, the Tyrrell six-wheeler abruptly

slowed, and after taking the flag pulled immediately off to the trackside.

Slumped in the cockpit, Depailler was on the verge of unconsciousness. In the last quarter of the race a fuel pipe had broken, and for twenty minutes a mist of petrol had been spraying into his face.

'For the last few laps I was on auto pilot, you know. I could not see from one eye at all, and I began to feel more and more drunk. For sure it was good the fuel was burning my skin — the pain was keeping me awake!'

In the races, Patrick's instincts may have been to charge, but there was enough sensitivity for him to become very adroit as a test driver. Scheckter was sceptical when Derek Gardner came up with the P34 Tyrrell six-wheeler, but Depailler was at once captivated. It was something new, *novel*. And I always think of the car in terms of Patrick rather than Jody.

Monaco 1978. Depailler waited a long time for his first Grand Prix win, and it was doubly sweet when it came at his favourite circuit. Behind the Tyrrell is Watson's Brabham.

Patrick was always good to watch! Here he aims the Ligier down Linden Drive at Long Beach in 1979. Andretti follows.

The P34 was never to measure up to Depailler's hopes of it, although occasionally right up with the pace. Through its development Patrick worked tirelessly, doing far more of the testing than his team mate. In 1977 he was joined at Tyrrell by Peterson, and enthusiasm invariably kept him ahead of Ronnie, who lost heart as the season wore down.

That this never happened to Depailler may be explained in part by a remark he made to me in an interview very shortly before his death: 'A lot of people hate to test, but I don't understand. How can they not be pleased just to be in a racing car? And *if* they are not, why are they doing this?'

Patrick's narcotic obsession with motor racing came before everything else. I remember his speaking sadly of the end of his marriage: 'She is a normal girl, you know? She is scared of what I do. How can I blame her for that? And how can I stop this?'

He had a vulnerability about him that women found

magnetic, and his face in repose often had a tragic quality — instantly dispelled by that lop-sided grin.

'Whatever he did,' Tyrrell recalls, 'you could never be angry with him for long. It was this schoolboy thing again. He'd look upset for a minute, then start to grin — and you'd burst out laughing! It was hopeless . . .'

During his five seasons with Ken's team Depailler finished 31 races in the points, but only one in the lead. At Kyalami in 1978 he led into the final lap, but the car was stammering with fuel pick-up problems, and in the final wheel-banging mile Peterson's Lotus went ahead. Patrick, again touching the hem of victory, was almost speechless afterwards.

That first Grand Prix win came, appropriately, at Monaco. It was the circuit he loved beyond all others, and he triumphed deservedly after a long scrap with the Brabhams of Watson and Lauda. It was one of those rare days when everyone in the paddock was happy with the result.

At the end of that year he left Tyrrell to join Jacques Laffite at Ligier, supposedly as joint number one. 'It was one of the most difficult moments of my life', Patrick said. 'Telling Ken, I mean. For me, it was like leaving a family.'

For all that, the decision seemed a wise one. Ligier's JS11 was the dominant car at the start of 1979, winning both South American races — in the hands of Laffite. Depailler placed second at Interlagos, quite sure there was a fundamental handling problem with his car. By the start of the European season he had been proved right, and all was well. At Jarama it was Patrick's turn to win, but at Zolder a fortnight before he and Jacques had lost a certain victory for Ligier by fighting between themselves, rooting their tyres.

'We had no team orders, no moving over to let the other past. I know many people thought that was a big mistake, but I did not agree at all. If you are a racing driver, you race.'

After Monaco came the hang-gliding accident, smack in the middle of what seemed certain to be Depailler's best season. The injuries to his legs were severe.

'It was not a dangerous day for it, but I was flying too close to the mountain. There was a lot of turbulence there . . . and, well, it just threw me against the mountainside. It was my lack of experience which caused it. If I'd had more I could probably have done something to prevent it, but . . .'

While Patrick faced several months in hospital, the reaction within racing to his accident was chillingly hard-nosed. In purely commercial terms it was understandable, of course, but I found disturbing — in human terms — the lack of sympathy for a man staring at the possibility of life in a wheelchair.

There were many who saw Depailler's predicament chiefly as an inconvenience to his team. He should not have gone anywhere near a hang-glider, they said. Why, a man can get hurt doing that! Ligier claimed that he had not only behaved irresponsibly, but had

Jarama in 1979 brought a conclusive victory. From the front row Depailler's Ligier led from start to finish.

On the rostrum between Reutemann and King Juan Carlos, Patrick stands for 'La Marseillaise' after winning in Spain.

also broken the terms of his contract. And that made Patrick very angry.

'I had no restriction in my Ligier contract, and neither did Jacques. I was not allowed to do things like that with Tyrrell, for sure. I waited five years to go hang-gliding while I was with Ken, and I started it the week after I left his team! But with Ligier I was free to do what I liked — and they knew what sort of man I was.'

True enough, Depailler's hobbies were always of the 'Action Man' kind. He went skiing and scuba-diving and sailing, and of course never lost his love of huge, over-powered motorcycles. He had two heroes, Jacques Anquetil and Eddy Merckx, both five-time winners of the Tour de France. 'Le sport dur!' he would stress. That was where the appeal lay.

Another driver once confided that he truly believed Patrick to have a death wish. Why else would the man be so attracted to anything dangerous? Was not his courage abnormal? Did he not ride motorbikes without a helmet? And what about hang-gliding?

There have been those who expressed similar feelings about Villeneuve, and I think they were right

about neither man. Patrick and Gilles, in my estimation, were exceptional in their love of life, and for that reason went to the limit — and beyond — in everything they experienced. Depailler, as we have said, liked to 'push things'.

It is one of racing's oldest clichés, resident in every movie script, that 'by being close to the possibility of death, we experience life more deeply', but I think it may have been true of these two men. It was not a death wish, simply that everything was sweetened by risk.

Interestingly, Depailler and Villeneuve had exactly similar views on safety in motor racing. They were concerned about cars rather than circuits, worried more about the unnecessary and additional dangers of the ground effect phenomenon than about moving a piece of guardrail five inches to the left.

'Give me a car that won't break', Patrick said, 'and it's my job to keep it from going off the road. There *are* circuits that have become unsafe — but only because cornering speeds have got so much higher. If you don't make changes to the circuits, you must keep cornering speeds down somehow. The safety

Left A typical Depailler stunt, during a break in testing at Brands Hatch in 1980. The Frenchman lost his life only six weeks later.

facilities should be relative to the speed. But it's crazy that tracks have to change all the time because of the stupid rules applying to the cars.

'I like circuits where the driver still has a big part to play, even in a poor car. But unfortunately those are the ones that have become very dangerous in this ground effect time. I think I am courageous, you know, but I am not mad.'

Like virtually all his colleagues, Depailler hated the ground effect cars: 'Everything about them is wrong. They are easier to drive, yet more dangerous.'

For Patrick the trauma of hospital came not from pain, but from fear of the future.

'The worst thing was lying there all those weeks, not knowing if I recover properly. For a long time there was the possibility of amputation, and I was very frightened. Not for five months was I sure to drive again.'

There is a widely held belief that drivers are never quite the same after severe leg injuries. But Depailler came out of hospital, soon discarded his wheelchair and signed a contract for 1980 with Alfa Romeo. After a couple of races it was apparent that he was driving as well as ever. Only the car's wretched unreliability kept him from several high finishes.

At the end of June the teams came to Brands Hatch for two days of testing, and there I taped an interview with Patrick. The conversation rambled over all kinds of territory, and we talked at length and with enthusiasm about two shared passions, wine and hero-worship of Jean Behra.

My childhood life revolved around Behra, and when I mentioned it Depailler's face lit up: 'No, really? I was the same . . .'

It came as no real surprise, for Behra was small, wiry, tough, unlucky and completely single-minded about motor racing. If he had a counterpart in modern racing I always felt it was Patrick, another man oblivious of the tinsel.

As he plucked yet another non-tipped Gauloise from his pack, I suggested that, while motor racing approves heartily of separating tobacco companies from their money, it does not care for its drivers to sample their products . . .

'Pah, that is rubbish', Depailler replied. 'I am driving a racing car, not running 10,000 metres. Others have smoked — Hunt, Amon, Cevert, Andretti sometimes. It makes no difference at all, and neither does drinking wine. Anyway,' he added, laughing, 'if I gave up cigarettes maybe I would start thinking about them during a race and lose concentration!'

Patrick recovered from the hang-gliding accident better than anyone expected, and was back to his best form with Alfa in 1980. It was on 1 August that he crashed at Hockenheim.

There was, as you can see, nothing of the ascetic about Patrick. But he was a shy and polite fellow, never pushy. At Paul Ricard someone introduced him to Nick Mason, and there was Depailler the schoolboy again. He adored 'Le Pink Floyd'.

A few weeks later I spent a morning at the Williams factory. It was 1 August, the date of Behra's death in 1959, and I was thinking about him as I drove to Didcot. On my way back, in the late morning, I heard on the radio the news of Depailler's accident at Hockenheim. Coincidence is sometimes disquieting.

'Today', Patrick had said at Brands Hatch, 'we are cornering so quickly that run-off areas and catch fences are necessary, *really* necessary. Without them,

every mechanical failure would mean complete disaster. And surely no one would want that.'

Something broke on the Alfa as it approached the flat-in-fifth Ostkurve, and the speed was such that, by the time he had registered that there was a problem, Depailler could do no more than hit the brakes. Horrifying black marks traced the car's path to its impact with the guardrail, against which it disintegrated.

It was a Friday morning, just a week before the race, and for reasons which have never been clear the catch fencing had been taken down. At the time of the accident it was neatly rolled up behind the guardrail.

JUAN MANUEL FANGIO
Maestro

It was the day after the Monaco Grand Prix in 1971. With time to kill before leaving for the airport, I decided to walk the circuit one last time, pausing for occasional refreshment in the sun. Strolling down from Casino Square I noticed a great clamour outside Rampoldi's.

Time has changed the sculpture of Monte Carlo, elegance in skyline giving way to jagged apartment blocks and high-rise hotels. The influence of Reno is much to the fore. But some things comfortably stay, and Rampoldi's is one of them, a wisp of Somerset Maugham's Côte d'Azur. Faded sign-writing and crisp, white linen. Around the walls are yellowing photographs of bygone races through the streets outside the door.

On this day, however, there were no racing cars passing by. Instead, vans were parked there, much to the displeasure of languid workmen who were taking up yesterday's Armco. I ventured into the restaurant and found a small crowd around one of the tables, arc-lights everywhere, people with heavy, shoulder-supported, movie cameras, a spectacular blonde with a clapper-board.

In the midst of all this, sitting quietly at one of the tables, was Fangio. Behind him was a framed picture of the famous multiple accident at Tabac in 1950, through which he threaded his Alfa to a famous victory. With knives, forks and several model cars, he was fighting the battle again. When there was a break in the filming, I asked him to sign my programme. An interview was obviously out of the question.

No subsequent opportunity arose until the great man came to England eight years later for the Gunnar Nilsson Memorial meeting at Donington. In London I was able to meet him at the Steering Wheel Club, an excellent interpreter bridging the sizeable gap between my Spanish and Fangio's English.

Outwardly, the years have been remarkably easy on him. Despite two serious heart attacks some years ago, he looks very youthful for one now into his seventies. The eyes are still mesmeric. He speaks quietly, the tempo increasing as he recalls events which gave him particular pleasure.

To put his career into proper perspective, you must bear in mind that Fangio was 38 before he came to Europe for the first time. In Argentina he was already the hero of countless long-distance races over the dirt roads of South America.

'They were hard, those races, very hard. The Gran Premio del Norte, which I won in 1940, was almost 10,000 kilometres, from Buenos Aires up through the Andes to Lima, Peru, and then back. It took nearly two weeks, with a stage each day, all on dirt roads. We were not allowed mechanics, so any work on the car had to be done by the driver and co-driver, and we were allowed only one hour for that at the end of each stage.

'I think I was eighteen when I raced for the first time, and I remember the car was a Ford taxi! It was borrowed from a friend, and we took the body off. After the race we put the bodywork back on, and it was then used as a taxi again . . .'

Fangio's Grand Prix career would conceivably have started very much earlier had it not been for the war years. Not until 1949 did he first arrive in Europe, financed by the Argentine Automobile Club. He would leave with five World Championships and 24 Grand Prix victories from 51 starts! The first title came in 1951.

'I have very good memories of my years with Alfa Romeo. In sentimental terms the Alfetta was perhaps my favourite car of all, because it gave me the chance to be World Champion for the first time. There were some wonderful races between Alfa and Ferrari. I had tremendous affection for Ascari, who led the Ferrari team for so many years. He and, later, Moss were without doubt the rivals I most feared. My team mate

Wet cobbles at Berne in an Alfa Romeo 159! Fangio made no mistake in the Swiss Grand Prix of 1951, the first of three World Championship victories that year which led to his first title.

at Alfa was Farina . . .'

Had I not read somewhere that Fangio had described Farina as a madman? He smiled. 'Si, si, loco! On the track he was not too bad, but on the road . . . aye, aye, aye. I hated to drive with him in traffic on the way to a race. Felice Bonetto was the same.' To illustrate the point he tapped his head, rolling his eyes at the memory of it all.

After tremendous success in 1951, the two seasons following were less triumphant. The formula had changed, Grands Prix now run for 2-litre F2 cars. Alfa Romeo had withdrawn, and Fangio spent most of his time with Maserati. But these were the years of Ascari and Ferrari.

Fangio also periodically drove the BRM V16, in the few Formula 1 events then being run. In 1952 he raced it in the Ulster Grand Prix at Dundrod. It was the day before the Monza Grand Prix, where he was down to drive for Maserati.

'I had given my word that I would be at Monza. Prince Bira had promised to fly me from Belfast to Milan in his own 'plane, but it broke down and I had to change my plans. I took a scheduled flight to London, hoping to get a connecting flight to Milan. But in London they told me that all flights to Italy were cancelled because of bad weather, so instead I flew to Paris and tried to get a sleeper train. But it was now

midnight, and there were no more trains.

'In desperation I borrowed a car and set off to drive to Monza, arriving only half an hour before the race. I had missed practice, of course, and there was no time even for a few unofficial laps. The race began at 2.30. By three o'clock I was in hospital, lucky to be alive.

'The accident happened on the second lap. I had had to start from the back, and was really forcing. But then the Maserati went into a big slide and, being so tired, my reactions were not quick enough. I can remember it all so clearly — going off the road, hitting the bank, taking off and turning over in the air, seeing the trees rushing towards me, being thrown out of the cockpit and landing on a patch of soft grass. I can clearly recall the strong smell of grass just before I passed out . . .'

For some hours Fangio hovered on the edge of life, his neck broken.

'When I regained consciousness, Farina was there by my bed, holding a laurel wreath. I thought he must be dead, also! Eventually I began to believe I was still alive, and realized that he had won and brought the laurels to me in tribute.'

It was Fangio's worst accident, and kept him out of racing for many months. But he never gave a thought to retiring, despite being already 42.

'My injuries were the most serious I ever suffered,

but morally my worst accident was at one of the long-distance races, in Peru in 1948. We went off the road and tumbled down a mountainside. Daniel Urrutia, my co-driver, was thrown out. When I found him, he was dying.

'Morally that was my worst experience. He was my best friend, and I thought for a while I would stop racing. But after the Monza accident I couldn't wait to get well so I could race again. It was completely different. But both times I crashed for the same reason, fatigue.'

In the course of his career, in fact, Fangio had very few accidents, his peerless ability keeping him from disaster many times. He still does not really understand how he steered his Mercedes through the holocaust of Le Mans in 1955 — 'There was green paint from Hawthorn's Jaguar on my car afterwards . . .'

There was also his avoidance of the carnage at Tabac in the Monaco Grand Prix of 1950, the incident which prompted the 'reconstruction' at Rampoldi's. Fangio led from the start, followed by Villoresi, but behind them was chaos as Farina spun. In an instant nearly a dozen cars were involved, the road blocked. On round his next lap rushed the Argentine, unaware of the commotion behind. As the Alfa sped on down to Tabac and apparent calamity, Fangio suddenly hit the brakes and stopped just short of the road block. Yet the accident had been out of his sight. It seemed like sixth sense.

'No, no', he shrugged, making light of it. 'It wasn't like that, really. I was lucky. There had been a similar accident in 1936, and I happened to see a photograph of it the day before the race. As I came out of the chicane I was aware of something different with the crowd — a different colour. I was leading, but they were not watching me. They were looking down the road. Instead of their faces, I was seeing the backs of their heads. So something at Tabac was more interesting than the leader — and then I remembered that photograph and braked as hard as I could . . .'

In the Italian Grand Prix of 1953 Fangio fought a pitched battle for the entire race with the Ferraris of Ascari and Farina. For much of the race his protégé and Maserati team mate, Onofre Marimon, was also involved. At the last corner of the last lap Ascari spun, involving both Farina and Marimon. Fangio, as usual, calmly made it through to win. But his abiding memory is of another incident altogether, and he remembers it with relish.

'My Maserati had a terrible vibration all through practice, and could not be cured. In every team I drove for, I always made sure of having the mechanics on my side. Whatever I win, I would tell them, you will get ten per cent. The night before Monza I again complained of the vibration, and for the race the car was suddenly cured!

'I have no idea how they solved the problem,' he chuckles ingenuously, 'but I know Bonetto's teeth fell out during the race . . .'

When Mercedes-Benz decided to return to racing,

The essence of calm and ease. Fangio rounds the old Gasworks Hairpin during the 1955 Monaco Grand Prix, securely in the lead with the Mercedes-Benz W196. In twelve Grandes Epreuves for the German team, however, this was his only retirement!

At Monaco in 1956 there were those who doubted that it really was Fangio in that familiar helmet. In the Lancia-Ferrari, here sliding at Massenet, he drove with uncharacteristic fury in his pursuit of Moss.

team manager Alfred Neubauer lost no time in signing Fangio. The reappearance of the Three Pointed Star was brief but devastating. It began at Reims in 1954, where three cars — all with 'sports car' bodywork — were entered. Fangio and team mate Kling cantered away from the field, which variously crashed or blew up in their wake. Every other Grand Prix car was suddenly obsolete.

'Well, with Mercedes there was always peace of mind. I drove twelve Grands Prix for them, with eight wins, one second, one third, one fourth and one retirement. They were amazingly strong, those cars.'

In terms of sophistication Mercedes were light-years clear of the opposition. Features such as cockpit-controlled rear shock-absorbers were hardly standard practice in the fifties. In 1954-55 Fangio was untouchable, and when Moss joined the team the two men frequently toured round at the front. Only at Aintree did the Englishman finish ahead, and Stirling says he has never really known whether or not Fangio simply allowed him to win. I mentioned it, and Fangio smiled.

'I don't think I could have won, even if I had wanted to. Moss was really pushing that day, and his car had a higher final drive than mine. It was quicker.'

There was no lack of conviction in his voice, but at the same time I was left with the impression that here was another example of the generous spirit which made 'El Chueco' the idol of his fellow drivers as well as the spectators.

On only one other occasion was he ever 'beaten' by another Mercedes driver in a Formula 1 race: at Avus in 1954 he finished a close second in the Berlin Grand Prix after leading for a long time. It can have been no coincidence that the winner was Kling, a German on home ground. Mercedes, remember, came back to Grand Prix racing to revive sagging sales on the automobile markets of the world. Public relations, whatever you may believe, is not a recent phenomenon.

Their purpose achieved, the Mercedes directors promptly withdrew the company from racing at the end of 1955, and Fangio went to Ferrari for a season which brought more success — a fourth World Championship — but little in the way of pleasure. He was never a political animal, working at his best in a relaxed and secure atmosphere. And in 1956 the Ferrari camp provided anything but that, positively encouraging rivalry between the drivers. If Fangio was supposedly the team leader, he had at his heels three young and determined chargers, Castellotti, Musso and Collins. All of whom worshipped him.

'Well, I must say the year with Ferrari was not happy, no. I never felt comfortable there, although I was on very good terms with all the drivers. The team manager I did not like. I had always had a mechanic exclusively on my car, but Ferrari had a different system. Halfway through the season I was able to arrange it, and then everything was much better. I won in England — for the first and only time — and on the Nurburgring . . .'

In 1956, of course, Scuderia Ferrari ran the brutish side-tank cars handed over to them by Lancia, who had abandoned racing soon after the death of Ascari a year earlier. Throughout the year they were officially billed as 'Lancia-Ferraris', but Fangio was at some pains to stress that, in his eyes, they were Lancias merely run by Ferrari. Clearly he has admiration for Maranello, but little affection.

Fangio thrived on oversteer, another reason for his general discontent with the Lancia-Ferrari, which always showed a pronounced reluctance to follow its front wheels. When the tail of the car finally broke away, it did so viciously.

For Monte Carlo it was far from the ideal machine, and at the Grand Prix in 1956 Fangio did not drive like Fangio. In terms of stamina and pace, the dimensions of his drive were staggering. But it was not like Fangio. He spun on oil at Ste Dévote on the first lap, taking off Musso and Schell. Catching up, he damaged the nose of his car against Collins's Ferrari. And, having got up to second again, he hit the wall at Tabac.

His own Ferrari now reduced almost to wreckage, Fangio stopped and took over from Collins, rejoining the race a minute and a half behind the leader, Moss. His pursuit of the Maserati was almost frightening, and only genius fended off disaster. He was on the edge of an accident for two hours. At the flag he was but six seconds behind.

'It was maybe the strongest race I ever drove. Even in those days, you know it was difficult to overtake at Monaco. And I did overtake a few, I can tell you . . .

'Many people have said it was not Fangio in the car that day, but they don't know what was going on in the car! For me it was the fastest way around that track in that car. May not have been pretty to watch, but it *was* the quickest way.'

For 1957 Fangio rejoined Maserati, with Moss moving on to Vanwall. It was a year of triumph for both men, Stirling giving Britain real Grand Prix success at last, Juan Manuel showing himself, at 46, still to be the best. Between them they won all the Grandes Epreuves that season.

Fangio, back in a car he could bend precisely to his will, was at his greatest and won the first three races of the year. Thereafter the power advantage of the Vanwall was usually too much for the Maserati, but the German Grand Prix produced what is generally regarded as Fangio's day of days.

The art of throttle control, seen here at Silverstone's Copse Corner in 1956. No, the Lancia-Ferrari did *not* clout the wall . . .

Fangio's last season was perhaps his greatest, and made him World Champion for the fifth time. Here he is, early in 1957, with Maserati team mate Behra, after they had won the Sebring 12 Hours.

The facts are too well documented to bear detailed repetition here. Suffice it to say that, after a long pit stop, Fangio made up well over a minute on the leading Ferraris of Hawthorn and Collins, breaking the Nurburgring lap record ten times on the way. The year before he had left it at 9 minutes 41.6 seconds. He had taken pole position with the 250F at 9 minutes 25.6 seconds, but in the race he finally put in a shattering lap of 9 minutes 17.4 seconds, taking the lead on the penultimate lap.

'Even now', he said, suddenly sitting up, 'I can feel fear when I think of that race. I knew what I had done, the chances I had taken. Without any doubt, the Nurburgring was my favourite circuit. I loved it, all of it, and I think that day I conquered it. On another day it might have conquered me, who knows? But I believe that day I took myself and my car to the limit, and perhaps a little bit more. I had never driven like that before, and knew I never would again. Aye, that Maserati . . . not very powerful, but beautifully

balanced, a lovely car to drive. I felt I could do anything with it . . .'

At Monza he and team mate Behra fought a rich battle with the Vanwalls of Moss, Brooks and Lewis-Evans, and again here was Fangio at his most majestic. On this ultra-fast circuit the Italian cars were not truly a match for the British trio. Tony Brooks says he learned a great deal that day.

'It was a wonderful place to race at that time, with none of these silly chicanes all over the place. Many of the corners were very quick — but not completely flat out. The Curva Grande was especially nice. We'd approach at about 175, I suppose, dab the brakes and go through at about 160.

'I thought I was taking this corner pretty quickly, and in the early stages I was dicing with Fangio for the lead. First time through, touch the brakes, turn in — *wham!* Fangio goes by on the inside, oversteering it on the throttle! Later in the lap I got past again, then next time into the corner — *wham!* Exactly the same thing again.

At Rouen in 1957 Juan Manuel was absolutely in a class of his own, so far ahead as to be able to indulge himself through the Rouen curves, steering the 250F largely on the throttle.

I don't know, maybe he wasn't braking at all . . .'

Everything changed at the end of 1957. Maserati, after a series of crippling financial blows, announced their retirement from racing. Later a skeleton programme was devised, this a matter of developing a lightweight 250F. If all went well, Fangio agreed, he would drive the car in four or five races. After many delays the new car appeared finally at Reims for the French Grand Prix.

'The clutch broke after only a few laps,' Fangio smiles with a touch of melancholy. 'I remember it was full of holes, that pedal, for lightness. I came into the pits and handed it to them! But they pleaded with me to carry on, so I went out again. It was very hard to drive like that, but I think I finished fourth. I remember feeling sorry for the crowds because I suppose some of them had come to see me race, and here I was, apparently driving like a beginner.

'But lots of other things were going through my mind — which should not happen during a race! I was thinking back over my career. I had intended to come to Europe for one year only, and never expected to win any races. Now I had raced Formula 1 for ten years, and suddenly I thought I was stupid to carry on doing it. I was already 46 years old and had accomplished a lot.

'All these things were in my mind that afternoon at Reims. When the race was over I got out of the car and said to my mechanic, "It is finished".'

Another Grand Prix career came to an end that same day, for Luigi Musso lost his life in an accident on the second lap. There were suggestions at the time that this played a part in Fangio's resolution to quit, but he says not.

'No, no, not at all. I saw the accident, but I did not know that Musso had died. My mind was made up before the end of the race, before I found out. You must in any case remember that during my time as a Grand Prix driver thirty men died. Always I was very sad, but I could not let it influence me. When another driver dies, you always believe he made a mistake, nothing more or less. Therefore it was necessary to concentrate on not making mistakes. If you think you are going to die in the next race, it is better not to race at all.

'I was never tempted to return afterwards. I was very tired, very content and I did not miss it. I loved my years in *Formula Uno*, but there had been great sacrifices — necessary if you are to remain on top, but sacrifices nevertheless. Racing is beautiful when you are full of enthusiasm, but when it becomes work you should quit. By the end of 1957 it was becoming work for me.'

Fangio enjoys his life today as much as ever. As President of Mercedes-Benz Argentina, he maintains a strong link with the company which enjoyed so many great days at his hand. At home he is a folk hero in the purest sense, and everywhere his name is spoken by racing people with what amounts to reverence.

'I know what these people are expecting of me,' he sighed as he looked out over Donington shortly before his demonstration in the Mercedes W125, 'and I just hope I have the nerve to do it.' At the end of an awesome display he came down the pit lane as he always did, cutting the engine and nonchalantly lifting his goggles with both hands before braking to a halt. He was 68, and it was still so easy . . .

ALAN JONES
My way

'There have been ups and downs', Keke Rosberg said of his four years with Williams. 'I joined the team after it had been through three great seasons — the tail end of the Cosworth era. And I got the drive because Jones had left too late for them to find another superstar for 1982. I think they felt they'd had enough of being messed around by drivers, and at the same time I felt they never really forgave me for not being Alan Jones . . .'

Williams-Head-Jones. Frank may rail against it, beat the drum that racing drivers are employees, nothing more, but the fact remains that the phoenix which rose in Didcot during the late seventies had three heads. Williams organized, Head designed, Jones drove. They sparked each other. Success was new and heady, the more so since it wildly exceeded any expectations.

'I can't say I saw Alan as a future World Champion when he joined us,' Frank says, 'and, by the same token, I'm quite sure he didn't see it in us. There was nothing in our past records to suggest it. What we needed for 1978 was a good, sensible, driver, who would finish regularly in the points. And that's what I thought I was getting. It was the same with Patrick. When I split with Walter Wolf, I decided he was the guy to have with me because he was the best available. That was all. I simply didn't appreciate his talents at that time. By the fourth race of the year — Long Beach — there was Alan in Patrick's first F1 car, FW06, pushing Reutemann's Ferrari for the lead. And then it began to dawn on me: "What have we got here?" It really was a revelation . . .'

Jones later hit trouble, as he was to do nearly every time out that summer, but he also was aware that something rather special was happening, something worth cultivating. He gave no thought to other offers at the end of the season.

'I'd previously driven for Graham Hill and John Surtees — and hated it', he says. 'I'd admired them as drivers, but both thought they were still drivers. They knew it all — they'd been there. There was nothing you could tell them.

'Then I had a reasonable year with Shadow, who took me on after poor Tom Pryce was killed. I even won my first Grand Prix with them, in Austria, but it was a bit of a fluke. The car was so heavy and slow in a straight line — if it had been a dry day we wouldn't have had a look-in . . .'

Until the start of the Williams era, I have to admit, my opinion of Alan's ability was much the same as Frank's. I saw him win at Zeltweg, and was impressed, as I had been by his drive in the Surtees at the Race of Champions in 1976. But at the back of my mind for a long time was the image of Tony Brise, Jones's team mate in the Hill days, shaking his fist and trying to lap him at Zandvoort in the rain. A novice Grand Prix driver is not easy to evaluate, unless he bounces lucky straight into a competitive car, a known quantity.

Compare, for example, the opinions of two former World Champions (admittedly a pair who rarely agree about anything). Stewart: 'I always liked Alan's driving very much indeed. He was forceful and intelligent in a car. I thought his natural ability was high.' Hunt: 'Overall he had a strong hand, but I wouldn't say he was the quickest guy around. He had a first class "motor racing brain", and always did a workmanlike job. But he wasn't the type who attracted attention from the day he arrived — he was never a natural super-talent.'

Whoever had doubts about Jones, however, Alan himself had none. From very early days he saw himself as a future World Champion, and through 1978 the Williams team fell into line with him. It was the year of the Lotus 79, the dawn of ground effect, obliging everyone to proceed down Chapman's path the following season.

So came FW07, one of history's great cars. By mid-season in 1979 it was the thing to have, Jones a likely winner every time out. One of racing's great ironies, though, was that its initial victory — Frank's first in eleven seasons of Formula 1 — was scored by Clay Regazzoni, who took over at Silverstone when Alan retired from a massive lead.

At that stage of the year Jones was immensely frustrated. Electrical problems had robbed him of the Belgian Grand Prix. At Dijon his fourth place grid position had been disallowed (officials claiming he had ignored a yellow flag), and this fuelled an already considerable animosity towards the French. On the pace everywhere, he had but seven points to show for it, and was becoming mighty irascible. 'Why are Australian racing drivers so well-balanced?' went a paddock joke of the time. Answer: 'Because they have chips on both shoulders'.

Alan himself later agreed. 'It's true, I was developing a bit of a persecution complex just then. I was burning to start winning races. The car could do it, and I knew I could do it, but something always seemed to go wrong.' The dam burst, finally, at Hockenheim two weeks later, not even a deflating tyre keeping Jones from victory. Then he won at Zeltweg, then at Zandvoort . . . During that period, indeed, his only

true opposition came from Villeneuve, the two men forging a bond of mutual respect through a series of classic battles, none better than that in Montreal, where the rest were incidental to the day.

Alan finished 1979 with four wins, more than anyone else, and all the Williams impetus went into ensuring his title the following year. And, as with Andretti in 1978 and Prost in 1985, justice was done. This time Jones took five, although Piquet ran him close.

'The win that meant most to him — to all of us — was in France,' Patrick Head relates with a smile. 'He's such a hard, competitive, animal in a racing car, and he really wanted that one. That business in Dijon the year before still needled him . . .'

'It was my best drive of the year,' Alan agreed. 'The Ligiers were definitely quicker at Ricard, and I won by keeping pressure on them, forcing them to screw their tyres. I love doing that, wearing someone down, inching up on them. It's really satisfying to know that what you're doing, lap after lap, is working. I had no personal grudge against Laffite and Pironi, but they were French in France . . .' To salt the wound, he waved a huge Union Jack from the cockpit on his lap of honour.

For me, though, 1981 was his greatest season, one

Mixed weather gave Jones the opportunity for an unexpected first victory, at the Osterreichring in 1977. This was Shadow's only Grand Prix win.

The second half of the 1979 season essentially trimmed down to a battle between Alan and Gilles Villeneuve. Here they are on the rostrum after a memorable fight in Montreal. A contented Regazzoni was third.

which should have brought him another World Championship. When they win the title, some drivers are blunted for a while, subconsciously relaxing that fraction which is the difference between winning and not. But this never happened to Jones. Indeed, we had seen that at the end of the previous year. He had locked up the championship at Montreal, but only a week later was stupendous at Watkins Glen. Off the road at the first corner, 12th at the end of the opening lap, yet into the lead soon after half-distance. A few laps from the end, for the hell of it, he set fastest lap. It was quicker than he had managed in qualifying . . .

That pace, that style, continued through the following year, and it says everything about Alan's strength of character that his driving was quite unaffected by two personal feuds, one with Piquet, the other with his own team mate.

'I'd never wanted Reutemann there in the first place,' he says, disarmingly straight as usual. 'We'd had a great year in '79 with Clay. He'd got a bundle of points for Frank, and he was totally unpolitical, quite content to be number two and good fun to be with. I really

liked him. When you've got a good picture on the TV set, why the hell change it?'

The two men had only their profession in common, and in this their styles were very different. Reutemann would go for the win on points, Jones always for the KO. Had I been choosing one to race for my life, I would have gone unhesitatingly for Alan and his Marciano approach.

They went through their first season together with a certain coolness, but no real animosity. 'The only thing was,' Jones mutters, 'that I got pissed off with people saying how much he'd helped me win the championship. In fact, it was quite the reverse. Lots of times I was annoyed when he just gave up, when I felt he should have been taking points from Piquet or something.'

Then came Rio, in early 1981. In the rain the Williams pair ran 1-2 throughout, Reutemann in front. Under the terms of his contract Carlos should have allowed Alan through, but in the closing stages the Argentine thought it through, and decided he wanted to be first. For the sake of appearances, Jones

The 1980 World Championship belonged to Jones and Williams throughout the year, and they clinched it properly, with victory in the Canadian Grand Prix.

perfunctorily shook his hand afterwards, but declined to join him on the rostrum. Privately, he raged.

'I'd like to think that when you shake hands and sign contracts on a cold December morning, the other guy doesn't pretend a couple of months later that it never happened. If he didn't like his contract, he shouldn't have signed it. If the same circumstances arise again, well, I wouldn't want to be Frank Williams, that's all. It's his problem, not mine.'

Considering the state of play between them, you might have expected Jones to erupt when he and Reutemann tangled on the first lap at Imola, Alan then having to stop for a new front wing. Not a bit of it. 'He chopped me, yes, but he had the line. It was fair enough.' That inclined you to take him as a man of his word.

This was the thing about Alan, you always knew exactly where you stood. If ever I wrote something which annoyed him, I'd know about it at the next race, which is far preferable to the sulkiness you get from some people. I know of no one indifferent to Jones. For a while I thought him truculent and overbearing, but eventually came to like him very much, not least because laughter is often hard to find in a Formula 1 paddock. Alan's one-liners scythe cleanly through flannel and cant. 'About as much use as an ashtray on a motorbike', he would say of one particular PR man.

Off hand Jones can certainly be when riled, but I remember an incident at Heathrow one evening, which served as a reminder that the world does not revolve around Grand Prix racing. We had recently landed after the flight from Amsterdam, and were waiting for our luggage. Hovering was one of those survey ladies, complete with clipboard.

'Where have you come from, sir?' she asked Jones.
'Er, where was it? Holland . . . yes, Holland.'
'And where is your place of residence?'
'Switzerland.'
'And the purpose of your visit to Holland?'
'Business.'

So it went on. The lady had no idea she was addressing the World Champion. I can think of holders of that title who would have ignored her, but Alan was patient and courteous, never giving any indication of who he was or what he did. 'My old man always drilled into me that good manners cost nothing — although if someone upset him he was quick with his fists, and that's something else I've inherited from him . . .'

As a driver Jones was always a raw competitor, one of those who habitually raced better than he qualified. More, he could make anger work *for* him, channel it into something productive. I happened to be in the Williams pit towards the end of practice at Zolder in 1980. Pironi was fastest, and Jones failed to come round. Finally he arrived on foot, disgruntled. His

The Didcot Triumvirate: Head, Williams, Jones. This is practice at Monza in 1980.

'No, really, Carlos and I are friends, (it says here) . . . ' A publicity shot to smooth troubled waters after the Rio controversy in 1981.

engine had cut out, and he looked around for the spare car. Had there been time, they would probably have drawn lots to decide who should break the news that Reutemann was out in it . . .

By the time Carlos came in to hand over, Alan was about ready to get the pole on foot, standing there like a bull in a pen as the mechanics swapped seat and numbers. There was time just for a couple of quick laps, and the second did the job.

He is a man of immense mental, as well as physical, toughness, and we saw that throughout 1981 as he dealt with Piquet and Reutemann. The grudge match with Nelson had its foundations at Montreal the previous autumn. There the two were to settle the championship, and at the first corner they touched. Now, at Zolder, the same thing happened, putting the Brazilian out. Piquet was almost apoplectic as he got back to the pits. What he wasn't going to do to Jones . . .

Alan, predictably, brushed the matter aside. 'It's just hysteria, isn't it? And you've got to remember he's a Latin. If I was upset with him, I'd tell him to his face, not do it through the press. To be honest, though, I

couldn't really care less. I haven't got time to mess with the Piquets of this world . . .'

Whoever encouraged Nelson in this line did him no service. If it were an attempt at intimidation, it was misplaced when aimed at a man like Jones. It did nothing to unsettle the Australian, merely ensured that if he could humiliate Piquet, he would do so. At Monaco he got the chance, sitting on the tail of the Brabham for a dozen chilling laps. In his anxiety, Nelson got more and more ragged, finally misjudging a lapping manoeuvre and sliding into a barrier. 'What's more,' Alan grinned maliciously afterwards, 'he'd hit the wall four times before he finally went off . . .' 'Don't fool with me', seemed to be the message.

Later in the race Alan was slowed by a mysterious misfire, which lost him the race. At Hockenheim it recurred, with similar result, and if ever there was visible evidence of a racing driver's ambition thwarted we saw it there. After the race Jones strode, face set, to the Mercedes waiting to take him to the airport. From some distance he hurled his leather briefcase into the open boot. I decided against chatting to him just then.

In Austria, though, he was very talkative, and in a manner which deeply upset his boss. 'Goodyear are letting us down — we need some proper qualifiers. If it was up to me, I'd go back to Michelin tomorrow . . .' Such remarks are often made by drivers to journalists, but invariably prefaced by 'off the record', or 'don't quote me'. 'Write it', Jones said. 'It might get someone angry — and then something might get done about it . . .'

That same day he spoke of an increasing disenchantment with Formula 1. 'They've allowed the cars to degenerate into bloody go-karts. To be honest, I just dread getting in these days, getting bounced all over the place, banging my head and spine. I don't enjoy racing these things at all. In fact, if they don't change the rules, I doubt that I'll continue.'

Many of them were saying that just then, but Alan, it transpired, was serious. At Monza the atmosphere in the Williams camp was on the frosty side, Frank and Patrick not at all amused that their number one driver had arrived with his right hand heavily bandaged: 'Just let's say it was, er, the result of an

Jones's Formula 1 return in 1986 was not a success. Here in Austria (about to be passed by Johansson's Ferrari), he finished fourth — but two laps down. The horsepower just wasn't there.

altercation with some black gentlemen in Chiswick High Road the other night. One of my fingers is broken, and I got kicked over fairly thoroughly from head to toe. I was outnumbered, but I think I gave a pretty good account of myself . . .' For all his discomfort, he drove beautifully to second in the race.

The chief reason for the coolness between management and driver, though, became apparent only a few days later, when Jones announced his retirement. 'I told Frank when I arrived at Monza — and I know I should have done it earlier. Problem was, every time I'd pick up the 'phone to tell him, I'd get butterflies and hang up! It wasn't that I was scared of facing the wrath of Frank, but because I just didn't want to face the decision.'

'Alan's indecisiveness always amazed me', Williams says. 'In a car he was incredibly positive, but out of it just the opposite. I told him to go home after the race and think it out, be sure he wasn't making a purely emotional decision.'

'That's exactly what it turned out to be', Alan recalls. 'It was my boy's birthday on the Monday. We all had party hats on and everything — and then it started to piss down! We had to go inside, and I thought, "Oh, bugger it, at least if we were in Australia now we could stay outside . . ."'

Jones being Jones, though, he wanted to finish on a high note. At Vegas he decided to go for it, and he led all the way. This was the day of Reutemann versus Piquet for the championship.

'Who are you rooting for?' I facetiously asked.

'Anyone but those two', was the prompt reply. 'I couldn't care less.'

'Will you help Carlos?' asked an American innocent.

'Of course I will', Alan said, his voice serious. A pause, then a giggle. 'I'll help him just as much as he helped me last year . . .'

I remember, too, the post-race interview with a very self-important Mark Thatcher, hired by NBC for the weekend. 'Did tyres play an important part today?'

'Oh, absolutely,' Jones replied. 'You see, they keep the wheels from touching the ground . . .'

Then he went home to Australia, to work on his farm, drink beer, barbecue steaks and live the good life that he believed was passing him by. I doubt that Frank and Patrick will ever allow another driver to become so central to the team. They were shattered when he quit, livid with him for what they considered a gross lack of consideration, and also sad that the triumvirate was being broken up. They loved going racing with Alan.

He is a restless soul, though, always on the move, easily bored. Back home he raced saloons and sports cars 'for fun', but found no satisfaction in it. 'I should have known better, I suppose. As soon as I've got my bum in a car, I only know how to try hard, close to ten-tenths, and I found I needed the professionalism that goes with topline racing. My attitude to Australia hasn't changed — I still think it's the best place on earth. But racing cars still aren't out of my system, and for racing cars you must come to Europe.'

There was a half-hearted return in early 1983, but it petered out when Arrows lost their expected sponsorship. Alan had no interest, he said, unless the team was in a position to compete at the top level. Eighteen months later, though, came another offer, and this time he was convinced.

'I've raced for Carl Haas before, in the CanAm, and I always said that his operation impressed me in the same way Frank's did. We've got the budget, and we've got the Ford engine. Carl will do whatever it takes to win, no worries on that score.'

The Hart-powered car, a temporary expedient for the last few races of 1985, was something of a disaster. And the following year, now with Ford's uncompetitive V6 turbo, Jones eventually lost complete heart with the Haas project, reviving suggestions he was bored, only back for the gelt. Even if there were a kernel of truth in both theories, Alan was still a prisoner of his own character. A *racer*.

And to the end the cynical humour remained out of PR reach. Jones would never suffer in silence. 'Could I interview you tomorrow?' asked a local journalist in the pits at Kyalami. 'Sure,' Alan said. 'Let's think, what time does the race start? Two-thirty? Right, I'll see you here about quarter to three . . .'

NIKI LAUDA
Short retirement urges sweet return

The old press room at Zeltweg was not a popular place. A tent — even one of circus proportions — without air conditioning could be immensely trying on one of those torpid August afternoons in Styria. I always preferred to work, typewriter on knees, in the car. At least you could wind down the windows. It was with relief, therefore, that we arrived for the 1985 race at the Osterreichring to discover a new purpose-built press centre in the paddock. And it was with curiosity that we saw on the notice board a request to present ourselves on Saturday morning for a Lauda press conference.

A Lauda *press conference?* Down all the years no one could remember such a thing. Formal gatherings were not Niki's way, never had been. What could he have to tell us? For some time there had been growing whispers that he was retiring again, but Lauda, surely, wasn't one to make an official announcement — especially not in Austria, where local journalists already hounded him as a matter of course. No, no, couldn't be that. If he were stopping, it would be like last time; step from the car, off with the helmet and on with the cap, that's it, finish — except that the one constant through Niki's twelve seasons at the top level had been his unpredictability. Who knew what he had in mind?

One journalist with a split personality — or, at least, a moonlighting *nom de plume* — had the luxury of hedging his bets, confidently predicting in one of his papers that Lauda would confirm the retirement rumours, in the other than he would refute them. Unhappily, the way the cards fell, his *alter ego* scooped him . . .

Niki did indeed announce that he would quit at season's end. 'I've devoted all these years of my life to the fascination of driving Formula 1 cars, which I still love. But this year I have the feeling of repeating myself, of not being able to find fresh motivation. So

I've decided it's time to do something else.' There followed a few words about Lauda Air, and the plans to expand it, and he concluded by thanking everyone from Ron Dennis down.

This he carried off with quiet dignity and style, if with typical lack of outward emotion. And at the end, from this usually cynical and world-weary gathering, there was a round of spontaneous and respectful applause. There is great affection for Niki, and the moment was briefly moving.

It was swept away by the nasal tones of his team owner. This being, in his opinion, a personal matter, Lauda had not wanted Ron Dennis at his press conference, but eventually shrugged and relented. Now Ron was asked for his comments, and for a couple of minutes we listened in embarrassed silence. This, we had thought, was supposed to be Niki's day.

Rather than pay tribute to a great driver, rather than thank him for a not inconsiderable part in building up McLaren International, for four years' work, several Grand Prix victories and a World Championship, Dennis chose instead to rebuke Lauda for paying insufficient tribute to John Barnard — 'the principle reason for our success last year . . .'

Yes, but what about Niki, and his retirement? 'We operate McLaren International principally to win Grands Prix, and next year we'll certainly have two drivers capable of doing that.'

Yes, but . . .

The moment was gone. Lauda made no visible response, and continued to answer questions. As he strode to the pits afterwards, however, he was bristling, most words in his conversation held down to four letters.

Through most of the 1985 season it appeared that Niki's driving had lost its bite. Never a good qualifier in the turbo era, he started the races far away from team mate Prost, and poor reliability — his car seemed

First year with Ferrari. Lauda wonders where Ickx is during the 1974 Race of Champions at Brands Hatch. A lap later the Lotus took the lead, and kept it.

to have a monopoly on McLaren problems — kept him from his forte, the stealthy and relentless climb up the lap chart. 'I wonder', Clay Regazzoni said to me that morning in Austria, 'what effect his anger will have on his driving. Will he take it into the car with him?'

Apparently he did, although, Lauda being Lauda, it was managed with discipline, channelled into something constructive. As well as that, there was perhaps the lightness of heart which comes from a major decision finally taken. Niki was going into the last half-dozen races of his career, and he wanted them to be good. That day he qualified third, and in the race was leading when a turbo failed.

'I want Prost to win the championship this year, and if I can do anything to help him at the end of the season, I will.' Lauda said that before the notorious press conference, and I wondered if the offer held good afterwards. He, after all, well knew that Dennis and Barnard wanted nothing more than a smooth run through to the title for Alain. And Niki could be bloody-minded . . .

'No, no, I wouldn't take it out on him,' he said, 'but it's not the end of the season yet, is it? For the moment, I want to win. Anyway, nothing has changed. For sure they very much wanted Prost to win the championship in '84. I felt that throughout the season, particularly in the last few races, after they knew I'd been talking to Renault. But I'm quite sure they never gave him any advantage with equipment. I think maybe they thought if he won, it would be a championship for McLaren, and if I did, it would be a championship for Lauda.'

Seething he might have been about Dennis's manners, but Niki had nothing but praise for his abilities. 'Ron was a mechanic, remember, and now he owns a team. He's come a long way, and he's a fantastic organizer — you know, getting Marlboro to sponsor him, getting TAG to pay for the Porsche engine, getting this, getting that. But not an easy man to work with. McLaren is not a team like Brabham, where everyone likes everyone else . . .'

A week later we went to Zandvoort, and in years to come people consulting reference books will see it as another McLaren benefit, Lauda heading Prost over the line by a couple of tenths. Why, didn't Andretti and Peterson do the same for Lotus in 1978? But behind similar results lay very different stories. Where Ronnie had played an obedient follow-my-leader role, Alain pulled every stunt he knew to get by.

True enough, he should have won, but a bodged tyre change had put him well behind. When Prost starts putting wheels in the dirt, you know he is trying very seriously indeed, but for the last eight laps Lauda held him at bay. Over the line they were separated by two tenths. And three points.

Niki's first win at Zandvoort had been rather more straightforward. As I watched him, the old Rat, up on the rostrum, grinning toothily, I thought back to that baking June day in 1974, to the young charger, baby-faced and unscarred, who was always in such a hurry then, eager and intense. He had led all the way, with Regga behind him in the other Ferrari.

Hard to believe now, but at that time Lauda was considered headstrong. The year brought nine pole positions, but only a couple of wins. At the Nurburgring he tried to put a move on Scheckter within a mile of the start, misjudged it and crashed. At Brands Hatch he pressed on in the lead, trying to

put a worsening rear puncture from his mind, and lost everything by pitting too late. At Mosport he lost certain victory in the closing laps when he registered too late there was dirt on the road.

The situation at Ferrari in 1974, indeed, was not dissimilar to that five years later. On each occasion we had a number two — in name, anyway — who was quicker than the team leader, but made more mistakes. And just as Jody finished up with more points than Gilles, so it was with Clay and Niki.

In 1975 Lauda equalled his own seasonal pole record (which still stands today, and probably for ever), but by now had become The Man. There was hardly a reasonable doubt that he was going to win the championship. The best driver was in the best car, and day follows night. He was untouchable, often reducing Grands Prix to Clark-like demonstrations.

It is a remarkable fact that, although Niki's 24 pole positions stand him third in the all-time list, all but one were set in his Ferrari years. 'Sure, the way we parted was not so nice,' he says now, 'but I don't remember Ferrari with any bad feelings now. I enjoyed my last season there the least — even though I won my

The story of the 1975 Formula 1 season: Lauda's 312T in front, the rest nowhere. This is the beginning of the second lap at Paul Ricard.

Six weeks after the horror at the 'Ring in 1976, Lauda, far from healed, somehow willed himself to return at Monza. He finished — astoundingly — in the points.

second championship. I was still upset with them for their attitude to me after the accident. Plus, I was happy with Clay as my team mate, and I didn't want Reutemann there.'

Lauda has mellowed these few years past. Early in 1977 I asked him about his new team mate. Was he looking upon Carlos as team mate or rival? 'Neither', was the swift answer, accompanied by a withering expression. They most assuredly did not hit it off. 'That year,' he says, 'I wanted only to win the championship, prove to them they were wrong — that I could recover from the accident — and get out, find something fresh, a new challenge.'

This last has always been vital to Niki. When he first went there, Ferrari had been dabbling with 'English technology' for a year, and were completely out to lunch, 1973 perhaps their worst ever season. Lauda's enormous capacity for work, together with a genius for method, galvanized them. His ambition was rampant. He was going to win races, become World Champion, so *they* were going to have to take him there. And he turned Ferrari around, made it his team as few have ever done.

Once that peak had been climbed, he searched around for something new, something novel. And the prospect of Gordon Murray's Brabham BT46, even though saddled with the Alfa Romeo flat-12 'sports car' engine, completely seduced him. With surface air cooling, built-in jacks, digital instrumentation, boundless trick stuff, there were so many things to go wrong! So many things he could help to put right . . . For there has always lain Niki's chief interest in motor racing.

It can only have been this which drew him into talks with Renault towards the end of 1984. Why else would a man with the best car in the business be prepared to squander it? 'It was like when I went to Ferrari', Lauda commented at the time. 'All the ingredients for success were there, but they needed managing. I helped to get them out of the shit, and I thought maybe I could do the same for Renault.'

A McLaren team member put forward a supplementary motive; 'He was pretty sure he was going to win the championship, and knew what it would do to Ron if he took his number 1 somewhere else!'

Gallic leaks to the press — perhaps the consequences of interfaction rivalry in Renault Sport —

killed the deal when it was close to signature, and elicited a classic response from the Rat: 'If Renault prepare their cars as well as they keep a confidence, I'm not surprised they haven't won a race this year . . .'

Had Niki gone to Renault, it is conceivable that neither team nor driver would have quit at the end of 1985. They might have made fine progress together, and in that event Lauda, certainly, would have been unwilling to leave a job half done. After climbing the summit in 1984, though, it was always doubtful that another year with basically unchanged McLaren chassis and Porsche engine would sustain his interest. The same ingredients had taken him to the title. Where was the impetus for another year?

I always had a pet theory that one contributory factor in Niki's 'instant' retirement in 1979 may have been that Murray's new car, the Cosworth-powered Brabham BT49, did nothing to excite him. It was clearly going to be the business, but essentially it was, well, mainstream. 'Often I had imagined that I might leave racing quickly, that it might suddenly seem pointless and boring,' he says, 'and, that morning in

Canada, it did . . .'

In the space of four months, then, Hunt and Lauda — the class of '76 — were gone from the sport, and it was in keeping that each left untidily, both being men who made their own rules, lived by no sort of convention. James had gone at mid-season, but Niki took the process a step further, quitting in the middle of a race weekend. He drove the BT49 during the first session at Montreal, then changed into civvies and announced he was off, leaving Bernie Ecclestone temporarily speechless.

Typically, he also left behind accoutrements such as helmet and overalls, items for which other men might have had a sentimental regard. But who needed them for flying, for running an airline? That was Lauda's future, and the future alone concerns him. It has always been that way. Silver cups went to a local garage in exchange for free car washes. Some were pressed into service as food bowls for his beloved dog. The only trophy in the house, indeed, is that from Jarama in 1974, his first Grand Prix win, and he denies any emotional attachment to it, says that its size and

---

In the Brabham-Alfa at Monaco in 1979. An unsuccessful season, and a time when Niki was growing bored 'driving round in circles'. At Montreal he turned his back on racing.

shape make it handy as a vessel for paper clips and rubber bands. From anyone but Niki that would come false, pretentious even.

Sante Ghedini, for long a close friend, packed the driving suit and helmet in his luggage when he left Montreal. If Lauda had no use for sentimental props, he felt differently. And a couple of years later Niki rang to say could he borrow them back for a while?

'I couldn't believe what had happened to the cars during my two years away', he says of that first McLaren test at Donington. 'When I came back, ground effect was coming to its peak, and it amazed me that the car was so horrible to drive — in fact, they were not cars at that time, not in any real sense. There was no warning when the limit was reached, because you couldn't feel any change in the car. If anything happened to alter the airflow under the car, it went crazy. This wasn't driving — not when your head was being smashed around, when you aimed at the apex and then hoped for the best. You were looking at the road out of the corner of your eye, with hardly any field of vision . . .'. Still, he had made up his mind to return. 'I wasn't fit, but that was no problem, like making a racing car reliable is no problem. I knew Willy

Dungl could take care of it. More important was that I was still quick enough.'

Dungl you wouldn't invite to a dinner party. During the four seasons of his comeback Lauda's diet was something to make any normal person blanch, a balanced selection of what looked like baby food, which Niki would eat at precisely the moment decreed by his guru. And his face, as he ground his reluctant way through it, suggested that it looked better than it tasted. In the same way he has always abhorred training, finding his daily four-mile run hard and tedious.

Who, though, could argue with the results? Lauda may have looked emaciated, but it takes considerable strength to drive a modern Formula 1 car, and in that — perhaps aided by an easy and fluent style — he was never found wanting. His stamina, too, you took for granted.

'I did the Marlboro PR tour with Niki one year,' remembered Keke Rosberg, 'and I was mighty impressed. He did all the flying himself, and never seemed to get tired. The other extreme was John Watson, who looked about sixty years old by the end of the trip!'

Victory in the 1984 Italian Grand Prix was Lauda's fifth of the season, and seemed to put a lock on his third World Championship.

Estoril 1984. The protagonists — and team mates — shake hands before the championship decider. Prost took the race, but Lauda's second place gave him the title.

Those years away undoubtedly changed Lauda in subtle ways. Economic problems of the time hurt the airline, and he was also subjected to a witch hunt by the Austrian tax authorities. 'I used to think', he says now, 'that I could never live anywhere else, but that's changed. Now I'm happy in Ibiza, and there I'm going to stay.'

He came back, of course, to a season of trauma. At the opening race, Kyalami, we had the drivers' 'Superlicence' strike, and Niki, typically, was at the centre of it. He won convincingly at Long Beach — only his third race — but then came the 'water tanks' crisis, which led to the FOCA boycott of the San Marino Grand Prix.

Lauda has ever been his own man. His team may have been absent, but he turned up at Imola to make very plain his opinion that the FOCA teams were acting stupidly. This willingness to sacrifice tact for honesty tells much about the man. At Zolder he was shattered by the death of Villeneuve, a man to whom he had grown close. Unhesitatingly he described Gilles as the best driver in the world, and while others spoke blandly of 'a motor racing accident, just one of those things,' Niki suggested it had been Jochen Mass's responsibility to keep out of the way of a faster car. That, in many quarters, was beyond the pale. Easier to blame a dead man. Lauda saw it differently: 'I was asked for my opinion, and I gave it . . .'

We should not have been surprised. This was, after all, the same man who went his own way at Fuji in 1976, finding the appalling conditions unacceptable. After two laps he packed it in, thereby perhaps tossing away the World Championship. This was but three months after the Nurburgring accident, and Mauro Forghieri, maybe believing that Lauda's nerve was gone, suggested they announce engine failure or some

such. Niki was indignant, stood by what he had done. He didn't care what people thought, only what he knew.

When you speak of Lauda, you speak truly of a legend. In his presence you feel that strongly, remember where he has been, what he has done. Days of his life are clear in my mind. I remember a soaking day at Oulton Park in the spring of 1972, when he ran away with a Formula 2 race, while others floundered and spun; or the opening lap of the restarted British Grand Prix a year later, when sheer *chutzpah* put his BRM between Peterson and Stewart; or races in his 'second' career, like Silverstone and Zeltweg in '83, when pureness of style — the art of not scrubbing off speed — set him a class above the other Cosworth drivers; or pretty well any race in his third World Championship season of 1984, when he put guile and experience to work against the blinding pace of Prost.

I remember, too, that dreadful day at the 'Ring, and driving back to the ferry afterwards and listening to the radio and expecting to hear that he had died. Five weeks later came there rumours, scarcely credible, that he might run at Monza the following Sunday. And there he was, qualifying fifth, finishing fourth. I was in the Ferrari pit afterwards, watching in silence as he gingerly peeled his balaclava from the fresh wounds.

'He had no right to be driving there', Jackie Stewart said, 'because he was nowhere near healed. It was the most courageous thing I have ever witnessed in sport.' Niki, no doubt, would offer a more pragmatic explanation for that weekend, but none exists. Everything of the man I have seen since has been coloured by those few seconds in the pits at Monza. Which is why I was so riled in the press room at Zeltweg.

STIRLING MOSS
The racer pure

A few years ago, at an Alfa Romeo lunch in Milan, I found myself seated next to Griff Borgeson. We had not met before, and I knew him only as a writer of earnest, historical books about cars. Mr Borgeson is one of those rather serious-minded expatriate Americans who weigh their words before giving them voice. There was little levity through the meal, and I made recourse with increasing frequency to the Chianti.

Conversation, I seem to remember, got around to record breaking, in particular to MG's assault on Class F records at the Bonneville Salt Flats in 1957. And here I thought to spot a point of contact between us, for the drivers had been Stirling Moss and Phil Hill. What, I asked, were your impressions of Moss?

Mr Borgeson paused. 'Oh,' he said, after two or three courses, 'you can't expect me to answer a question like that. I mean, I'd want to think that through for quite a while before committing myself . . .'

I gave in then, and reached once more for the bottle. Mention of Stirling Moss usually guarantees a flood of anecdote.

He was always 'Stirling', wasn't he? — even to people who had never seen him race, nor wished to. His charisma reached far beyond the narrow world of motor racing. In April 1962, as he lay in hospital, battered and unconscious, broadcasts and front pages put aside mere political crises, earthquakes and strikes. Stirling Moss's life was in danger. At sixteen, I was among the countless who tremblingly awaited the latest bulletin from the Atkinson Morley Hospital.

In time, of course, Stirling recovered, and it was assumed that eventually he would return. Had he not, after all, broken his back at Spa in 1960, yet won in Sweden only six weeks later? Moss's love of competition was so strong that he would surely come back . . .

Perhaps, if it had been a little less of an obsession,

merely a means of making a good living and having fun, Stirling might have returned. But the perfectionist in him was dissatisfied. In May of 1963, away from the gaze of the press, he returned to Goodwood, went out in a Lotus 19 sports car, even turned in competitive times. But at the end he stepped out, his mind already made up. He would not race again.

'I went out and I did the times all right,' he remembers, 'but I realized that I'd done them purely by experience and know-how. When you're racing, everything — where you brake, turn in, squeeze the throttle and so on — has to be automatic. It had always been that way for me and now, suddenly, it wasn't. At that time my concentration had completely gone, you know, to the point that I could be having a conversation with someone, and forget what we were discussing.

'Now, at Goodwood I'd come into a corner, and everything was all right because I still had the ability to handle it. I knew what I was doing. But then I'd get out on to a straight, and find that I was looking at the side of the road or something. Then I'd look back ahead and — my God! — here's a corner! So I could see that I could kill myself quite easily. The times I did that day were in spite of the problem, not because the problem had been sorted out. And it would have been absolutely impossible for me to have concentrated for two or three hours in a race.

'So this was an intangible problem, you see, and that's what forced me to retire. To fight something you have to think about it, confront it, concentrate on it — which is precisely what I couldn't do . . .'

Moss says that his memory has never been particularly good. 'Now when was it? Sixty-two?' he murmurs, looking for his diary covering the time of the accident.

He has always kept a diary, meticulously noting details of his day, and there is something eerie about

A youthful Stirling Moss poses with Alfred Neubauer for Mercedes-Benz publicity shots in late 1954, after signing a contract to drive number two to Fangio.

the great white void which was his month of coma.

'Saturday, April 21 . . . that would have been practice day, wouldn't it?' he says, looking at the last entries before the shunt. 'Yes, here we are . . . "Up at 10 o'clock, went off to Goodwood. Wet all day. Ferrari (250GT) fantastic on D9s. Lotus feels fair, and the 19 good. Cocktails at the Duke's. Party in evening. Bed at three o'clock . . ." Next day, Sunday, I see we went to another cocktail party, and the day after, of course, there's nothing . . .'

It was not until 4 June that Stirling was able to resume his notes, a yonderly and child-like scrawl recording simply: 'Feeling very tired. Later Innes [Ireland] came round for a while'.

That Moss recalls nothing of the accident, nor of the hours before it, is a well-chronicled fact. He hoped, he says, that going back to Goodwood for the first test run afterwards would trigger something in his memory, but nothing came back. Many times since he has tried to piece together what could have led to the circumstances of the accident.

'I've seen the movie of the shunt, and formed one or two theories. Where the accident happened, at St Mary's, is very quick, but if I had high speed shunts it tended to be because wheels fell off. If I was really chancing my arm, I always reckoned to do it on slow or medium-speed corners.'

Graham Hill always said that he clearly recalled Stirling's car overtaking him on the left, the Lotus already on the grass. Thereafter it plunged onward towards the bank, with no attempt by Moss either to brake or scrub off speed by spinning it. This, surely, points to some sort of mechanical failure?

'Yes', Moss agrees. 'I must say I've always believed that something broke — either before or after I got on the grass — because I always did everything possible to minimize the effects of a shunt, and here I appear to have done nothing. I reckon the most likely failure was in the front suspension or steering. After all, if it had been something like brake failure or a jammed throttle, I could still have spun the thing . . .'

The photographs bring back the full horror of the rescue — Stirling was trapped in the wreckage for forty minutes — and also serve to remind us of the implications of a high-speed accident in a space-frame car. The front of the Lotus simply folded over, like the blade of a pen knife. It was a particularly dangerous time to be a racing driver.

If Fleet Street paid full heed to Moss's accident, and what it meant to the public, the specialist magazines did not. There was no weekly news of his condition, no impression that racing's greatest figure was fighting for his life, but merely the same old nonsense about Mr and Mrs So-and-so's 'new model, which weighed in at 7 lb 4 oz . . .'

Stirling drifted in and out of consciousness for almost a month. 'I got a big shock when they told me the date, I remember that. And I couldn't move my left arm, which I assumed was broken. In fact, the whole of my left side was paralysed, thanks to the bang on the head . . .'

That, I suggested, must have come as a terrifying realization. 'No, not really', answers Moss. 'A friend of mine told me, and the full implication of his words didn't dawn on me. It wasn't like being told I'd lost a leg or something. Everything was still there. I had something to work on. If it was simply a matter of my head sending the wrong messages, then I'd change the messages!'

After a year, though, Stirling felt sufficiently physically recovered to undertake that fateful Goodwood test, where he discovered fully his loss of concentration. Looking back, he now bitterly regrets his decision.

'By the end of '64, my concentration had come back completely, and there is no doubt in my mind that I should have left the test until then. But this was nearly two years after deciding to retire, and I decided that a comeback to Grand Prix racing then simply wasn't on. And frankly I never considered going back simply to race sports cars or something, although I always enjoyed them. I'd made up my mind, and I think you should always stick by a decision.'

We then discussed a later, hypothetical, career. At the time of his accident Stirling was only 32, and without the slightest thought of retirement. In moments of reverie I have often taken him forward five or ten years, imagined him in Rob Walker's Lotus 49 or a factory Porsche 917 . . .

'Without the shunt,' he says, 'I obviously wouldn't be racing today, but I tell you what, I wouldn't have given up that long ago. Fangio, for example, was World

The straight-arm driving style, Moss said, was modelled on Farina. Stirling looked set for his first Grand Prix win here at Monaco in 1955, but the W196 blew up late in the race.

One of Moss's finest races was the Italian Grand Prix of 1956, when his Maserati 250F took on — and beat — the might of Ferrari. At the finish Fangio was less than six seconds behind.

Champion at 46. Now I know a lot of people say it wasn't as difficult then — with which I don't agree, incidentally — but Fangio was extremely fit. Races were longer, and we had tremendous heat problems to deal with. I think if you go along with the game, you keep yourself as fit as you need to be.

'The physical effort may be more now, but I don't think it's that much more. And I think if you're part of the game when new things arrive — wings, slick tyres, skirts or whatever — you keep up with it because everything comes in small increments. I really don't believe that would have been a problem for me.'

Three weeks to the day before the Goodwood shunt Moss was in Maranello, a matter given astonishingly scant attention by the press of the time. How had that come about?

'I simply got an invitation from the Commendatore. Now I'm the sort of person who does stupid things sometimes, and I'd always vowed that I would never drive a Ferrari. That went back to a time in Bari, early in my career, when he offered me a drive, then changed his mind. I got there and found there was no car for me, which really pissed me off. Thereafter

I often drove other people's Ferraris, and I built up enormous respect and admiration for the man, and what he had done.

'Anyway I went down to see him, and he asked me to tell him exactly what I wanted from an F1 car, and he would build it for me. Incredible. He wanted me to drive for the factory, of course, but I'd already spoken to Fangio about that, asked his advice. "By all means drive the car", he'd said, "but don't drive for the factory".

'Now I already knew that Ferrari played his drivers off against each other. I'd seen people like Collins, Musso, Hawthorn and Castellotti — all people of a similar standard — being messed around there, so I told Ferrari I would drive one of his cars — but only in Rob Walker's colours. And he agreed . . .'

Enzo Ferrari has never made any secret of his high opinion of Moss, whom he classes, with Nuvolari, as the greatest driver of all time. This willingness to prepare a separate car — in dark blue! — for Stirling illustrates the extent of his esteem.

'It was all arranged. I was to have a factory car, prepared at Maranello, but entered and transported by Rob Walker. Looking back, I suppose it was a fairly astonishing concession! But just after that, of course, I went and nearly killed myself, so unfortunately it didn't happen. But it was all looking great from my point of view: I could race for Rob, which I always enjoyed — and have what was effectively a factory Ferrari! Of course, the big thing would have been to try and beat the factory cars . . .'

You can say with a degree of certainty that Stirling *would* have beaten the factory cars. That being the case, however, would the Moss-Ferrari agreement have lasted long?

'Well, I think the factory drivers might have objected, but I don't believe Ferrari himself would have minded. He doesn't really care about his drivers — he cares about his *cars*. So long as a Ferrari had been winning, I don't think he would have cared about its colour or its driver, quite honestly. I reckon that he always allowed different drivers to win different races by giving them better cars sometimes, because it gave the impression that the driver didn't count for anything, that it was the *car* which won the race. So if I had beaten the factory drivers, he would have been able to use that against them . . .'

When Stirling says that, accidents apart, he would have continued Grand Prix racing into his late forties, is he making allowances for other factors which have entered the sport since he retired? He liked to race outside of Formula 1, for instance, a practice which has all but disappeared among the top drivers of today.

'No, I wouldn't have liked that — in fact, I wouldn't have accepted it. If it had reached the point where all the F1 teams prohibited their drivers from doing anything else, I would have left F1 and carried on with everything else — primarily out of cussedness. I would never have allowed anyone to dictate to me like that.

'That might have driven me out of Grand Prix racing. I would certainly have left it voluntarily as and when I knew I was getting slower, being beaten by people who shouldn't have been beating me. And I think the developments of the last few years would have lessened my interest in it. The sport has become dehumanized because of the increasing importance of the cars.

'I'll tell you, I feel very sorry for today's drivers. I reckon the top ones are as good as they have ever been, but if they're not with the right team at the right

In torrid heat Stirling's Vanwall won its second Grand Prix of 1957 on the magnificent Pescara road circuit. Musso's Ferrari strives to keep up.

After the Vanwall withdrawal, Moss drove for Rob Walker's private team almost exclusively for the rest of his career. Indifferent reliability with the Cooper-Climax kept his Grand Prix tally down to two in 1959.

time they can't show it, which is very sad. A guy might have all the talent in the world, but his contribution now is not enough. To me it's a sport, not a technical exercise.

'You know, people are always saying that racing's more competitive now than it's ever been, but I don't reckon that's the case at all. They might be closer, on time, but that's not the same thing at all — not when overtaking is virtually impossible. The cars, I know, are incredibly sophisticated these days, but I don't believe the *sport* is . . .

'Perhaps the cars are just too efficient. I'm sure that if narrower rim widths — and I'm talking about eight-inch rims, not twelve — were made mandatory, the racing would improve. I know they couldn't handle 700 horsepower, but I'm sure the *racing* would be better. The art of throttle control would come back, overtaking would be easier, and the real artist would stand out again. Sheer speed isn't worth a thing when you have processions all the time. In '61, you know, I beat the Ferraris twice, at the 'Ring and Monaco, and they had 20 per cent more power than my Lotus. I don't believe that anything like that could happen now — not even with a Fangio driving. And that's sad for the drivers.

'I also think there's probably too much money in racing now. Now I always reckoned to get my fair share of it when I was racing, don't get me wrong, but my best year financially was 1961, when I made £32,700. I had to pay a manager, travel and hotels, so that in the end I probably paid tax on about £8,000 and finished up with about £5,000. Now that was a lot of money then, you know, as much as a top surgeon was making. But I suppose if I were racing today as successfully as I did then, I would be earning a million or something. Frankly I don't think that's beneficial. I think it's gone too far. Perhaps a lot of it is paid in incentives, I don't know, but a real racer shouldn't need incentives to win. A driver, yes, a racer, no. To me, the most important race was the one I was in that day.'

Moss, of course, never won the World Championship, a fact which in itself denigrates the importance of the title. In 1958 he won four of the ten Grandes Epreuves, yet lost the championship to Mike Hawthorn, who scored one victory.

'If Stirling Moss had put reason before passion,' Enzo Ferrari has said, 'he would have been World Champion — he was more than deserving of it.'

Stirling shrugs at that. 'To me, the idea of driving for points goes against the whole point of racing. That's why I so admired Villeneuve's approach. If you're not trying to win the race at all costs, what on earth are you doing there? As far as I'm concerned, boy, any driver who's worth the name tries to win every race he runs. Eventually the World Championship ceased to be very important to me.'

The enjoyment, the sheer pleasure of race driving, was always paramount for Moss. The cars for which he felt most affection were not necessarily those which brought him the greatest successes.

'All round, my sentimental favourite was the Maserati 250F. I enjoyed the Mercedes W196, but for a different reason — I knew that if I didn't go off the road, I was either going to win or finish second to Fangio. It was *much* more reliable than the Maserati, but the 250F was a lot more fun because you could overdrive it. And I always enjoyed cars like that. When things got really tough you could throw it around, and it responded beautifully and came back for more.

'It was the same in the early rear-engined days. The Lotus was a much better car than the Cooper, but nothing like as nice to drive *because* it was better. And I suppose it gave the individual driver less scope . . '

When drivers quit, they go their different ways. Some stay involved, others not. Moss, now very much the family man, continues to live in his hi-tech house in Mayfair, racing for fun occasionally, promoting this, writing about that. Once in a while he shows up at a Grand Prix, as also does the man he unforgettably beat at Monte Carlo in 1961.

Richie Ginther, by contrast, has dropped out. Always a free spirit, he has enough money, he figures, to see him through if he takes care. And he lives in a motorhome, a gypsy by choice.

'What do I do now?' he laughs at my question. 'Why, nothing at all — and I love it! I do whatever comes to my head.'

Memories unite. When I ask him about Moss, he rolls his eyes. 'That race at Monaco was undoubtedly the best of my life. It was one hundred laps then, and going on three hours. I was right on the limit all the way, and I think Stirling was, too. He and I were first and second in qualifying, you know, and in the race we got three seconds under that, incredible as it seems now.

'In the Monaco programmes they credit me with the lap record that year — but he equalled it the very lap after I did it! That's why he was so discouraging to race. Any time you did well against him, hey, you knew you'd *really* done something.

'Stirling compromised himself by not joining a factory team. If he had, he'd have been World Champion who knows how many times.'

Was Moss the best driver he'd seen? Mr Ginther shares only nationality with Mr Borgeson. He hesitates for at least half a second before answering.

'Oh yes, he was. Without a doubt. And by a long way. As far as I'm concerned, there's never been anyone close . . '

The pose is relaxed, yet Stirling is driving the race of his life. At Monaco in 1961 Moss in Walker's Lotus 18 fought off constant assaults from the more powerful Ferraris.

RONNIE PETERSON
Innocent abroad

Michele Alboreto is a sanguine fellow, a hard racer when he chooses to be, but foremost a man who drives with his head. At the end of 1983 he became the first Italian to join Ferrari in a generation, but it did not especially move him. Alboreto is a professional sportsman of the eighties. Enzo's offer, he said, was the best he had received.

An Italian of unusual cut, therefore, analytical and invariably calm. You might expect him to cite Stewart, the paragon of orderly genius, as his own hero. Instead he unhesitatingly names Peterson as the man who shaped his ambition. 'I worshipped him', he says. 'That's why my own helmet is blue and yellow.'

Ronnie! That name — no one ever talked about 'Peterson' — set you tingling. By word association I think instantly of a black Lotus 72 skittering through the old Woodcote. It was worth going a very long way to see Ronnie through there. For he was one of those very few who ventured constantly into the outer reaches, beyond accepted limits, and could be seen to do so. Rindt was out of the same cast.

In personality these two were utterly different, but the parallels between their careers border on the uncanny. Similar styles apart, each quite dominated Formula 2, but took years to translate that native ability into similar success in Formula 1. Both achieved it with Colin Chapman. And both died, sadly, in Lotuses at Monza.

If ever you witnessed the sight of Rindt bawling at Chapman, you were not surprised that he sometimes drove as he did. There was a turbulence in the man which he took with him on to the track. Some of his greatest drives — as at the British Grand Prix of 1969 — were rooted in fury and frustration. Only in his final season, when victories at last came easy, did he find some serenity in Grand Prix racing.

Ronnie, though, was a quiet man, and gentle. There was none of Jochen's overt arrogance, but neither was there the degree of vulnerability one often sensed in the Austrian. During his last months Rindt, for all his success, fretted increasingly about the risks of racing, and talked of quitting. But Peterson looked ahead only to years and years of Formula 1. 'I never give any thought to retirement', he would say. 'If I could, I would race for ever.'

Ronnie won perhaps the most exciting race I ever saw, the Formula 3 curtain-raiser to the 1969 Monaco Grand Prix. He and compatriot Reine Wisell made it completely their own, swapping the lead until Reine went down the escape road at the chicane. Ronnie's fastest lap stamped him as someone for the future, two full seconds inside his own pole position time. A year later he made his Formula 1 debut at Monaco, and twelve months after that was beaten only by Stewart in the Grand Prix.

At that time he was very much the prodigy, the man of infinite speed, for whom all things were possible. In 1971 he was second four times with the 'tea tray' March 711 (losing the Italian Grand Prix to Gethin by only a hundredth of a second), but then, as so often happens with an overnight sensation, his career faltered. Through most of the following season he was scarcely a factor.

In absolute terms, this was hardly Ronnie's fault. The March 721X, one of Robin Herd's few fiascos, understeered grossly and never looked a winner. What it brought to light, however, was Peterson's sole major failing — he was a dreadful test driver. The youthful Lauda was his team mate that year, and from the start Niki pronounced the car undrivable. Ronnie, by contrast, initially thought it wonderful, its potential boundless. He would later say the same of Chapman's disastrous Lotus 76.

His particular ability perhaps militated against ever being able to 'sort' a car. So consummate was his car control, so instinctive his reflexes, that he could to

Barcelona 1971. In the odd March 711 Peterson was a serious contender throughout the year. There were no wins, but four second places helped him to the number two spot in the World Championship — albeit a long way behind Stewart.

some extent mask a car's shortcomings, drive around a problem. In changing circuit conditions during a race — such as at Zeltweg in 1978, his last victory — this was a boon, of course, but in testing it was anything but. Ronnie was never much help to his engineers.

'He was amazing in that respect', Chapman said. 'You could change the car really quite fundamentally — and he'd still turn in the same sort of times! So you'd ask him how it felt different from before, and he'd say, "Ummm, slides a bit more . . ." Where? At the front, the back, both ends? And he'd say he wasn't really sure! Made me tear my hair out. Then, of course, he'd go and put the thing on pole position, so you couldn't really get too mad with him . . .'

Certainly it was a fact that Peterson was at his greatest when teamed with a fine test driver like Fittipaldi or, particularly, Andretti. And it must have been supremely frustrating for these two to work away at perfecting a car, then have Peterson climb in and drive it quicker! It says much for his ingenuous

character that Ronnie's devastating pace was never resented by Mario (although there were times when Emerson failed to see the funny side of it . . .).

At Brands Hatch in 1978, Ronnie took pole position — and did it on race tyres. During the final session Mario used up nine sets of qualifiers trying to better it, and afterwards there were murmurings of a 'crisis' within the Lotus team. Peterson, people said, was number two to Andretti, and not supposed to do that sort of thing. Mario was indignant.

'Where's the mystery, for God's sake? Ronnie was quicker than me, and that's all there is about it. Yeah, I was going through qualifiers like Carter's Little Liver Pills, but it's no dishonour to be slower than Ronnie Peterson. People are talking about him like he's a rookie or something, suddenly appeared from nowhere! Let's face it, the man's a very great race driver.'

Memories are short in Formula 1. Peterson went to Lotus in 1973, soon proving faster than Fittipaldi, the team's resident World Champion. He won his first

Grand Prix at mid-season, and followed up with three more. Emerson promptly left for McLaren, and that made Ronnie team leader for 1974.

He had three top-drawer victories that year, but my clearest memory is his drive at Jarama. The Lotus 76 had not yet been officially designated a disaster area, and for twenty unforgettable laps Peterson led in the rain, a shambolic tyre stop putting him out of contention. Futile heroism.

Soon afterwards the old 72 was resurrected, and at Monte Carlo Ronnie won with it, a victory repeated at Dijon and then again at Monza. By 1975, though, the legendary car was an embarrassing also-ran. Only in the rains of Zeltweg was the world's fastest driver seen to advantage. And when Chapman's 'all-adjustable' Lotus 77 flopped at the start of the following year, Peterson returned to March, scoring a solitary win — at Monza again. These were the years of Lauda and Hunt, and a dreadful season in Tyrrell's blind alley six-wheelers dropped Ronnie's stock still further.

'It was no time to be proud', he said. 'I looked at what Lotus were doing, what Mario had managed to achieve with the 77. That car was dreadful when I left, but by the end of the year he and Chapman had made a winner out of it. Then I saw the 78, and I knew somehow I had to get back there.'

It seems absurd, with hindsight, but Peterson was hardly in demand by then. In Formula 1 you're only as good as your last picture, and three indifferent seasons with poor cars had swept away all that went before. Ronnie, people said, just didn't have it any more. He was podgy and unfit, not at all the charger of old. Pity, they said. And, true enough, he was not as quick as he should have been, as he *had* been. At Tyrrell, Depailler out-qualified him more often than not.

Peterson admitted that the spark was temporarily gone. 'I got very depressed, and it affected me. It was another season wasted, and one I'd expected to be good. I knew that if Chapman took me back it would

---

Ronnie and Lotus 72 in typical pose. By 1974 the car was getting a little long in the tooth, but Peterson nevertheless won three races with it, including this one at Dijon.

A year to forget. Peterson never really got along with the Tyrrell P34 six-wheeler, and by the end of 1977 found it necessary — absurdly — to buy his way back into Lotus.

be entirely on his terms. Okay, it was worth it.' Indeed it was, for Ronnie also knew that a year with Lotus — at that time coming to one of their periodic crescendos — would be enough to re-establish himself.

So he went, cap in hand, back to his old boss. In the cap was a cheque from Polar Caravans and another from Peterson's personal sponsor, Count Zanon. And Colin began to see the attraction of running Ronnie alongside Mario in 1978.

Initially, it must be said, Andretti did not. 'Tell me where it's written we need two stars in this team', he growled at Watkins Glen, where the news broke. 'When Ronnie ran with Fittipaldi at Lotus in '73 they won a whole bunch of races — and neither one won the championship. I don't want that to happen again. I've signed as number one, but I feel bad that a guy like Ronnie has to accept number two, because that's not what he is.'

By and by, though, it ceased to be a problem. In their few months of working together, their friendship became as firm as any I have known between Grand Prix drivers — particularly remarkable since team mates are always, in fact, strong rivals, each a yardstick for the other. Andretti frankly admitted he had

reckoned without Peterson's complete honesty — 'Something you don't find too often in this business . . .'

Ronnie was reacquainted with Lotus on a winter's test day at Paul Ricard. He drove the 78, and was stunned. 'This car', he said, 'gives me back my inspiration. What the 79 will be like I can't imagine.' And, for the first time in his life, he set to work on a fitness programme. By the beginning of the season he was in fine shape.

There were those who predicted that, from the first, he would blow Mario aside, but such was not the way of it. At Buenos Aires it was Andretti on the pole, Andretti who won. In Rio Ronnie qualified fastest, and at Kyalami took a dramatic victory, passing a hobbled Depailler during a wheel-banging final lap. Generally, though, Mario had the upper hand through the first half of the season.

'That's why', Peterson maintained, 'he deserves to be World Champion this year. And that has nothing to do with the contracts we signed.' At Brands, where Ronnie took the pole, Mario took it upon himself to explain those contracts to the press. The deal, he said, was that if the two of them were running at the front, with no problems, then he was to win. 'Out of fairness

Ronnie and Colin Chapman had their ups and downs, but through 1978 got along fine, despite the team's push for an Andretti World Championship.

to Ronnie, I didn't want anything to be artificial, like people thinking I was passing him because he couldn't keep me back. I don't think either of us felt bad about it, and I wanted it to be in the open.'

In Holland, though, Andretti was untypically edgy. In Austria he had crashed on the opening lap, and Peterson turned in as great a drive as we ever saw from him, running away in the dreadful conditions. The win moved him to within nine points of Mario, with four races left. His integrity faced a stern test, the more so since it was now becoming clear that he would not be staying at Lotus for 1979.

'If I were Ronnie,' one of the lesser lights (British, I regret to say) suggested before the Dutch Grand Prix, 'I'd just go for it from now on. What's he got to lose?' But Andretti had a higher opinion of him than that: 'I had no doubts on that score. I was just scared the car wouldn't last — hell, I couldn't expect him to retire if I did!'

On race morning at Zandvoort I talked to Peterson about the state of play. 'I'm going to McLaren next year', he said. 'It's not anounced yet, but Mario knows. Some of these people,' he sighed, 'who say I should forget our agreement now . . . I don't understand them. I had open eyes when I signed the contract, and I also gave my word. If I break it now, who will ever trust me again?'

The afternoon brought another race he could have won. His brakes were failing, but Andretti's car broke an exhaust and lost power. Ronnie dutifully followed him over the line.

I spent a lot of time in the Lotus motorhome at Monza that year, having agreed with Mario that we would do a book on his World Championship year. The man from Nazareth had shed his Zandvoort blues now, but even so there was a tension in the air, perhaps amplified by the extra pressures which are inherent at Monza. Andretti and Peterson lolled around in the motorhome for long periods, keeping clear of the crazies outside, but there wasn't much talk.

Ronnie was never a man to show much emotion, in that way very much a child of his race. At Anderstorp, where Patrese had blatantly blocked him during the last few laps, he was positively shaking with rage afterwards, but there was no display of histrionics. Now, at Monza, he was uncharacteristically worked up about the changing ways of Grand Prix racing.

'There are some members of my Swedish fan club here. They have a competition every year, and the winners come to Monza. I always show them round the paddock. Now, for the first time,' he scowled, 'I can't get any passes for them. Ecclestone said no.'

Mario nodded sympathetically. 'Yeah, I know how it is. I had to fight to get one for my own wife! The race is incidental in this goddam place. What wears you out is getting a pass . . .'

Silence again. Andretti lit one of his rare cigarettes and stared out of the window, while Peterson searched for a lost pair of sunglasses.

'Later I thought a lot about that weekend', Mario said. 'I was quite relaxed again, but Ronnie was more uptight than I'd ever seen him. We always used to level with each other before a race, but at Monza we never did that — hardly said a word, never wished each other good luck or shook hands before the start, which we'd always done before. Exactly what was happening there between us, I don't know. It was nothing bad, just something of the moment, but it bothered me at the time, and it has since. The guy was so different that day, and the outcome so disastrous. Just like there was something in the air.'

On race morning Peterson had an accident in the warm-up, the 79 mowing down several layers of catch fencing and finishing up against a tree. That meant using the old 78 for the race.

'Bloody rear brakes again,' he said to Andretti. 'Just like yesterday — and at Zandvoort . . .' 'You okay?' Mario asked. 'Yes', Ronnie said, rubbing his leg. 'Just

Back to the front. At Kyalami in 1978 Peterson took the Lotus 78 to a sensational last-lap victory, passing Depailler's hobbled Tyrrell within a mile of the flag.

Ronnie's last Grand Prix victory was perhaps his greatest. At Zeltweg in 1978 he toyed with the rest in appalling conditions, never facing any serious challenge.

bruised.'

How different was the scene in the motorhome a few hours later. Andretti was champion, and everyone was drinking champagne. But all conversation, such as there was, centred on Peterson and the accident. How had it happened? Who caused it? There were as many opinions as voices. 'It's been a long, confused, day.' Mario muttered. 'Thank God he's going to be okay, that's all. What's the story on Vittorio?' At that stage the man at risk seemed to be Brambilla, one of nine other drivers involved in the fearful accident.

I should have flown back to England that night, but obviously that plan went by the board. The following morning we landed at Heathrow, and I waited by the luggage carousel for a colleague to ring his Fleet Street office. He came back, shocked, and said that Ronnie had died during the night.

'At the Glen', Andretti said, 'there was this sign by one of the barriers: "Mario — win this one for Ronnie". I tell you, there was never anything I wanted to do more. I missed him like hell. He was something unique in my experience — this innocence he had about him,

even after all those years in racing. There was nothing false in the man.'

'Everyone loved him', Jackie Stewart agreed. 'He was one of those people you could never get angry with. I don't think he ever had the mental application that a complete racing driver needs, but I admired his ability tremendously. Any number of times, particularly in 1973, I'd follow him into a corner and think, "Oh-oh, Ronnie, this time you've overdone it, you're gone!" But he always seemed to get it back somehow. It never surprised me the spectators loved him — he was exciting to watch from where I was, too!'

'Mad Ronald' (as Mike Hailwood used to call him) had not an enemy in the business. People smiled and shook their heads as they listened to his fragmented English, waited for that sheepish grin which would come over his face as he struggled with a word like 'development'. How they wondered, had he failed to pick up the language after so many years in the country? 'I'm lazy', Ronnie would say. 'Except when I'm driving, I'm lazy . . .'

NELSON PIQUET
Changing times

'I think about Pele and Garrincha sometimes,' Nelson Piquet said, 'and how they finished their playing days. In Brazil — everywhere in the world — they were superstars, and they finished their playing days with *nothing*! Pele had to go to the New York Cosmos when he was an old man for football, to make some money, so now he's OK, but otherwise . . .

'I tell you one thing,' he went on. 'That's *not* going to happen to me.'

We were in the paddock at the Osterreichring after first practice in 1985, and it was obvious from his uninhibited remarks that Piquet had firmly and irrevocably come to a crossroads in his career. Conversations of this kind with most drivers are usually prefaced by 'Off the record . . .'. Nelson, typically, laid bare his soul before saying, as an afterthought, 'No writing for now, huh? Not until it's settled.'

The month of August is traditionally a time of gossip in Formula 1, the emphasis on who's going where next year rather than who's doing what this weekend. In previous seasons, though, Piquet had never figured seriously in the speculation: he was going to stay with Brabham, as always, a fixture as Clark had been at Lotus.

Actually, this was not quite true. Towards the end of 1981 Nelson spoke seriously to Frank Williams about a move, their discussion coming to nought only because he was unwilling to be team mate to Alan Jones, with whom he wasn't hitting it off at the time. In the event, of course, the Australian later quit at very short notice, but by then Piquet's name was on a fresh Brabham contract.

Renault, too, had made efforts to land Piquet, first when Prost was threatening to leave in the autumn of 1983, then again twelve months later, when Nelson was reeling from the news that Ecclestone had contracted Brabham to Pirelli. This decision by Bernie crucially affected Piquet's attitude both to his team and his future.

Now, several months on, the Brazilian leaned against a motorhome in the Zeltweg paddock, and talked about money. 'I have a name, I know, for not caring too much about it. Everywhere I read that "Piquet has simple tastes, just loves to race, doesn't need to earn a lot." Bah! I've been screwed around on money for seven years.

'When I started with Brabham, you know, I got paid so little I *had* to race those Procars. OK, I enjoyed them, but that was where I earned most of my money at that time. And I didn't mind too much — I was straight from Formula 3 into one of the great teams. It was my big chance. I knew that, and so did Bernie.

'Since then I've been World Champion twice, stayed loyal to one team — and Prost is earning three times as much as me. I don't know how you rate drivers, but for sure Alain isn't three times as good as I am!'

Prost himself has often suggested that Formula 1 retainers have ceased to mean very much. Rich is rich. But they have in recent years taken on a symbolic value, he says, an indication of worth. Not necessarily a good thing, he shrugs, but a fact. And clearly a fact which had come to mean something to Piquet.

'During that last season with us,' one of the Brabham mechanics told me, 'Nelson was different. We started to think he was doing it mainly for the money. Little things changed. He spent less time in the pits before and after practice than he'd always done before, didn't seem as dedicated to it. Even so, we still thought he was the best driver in the business, and it didn't change the way we felt about him — everyone worshipped him. He always treated us as friends. We were all shattered when he told us he was going . . .'

The Brabham team, in the Piquet era, was close-knit like no other. Several mechanics told me over the

Broken exhaust or no, Piquet served notice of intent to the Grand Prix world with a superb drive in the Brabham-Alfa BT48 to second place, behind Villeneuve, at the Race of Champions in 1979.

Semi-comatose in the late stages of the race, Nelson somehow kept the BT49 away from the walls to clinch his first World Championship at Las Vegas in 1981.

years that they would have left long ago had it not been for their devotion to Nelson. Certainly, they said, the money wasn't good enough to keep them. And, in the end, it wasn't enough to keep Piquet, either.

At the base, he *is* a simple man. And, by his own admission, a lazy one. His interest in racing stops with the driving. Many drivers have a distaste for the PR fringe work which now goes with the job, but Nelson's position is rather more trenchant: he won't do it. Love me, love my attitude. I'm here to drive.

Parmalat was the perfect sponsor for Nelson, making absolutely no demands of him beyond driving a race car faster than anyone else. For all the years of their involvement, both parties were well satisfied with the arrangement, and Piquet admits he was lucky to be so spoiled.

Parmalat, though, was not typical. The law of the eighties, difficult to refute in the light of some drivers' telephone-number retainers, is that winning Grands Prix, even World Championships, is not enough. You have to put out for the company that keeps you. It's showbiz money, so provide the showbiz.

This Nelson will not accept. 'I spoke to Ron Dennis about going to McLaren, and he mentioned so many days a year working for Marlboro, five for this, six for

that . . . forget it, I lost interest. I won't spend my life talking to people who don't understand racing.' Prost and Lauda, I said, care little for personal appearances and so on, but do them because they know the sponsor is paying for a star — out of the cockpit, as well as in it. Nelson shrugged, made a face.

Some of his colleagues reckoned his attitude to be unrealistic. At the other end of the scale, of course, we had Rosberg, the man who *did* go to McLaren, the man whose place Piquet filled at Williams. Keke positively embraced PR, having the outgoing personality sponsors dream about — as well as a healthy irreverence which can make team managers wince. He always sought out personal backers to bolster his income, anathema to Nelson.

'It's true that I could have made much more money if I'd been prepared to do that, but I wasn't. When I'm not at a track, racing or testing, I like to get back to my boat and disappear,' he said. 'I swim and ski, watch a lot of TV, lie around and do nothing. That's the way I am, and when I turn up at a race I feel fresh. Away from it, I ring the factory once a week to find out what's going on, and that's it . . .'

He knows only racing, and never talks of retirement. Throughout his career he has been fond of saying that:

'What else would I do?' But recently there have been signs of a slight wavering. Perhaps there *are* other things in life; maybe he will quit in the foreseeable future, after all.

He nearly did at the end of 1983, that stunning season when he whisked away Prost's title at the final race. 'I was very tired, it was that simple. Not of racing, but travelling. I couldn't stand the thought of another airport queue, another delayed flight. And if it hadn't been for Niki, I probably would have retired then, yes. He persuaded me that the answer was not to quit, but to get my own plane — my own *jet*. And he arranged everything for me.

'So that much has changed. I can race in a Grand Prix in Europe, and by seven o'clock on Sunday evening I'm back on the boat in Sardinia, Corsica, Ibiza or wherever we happen to be.'

The Lear, he adds, may have changed his life, but it also significantly changed his bank statements. In 1985, he estimates, at least half of his total income was spent on the business of simply being a Grand Prix driver, on travel, hotels, fuel for the aircraft. And much of the travel was necessary, Nelson goes on, because of Ecclestone's agreement with Pirelli,

who had relied on him almost exclusively for testing work.

'Since Brabham went with Pirelli,' he said, very serious now, 'I've done the equivalent of 75 Grands Prix in testing for them. Forget the PR appearances. *That* is real work for a racing driver, and that's why I should get what I'm worth. For sure a Brabham-BMW can win the World Championship in '86, but if I stay another year people will think I'll never leave. Bernie thinks that now . . .'

Such was undoubtedly the case. Ecclestone recognized that some aspects of his team were uniquely attractive to Nelson, and growing more so by the year. Brabham was not a PR-minded organization, first of all. Since 1979 Piquet had built up with Gordon Murray what amounted virtually to a telepathic working relationship. Nelson usually had a highly competitive car, always an ultra-safe one.

And it was a team which could *respond*, at all levels, to a changing situation. Towards the end of 1979, Piquet's first season there, Ecclestone gave Murray the nod to get on with a Cosworth car. Gordon, hamstrung by Alfa Romeo engines for long enough, was happy to comply, and just eight weeks later there

---

The joys of the ground effect era. Almost alone, Piquet claimed to enjoy the cars of that time, but they took a horrible toll. Here Nelson grabs at Rosberg and Prost as he prepares to pass out at Rio in early 1982.

A brilliant victory with the BT52 in the 1983 Grand Prix of Europe at Brands Hatch put Piquet within striking range of his second championship.

were three new BT49s in the pits at Montreal. Nelson, captivated by the car, was deeply impressed. Four years later Brabham and BMW 'kicked' in the second half of the season while Renault played safe — and Prost lost the championship to Piquet.

So these factors counted for a lot. Bernie, ever the gambler, reckoned that they had kept Nelson on board for seven years, and would be good for an eighth.

Piquet is remarkably frank about money: 'I was getting $1m from Bernie, and I asked for double — which was still a lot less than Prost. He offered me $1.6m, plus a thousand dollars a point, thinking that would be just enough to keep me. I wasn't prepared to get into an argument over it and immediately told Williams I was ready to sign. Frank's offer was $3.3m . . .'

In the days following, Nelson made a practice of sneaking up behind Brabham personnel, whispering 'Money, money, money!' in their ears. They laughed and were happy for him, but deep down they were heartbroken that the family was splitting. It had been a couple of Brabham mechanics, remember, who set up the Nelson Piquet Fan Club in 1983.

The length of their association has much to do with it, of course. In seven seasons, well over a hundred

Grands Prix, Nelson and the team went through a lot together. He first drove a Brabham in Montreal at the end of 1978, and they remember how he was in those early days. At 26, he looked far younger, and suffered so badly with his nerves that he often doubled up with stomach cramps. It was not — as was the case of one fleeting star, who used routinely to vomit before a race — a matter of fright, for Piquet says fear of an accident never comes into his mind. No, for Nelson it was worry about doing a good enough job.

He won his first Grand Prix in 1980 (at Long Beach, ironically, for he hates street circuits, preferring fast, open tracks). And by September, with only the North American races left, he led the championship by a single point from Alan Jones.

The matter was resolved at Montreal, where the Williams and Brabham touched at the first corner after a particularly muscular manoeuvre by the Australian. On the restart Nelson, now in his spare car, led for as long as his engine lasted, and Alan went on to take race and title. A grudge match between the two — and their teams — was under way.

It was resumed at Zolder the following season. Again there was a coming together, and this time Piquet was out on the spot, walking back to the pits in a towering rage, where he made a variety of colourful, if ill-advised, threats against his rival. I was not alone in thinking that Nelson was at that time being subjected to the 'get out there and kill 'em' philosophy of the late Vince Lombardi, one-time coach of the Washington Redskins. In Formula 1 terms, that was a lethal creed, and there was a sigh of relief in the pit lane when certain management changes were made at Brabham.

Jones made Piquet pay for that outburst at Monaco, subjecting him to the fiercest pressure for lap after lap. Finally Nelson hit the barrier at Tabac. 'I don't often piss myself laughing in a racing car,' Alan remarked, 'but I did when I saw that . . .'

By the end of that year, though, the two men had patched up their differences. Jones won his last race before retirement, at Las Vegas, and an exhausted Piquet won the World Championship — which also pleased Alan, for it was at the expense of team mate Carlos Reutemann, with whom he had passed a difficult season.

That afternoon in Vegas was unforgettable, not because the tin-pot little track in the car park gave us a great race but because it provided a test of endurance, courage. This was the season of hydraulic suspension, the zenith of recent Formula 1 absurdity,

when cars were raised to pass an arbitrary ride height test in the pits, then lowered, in the interests of ground effect, once out on the circuit. Cornering forces were very high, and there was no discernible suspension movement. The drivers took a battering, and for the last 20 laps Nelson's head — neck muscles spent — lolled to the right. Not even he knows how he made it to the finish, a distant fifth.

They had to lift him from the car afterwards, and briefly there was genuine concern from the medics on hand. He was into the far reaches of exhaustion, it seemed, but eventually he rallied and took his place on the podium, an undignified Caesars Palace 'crown' on his head. There he embraced Jones. The world was coming back into focus, the title won.

At Rio the following year he was in the same state, this time collapsing on the rostrum and needing support from Prost and Rosberg. Ground effect was exacting ridiculous dues, yet Piquet is the only driver I have known regret its banning. 'They were faster, those cars, that's why I liked them. There was less reaction time for the driver.' It seemed a surprisingly shallow attitude to a complex phenomenon which was threatening the whole future of the sport. There again, Nelson *was* in a Brabham, a good ground effect car. And a strong one in the event of a shunt. Others were

A discussion about money? A wry Gordon Murray looks on as Piquet makes a forcible point to Ecclestone. Gambling to the end, Bernie lost Nelson to Williams after seven years.

Piquet lives in Monaco, but loathes the circuit. His Williams-Honda years produced a World Championship and seven wins, yet still fell short of Frank's expectations.

less fortunate.

His second World Championship was more satisfactory than the first, which I always felt he rather lucked into. After the Austrian Grand Prix of 1983 he stood 14 points adrift of Prost, with four races left, yet spoke of his absolute confidence in winning the title. He was relaxed about it, but you had to take him seriously. That period was a highspot in Brabham history.

By 1985, though, Piquet's relationship with the team was burned out, and both parties knew it. He went to Williams the following year, quite sure in his own mind he would blow aside new team mate, Nigel Mansell. It would be business as it had always been: everyone working for our Nelson. It wasn't, though. For the first time in his life Piquet found himself confronting a genuine yardstick of his pace and effort; found himself, too, in a team without a caste system. Jones and Reutemann had taught Williams a big lesson in that direction; in theory, by virtue of his reputation, Nelson was the number one driver, but in practice they liked the man who won races for them. And, more often than not, that was Mansell.

By mid-season the hostility between the two was undisguised, and the situation was scarcely helped by the absence from the races of Frank Williams, then recovering from his dreadful road accident. Nigel and Nelson went to Adelaide for the championship showdown — and the title was stolen by Alain Prost.

Throughout the following year the situation continued. Piquet was fortunate to escape without serious injury in a huge shunt at Imola, and rarely looked an obvious race winner for the balance of the season. But he racked up the points as never before — 18 of them from a couple of inherited victories — and finished the year with a third, not particularly distinguished, World Championship. Then he left for Lotus, guaranteed star treatment, with journeyman team mate once more.

Peter Warr, his new boss, stuck by him through 1988, bravely brushing away the tears at the thought of all that money for a series of undistinguished drives in, it must be said, an undistinguished car. Nelson, he said he had come to realize, was not motivated like most drivers: what he needed to give of his best was an 'unfair advantage'.

It won't do. Not in itself. Piquet had precisely that in his two years with Williams-Hondas. Trouble was, so did Mansell. And what Nelson no longer had was Nigel's willingness to brush barriers, go for it.

'I don't want to finish up like Garrincha,' he had said. And no more will he, happily. But neither, following his post-Brabham years, will he be remembered like Fangio.

DIDIER PIRONI
Summer of '82

'I remember so clearly,' Harvey Postlethwaite said to me, 'that Saturday morning in August of 1982. I got a call asking me to go to the Old Man's office, and he told me that Pironi had crashed at Hockenheim. "Addio Mondiale," he muttered. Goodbye World Championship . . .'

A few years ago I was asked by a publisher to consider writing a novel with a motor racing background, and the idea has been in cold storage ever since, although it is my intention one day to revive it. Works of fiction about this sport are nothing new, but so far none has been written by anyone closely involved in it. And that has been the inhibiting factor: coming up with a plot at once engaging to readers and at least semi-believable to myself.

There are the beginnings of it, perhaps, in the last few months of Didier Pironi's career as a Grand Prix driver, although hindsight suggests that much of that summer of '82, chronicled in novel form, would beggar belief. Hockenheim was the end of a remarkable saga.

Pironi was as enigmatic a man as I have ever met, a creature of contrasts, in many ways the Varzi of his time. He had about him an aura of almost ethereal calm. I never heard him raise his voice, whatever the circumstance. French journalists, with whom he was not popular, put this down to native arrogance. Pironi, they said, was the son of privilege and wealth, and it showed.

'It's not true,' Didier insisted when I raised the subject with him one day. 'I am not aloof, but *timide* . . . shy, you know.'

We were talking exactly a year before the accident, after final qualifying at Hockenheim in 1981. Ferrari were off the pace, but Pironi was not too concerned. It was his first year with the team, their first with turbo engines. The right rewards, he was sure, would follow in due time.

I had spoken briefly with him immediately after the session's end, an hour earlier, and was now struck yet again by the transformation in his appearance. Didier Pironi was never one of those who stepped from a race car with a dry brow. When he had really been going for it, you knew. Red in the face, almost pumping with sweat, hair dishevelled, a little breathless, he clearly put huge effort into his driving.

The contrast with Villeneuve, his team mate, was always striking, for Gilles would rarely betray any outward sign of fatigue or stress. Through that summer a French medical research team conducted a series of experiments designed to assess the general strain exerted on a man by Grand Prix racing. At Monaco Pironi's heart was monitored throughout the race, registering a low of 185 beats a minute, a high of 207. His normal count, at rest, was just 60.

By way of comparison, a similar test on Villeneuve at Dijon revealed a norm during qualifying of 127 and a flash high reading of 165 — that while having an accident at a fourth gear corner . . .

Clearly, therefore, Pironi had to put an awful lot of himself into his work. But a few minutes later, showered and changed, he would revert to his languid self, the faintly mocking smile on his face once more. And he was just so this particular day.

For all the softness of his voice, however, Didier's steel ambition was never in doubt. Where a Depailler or Regazzoni would tell of the simple joy they felt from driving a Grand Prix car, Pironi's motivation seemed to come almost exclusively from thoughts of the title.

'The only thing,' he remarked, 'that interests me in Formula 1 is the World Championship. If, for any reason, I began to think that I couldn't win it, I would stop racing. I don't want to spend my life in Formula 1 for the sake of it.'

That said, he went on to speak about his association with Ferrari, recalling intense nervousness when about

Like so many others, Pironi got his start in Formula 1 with Ken Tyrrell. His second season with the team, 1979, was a rough one, however, with several car failures, and at the end of it he left.

to meet the Commendatore for the first time.

'It's not like being with any other team. Psychologically, you have the feeling, when you drive, that you are doing it for *somebody*, you know, rather than some *thing*. For me, that's very important — to feel that there is someone behind me, with the same passion as me, someone who is interested in what I can do, in the results I can get. And that is completely different from being with Tyrrell or Ligier . . .

'I rarely regret decisions I make, and I don't regret coming into Formula 1 with Ken, because he knows very well how to teach a new driver and I learned a lot from him. But in my second year I felt I was ready to win races — if I had a good car. Maybe I was wrong, but I talked to Ken about getting some new engineers because I never felt they understood much about aerodynamics. For 1979 they just copied the Lotus 79, so we were a year behind already! They were just too conservative.'

Clearly, I said, you were not a man to suffer in silence . . .

'No, there is no time for that in Formula 1. But there was something else wrong when I was with Tyrrell. I had seven or eight accidents, because of things breaking, and I began almost to expect it every time I got in the car . . .'

Pironi's phlegmatic attitude to accidents was always astonishing. During practice at Dijon in 1979 he crashed twice, thanks to wheels coming adrift, and each time he immediately got into another car and went out again. In the race he had to pit twice — to have wheel nuts tightened.

'The accidents were not a problem. They happen, but I am never affected by them. What did affect me was Ken's behaviour afterwards. There was never any apology when the car had broken, and when the boss doesn't apologize no one in the team feels they can, either. I was disappointed by Ken's attitude — especially as for sure he will tell you if a crash is *your* fault!'

Pironi had a single stormy season with Ligier, during which he emerged as a world class driver, usually quicker than established team leader Jacques Laffite. He won at Zolder, dominated most of Monaco. And his comeback drive at Brands Hatch was not less than stunning.

It was not an easy year, for the relationship between Pironi and Ligier was scarcely a meeting of minds. Didier's chilling self-control failed to melt before his boss's fire breathing, and when Guy learned — from reading *Autosport* — of Pironi's forthcoming move to Ferrari there were those who worried seriously for his blood pressure.

For all his claims of shyness, Didier always struck me as a very dispassionate and calculating sort of man. It came as no surprise to learn that his own sporting heroes were Stewart and Borg. Following the BMW Procar race at Hockenheim in 1980, an apoplectic Stuck had to be dissuaded from reworking Pironi's features after a particularly muscular display by the Frenchman. While a scarlet Hans-Joachim stood and bawled abuse, Didier looked on without emotion. Who, me?

'Perhaps I am too fiery in a race,' he quietly allowed. 'Sometimes over the limit . . .'

I have always believed that Pironi's move to Ferrari, once through the initial euphoria, set him psychologically back. Without a doubt he went there in the belief that he was now the fastest driver in the world, quicker even than Villeneuve, and the discovery that this was not so was hard to accept.

As well as that, the uncomplicated Gilles was adored at Ferrari, worshipped by the public. Although the two men were always given equal equipment, it was impossible for Didier — however he fought against it — to feel like anything other than a number two.

At Monte Carlo Villeneuve qualified second and finished first, lapping fourth-place Pironi in the process. At Jarama Gilles won again, with a troubled Didier nowhere. These were unsettling times for the Frenchman, but he showed his class at Imola and Zolder, leading for a while with the unruly 126C.

In Belgium he also demonstrated coolness and

Didier was scintillating at Brands Hatch in 1980, leading from pole position until an early pit stop. Thereafter the Ligier came back from 21st to fifth in 34 laps, setting a lap record which stood for more than five years.

'Sorry, but we've bad news for you . . .' Pironi was first over the line at Montreal in 1980, but officials docked him a minute for jumping the start.

common sense. This was the race in which Stohr hit an Arrows mechanic on the grid. The ensuing rescue operation filled up half the width of the track, yet idiotic officials did nothing to stop the race. Twice Piquet blasted past the scene in the lead, with a more circumspect Reutemann behind him. Pironi, third, took it upon himself to halt the madness, slowing and raising his arm. Those behind followed his lead.

Thereafter, Didier was to play an increasing part in safety politics, taking charge of the newly-formed Professional Racing Drivers Association (remember it?) the following winter. Perhaps, as he always claimed, his motives were never other than altruistic. Be that the case or not, there were those who developed a strong personal antipathy to him at that time. And their feelings never changed.

If he felt jealous of Villeneuve through 1981, Pironi hid his feelings well. 'Everything is fine between us,' he would say. 'We collaborate absolutely. What is important is that *Ferrari* win . . .' I almost believed him.

The following year was perhaps the most traumatic Ferrari has endured. In pre-season testing Didier

survived a colossal accident at Paul Ricard, his car coming to rest finally in an empty spectator enclosure. At Rio, shortly afterwards, he was off the pace.

Soon after practice Villeneuve asked for a quiet word. 'When you write your report, go easy on Didier,' he said, 'Believe me, that Ricard shunt was *something*, and he's a bit shaken up. But he'll be fine at the next race . . .'

The next race was Imola, and I have often wondered if Pironi ever realized just how much of a friendship he tossed away that day. With the two Ferraris cruising to victory, Didier ignored team orders and sprinted past his unsuspecting team mate on the last lap.

Pironi always maintained — despite overwhelming contrary evidence — that he believed himself to be in a *race*, which suggestion Villeneuve found both farcical and dishonest. Only Didier *knew* what was in his mind when he made that frenzied last pass. What is certain is that Gilles went to the grave hating him for it. The chord of trust had been broken. At Zolder the two did not exchange a word, and after the French-

Villeneuve and Pironi at the Silverstone tests in June 1981. Until the controversy at Imola the following year, the two team mates were on excellent terms.

Canadian's fatal accident, Pironi was given to understand that his presence at the funeral would not be welcomed.

Who knows how a man deals with circumstances as unimaginable at these? Two weeks later came Monaco, where Didier would have won had not a fuel pressure problem halted him on the last lap. Ferrari had been in two minds about entering for the race, leaving the decision to Pironi — who opted to race. Not to have done would have served no purpose.

In Montreal he put the Ferrari on pole position, afterwards mournfully dedicating it to the memory of Villeneuve. And in the race there was more tragedy, for he stalled at the start, and was struck horrifyingly by the inexperienced Paletti, who died of his injuries. Two hours later Pironi took the restart in the spare car, and drove it quite brilliantly. It was during that murky evening that I began to see him as the 1982 World Champion.

He won superbly and without problems in Holland, scored well elsewhere. Curiously, however, the races were the eye of the storm. All around him was turmoil.

In April he had married his longtime girl friend, yet was now involved with an actress. A second major testing accident at Ricard left him unhurt, and this time unmoved.

'Something very odd came over Didier in the weeks before Hockenheim,' Harvey Postlethwaite reckoned. 'He went very strange. He had big personal problems, I think, but he became *extremely* arrogant about everything, about the car and the fact that he was going to be World Champion.'

Certainly, it looked that way. Whatever the circumstances which led to his Ferrari team leadership, Didier's confidence blossomed. 'I feel that I am beginning to touch the World Championship,' he said to me at Brands Hatch.

On the opening practice day at Hockenheim he was a second clear of the field. The following morning, in only four laps, he set a time which remained unbeaten through the torrential session. The fifth he did not complete.

I have witnessed many motor racing accidents, but none stays in the mind more vividly. I was a little late that dreary morning, glancing at the circuit as I locked up my car. Momentarily the Ferrari seemed frozen, thirty feet off the ground, nose pointing straight up into the grey sky. It landed tail first, mercifully, then cartwheeled to the side of the track. In the cockpit Pironi was moving a little, and that was hard to believe. His face was bloody, and seemed contorted with agony, but he was later to say that he felt nothing.

'In the few minutes after the accident I had no pain. It was just like all my accidents before, when I had no injuries. All I could think about was the car, that the spare didn't work as well as this one, and I would have to use it for the race . . .

'Then I saw my legs and thought maybe I would not be doing this race, after all. In the helicopter they began to hurt very seriously. But if I was going to have this accident, it was lucky for me that it was in Germany and not in a more primitive place . . .'

This ordeal he faced was terrifying, and there is little doubt that in some countries they would have immediately amputated his right foot. Wonderful work was done in Heidelberg and later in Paris. Didier soon announced his intention eventually to return, and Enzo Ferrari confirmed that, as and when, there would be a car for him.

Twelve months later we were all back at Hockenheim, and so also was Pironi. A year to the day after his accident he made his reappearance, still needing sticks but looking well — remarkably so for one who had undergone more than thirty operations, more than forty general anaesthetics.

No, he shrugged, he felt no emotion at returning. Time and place were a matter of coincidence — this was the first race he had been fit enough to attend. He had already started driving his Ferrari Boxer again, and the Commendatore's offer still stood. He was going to take it easy, do a little private testing in his own Martini F3 car, come back in his own time when he knew that all was well.

Pironi showed signs of agitation only when I mentioned remarks critical of him from some team managers in the immediate aftermath of the accident.

Didier celebrates after finishing first in the 1982 San Marino Grand Prix. Gilles's expression tells its own story . . .

By Hockenheim Pironi looked on certain course for the 1982 World Championship. Here, on the opening day of practice for the German Grand Prix, he and the Ferrari 126C2 were comfortably fastest. On Saturday morning came disaster.

'He was a fool,' Teddy Mayer had said. 'He was going to walk the race, anyway. Why was he going so quick in a wet untimed session?'

'I wasn't going that quickly,' was the instant response. 'Just more quickly than anyone else. The car felt unbelievably good in the rain, and I wasn't driving it particularly hard. I had different wet tyres to try that morning — after all, we could have had a wet race. I was doing my job, not taking crazy risks . . .'

Through the following season Didier showed up at the circuits occasionally, now walking without sticks. But there was no word of a return to the cockpit. 'My only problem,' he insisted, 'is that the right ankle is still not strong enough for hard braking . . .' In the autumn he suffered another leg fracture, this time in one of his beloved powerboats.

When I think of Pironi now, I remember a Sunday in the spring of '82 — just a week before the controversy at Imola — when I dropped in at Montlhery on the way back from holiday. Didier was to drive David Piper's sublime Ferrari P4, something very far removed from the dreadful kart-like Grand Prix cars of the time.

'In this car,' he enthused, 'I have rediscovered the pleasure of driving. No one can pretend that he actually *enjoys* driving the Formula 1 car of today, but this is pure pleasure. The P4 rides beautifully, slides progressively — and you can steer it on the throttle. I haven't enjoyed a racing car so much for years . . .' This was an emotional side of Didier which I had never suspected, and which I never saw anywhere else.

And I remember, too, a photograph of Pironi's room in the Paris hospital. He is holding an elaborate Prancing Horse trophy sent by the Commendatore, and he would describe it as his most prized possession. It bears the inscription 'Didier Pironi — the true 1982 World Champion'.

Five years on, his return to Formula 1 seemed firm at last — although it would not be in a Ferrari. Instead, Didier reached agreement with Gerard Larrousse, but only days later, one Sunday morning in August 1987, he was drowned in a powerboat accident in the Needles Trophy. There was severe wash from a tanker recently passed, other drivers said. They backed off for it. Pironi — just as at Hockenheim — did not.

ALAIN PROST
Not without honour

Prost, I always think, looks more like a scrum-half than a Grand Prix driver. He is short, with a crooked nose and curly hair. His forearms are like hams. I remember once seeing him in a paddock somewhere, chatting with Jabouille (himself a dead ringer for Jean-Pierre Rives), and thinking they belonged more in the Parc des Princes.

I first met him towards the end of 1979. A rather diffident fellow he was in those days, smiling shyly at everyone, hanging around in the Elf motorhome, worried about being in the way. He had easily won that year's European Formula 3 Championship, and now came to the Grands Prix like an extra on a film lot, hoping to be offered something. The best hope seemed to be Ligier, but they wanted money, and that he didn't have. There was a slight possibility of Brabham or Lotus, nothing more. Then came a surprise. Marlboro were interested, and out of nowhere came the offer of a McLaren — a third car — in the final race of the year, at Watkins Glen.

Then came more of a surprise. Alain turned it down. He did it politely, of course, but that was rather wasted on Teddy Mayer, a man to whom all china shops should perhaps be out of bounds. Prost smiles, remembering it now. 'Yes, he was a bit surprised, I think, but it was the right decision — one of my better ones. Already they had two cars entered, and I had never even sat in a Formula 1 car. Bad for you, bad for me was what I said. Instead I asked for a test at Ricard, and I went there with John Watson and Kevin Cogan, who was also being considered for 1980. It was a nice test. I was quicker than both of them . . .'

That decision to skip the Glen aroused a lot of interest, setting Alain already as a man apart. How many in his position would have had the sense — the *confidence* — to say no to McLaren? After the Ricard test came a swift offer for the following season. This Prost accepted, but many were the times when he

wished he had said no to Mayer on this, too. Talk about baptism of fire . . .

'The car was not very competitive, but you have to live with that, work on it, no problem. That year, though, I had six or seven serious accidents. You know,' he adds, always delightfully downbeat in his throwaway lines, 'if your car loses a wheel in each race, I think it's not good . . .

'I scored points in my first two races, but next was Kyalami. Two accidents in two days. Suspension failures. I broke my wrist. The car was *always* breaking, and when that happens you lose confidence and it's finished. In practice at Watkins Glen it broke again, in a fourth gear corner. I hit the wall very hard, got a big bang on my head. And still they wanted me to race the next day! I was in bed for two weeks . . .'

This it was which gave rise to 'The Prost Clause', not a new Robert Ludlum novel but a passage now standard in driver contracts, dealing with switching teams ahead of time. Alain left McLaren after a single season, despite having signed a three-year contract, and mention of 'Renault' makes E. E. Mayer apoplectic to this day. Mention of the clause bearing his name makes Prost angry, too.

'I did *not* leave McLaren because I had received a better offer from Renault! When I sign a contract, I give my word, I mean it. I wanted to leave, sure, but until the accident at the Glen I felt I should stay because of my contract. Then the suspension broke, and I crashed. It was becoming normal, *hein*? But I got back to the pits to find people in the team talking about driver error, even going too fast on cold tyres — I had already done eight laps! Okay, I said, if you want to speak like that, it's finished. And if you don't release me, I stop Formula 1. I don't drive.

'They accused me of moving to Renault for money — but if I had been willing to break my contract just like that, I would have done it months earlier when

Teddy Mayer with Prost in 1980. The Frenchman's first spell with McLaren was not a happy one, and at season's end he departed in controversial circumstances.

Ferrari spoke to me. They wanted me to go there with Gilles in 1981.'

If the McLaren had not broken so often, though, Alain doubts that he would ever have left. The painful Renault saga, he says wistfully, might have been sidestepped. But at the time he had to get away, regain his confidence. He went to Renault as number two, and immediately his talent presented problems. As with Watson at McLaren, now with Arnoux at Renault. Prost, from the start, was quicker than the team leader. He won his first Grand Prix at Dijon, followed up at Zandvoort and Monza. René won nothing. The contracts were very different for 1982.

Alain says he hated that year in every way. 'There was the personal problem with Arnoux, of course, but it was the season when we had no suspension. There was no pleasure in driving. Our reliability was terrible. René refused to do much testing, leaving it to me. I got tired. I didn't drive anywhere near my best in 1982. Twice I have nearly quit Formula 1 for good, and each time it has been because of a reaction against me in my own country. I am not so popular in France. For sure they like me much more in England. When I win at Silverstone in the McLaren — fantastic! I never got cheers like that when I won in France in a Renault . . .'

'Retirement was seriously in your mind?' I questioned. 'When was this?'

'After the French Grand Prix in 1982, for a couple of days I decided absolutely to stop at the end of the year.'

This was the race, of course, in which Arnoux went back on his word, promising to play a supporting role to Prost, then marching off with the race.

'But that wasn't the reason for thinking about retirement', Alain insists. 'I'd been duped by Arnoux, okay. Stupid of me to trust him. I looked at the problem with Villeneuve after Pironi passed him at Imola, and learned a lesson . . . No, I was disillusioned because the whole of France seemed to take his side. *I* was the one had been conned, and the French journalists were talking about poor little René, how he had fought for this, how unlucky he was, always a martyr. Ever since Joan of Arc, you know, the French have loved martyrs . . .'

He laughs about it now, but admits it was less amusing at the time. 'French mentality is odd in some ways, you know. When I went to Renault the journalists wrote good things about me, but by 1982 I had become the bad guy. I think, to be honest, I had made the mistake of winning! The French don't really like winners. They prefer the second, the man who loses gloriously . . . I was furious, like Gilles at Imola, that my team did not back me up as they should have done afterwards. For me *that* is the wound which has never healed. René and I don't have a problem these days.'

It may sound like a bunch of sour grapes, but the words come across in a matter-of-fact tone. A set of circumstances, Prost feels, were misinterpreted — perhaps deliberately — to his detriment. He felt the same way at Kyalami in 1983, when Piquet flicked the title from his grasp.

'Okay, we lost the championship. It happens. And I thought it was Renault's fault because they were too conservative, refusing to change things on the car. I warned them that you couldn't beat Gordon Murray and Nelson Piquet that way, but . . .

'You know what? Every week there is a house newspaper in the Renault factories, and it said I stopped at Kyalami because I was running only third and didn't want to look bad! And some French journalists wrote the same kind of thing. You can't imagine how a driver feels about something like that.'

Two days after the debacle in South Africa came the bombshell from Paris: the Régie had shown Prost the door. And Alain, it should be added, positively ran through it. Within days his name was at the foot of a McLaren contract. He needed a top drive, and they knew it. They got him cheap, and he knew it. No matter. Now he could seriously go racing; the big money would follow with the results. McLaren by this time had fundamentally changed. The old regime had gone, replaced by Ron Dennis and John Barnard. Under way was the Porsche engine programme (paid for by TAG), and Barnard was in the process of designing one of history's great Formula 1 cars.

'It was impossible to compare McLaren then and when I had been there before', Prost says. 'Really, only the name was the same. The first time the MP4/2 ran, I broke the Ricard lap record with it. Barnard and Dennis are not easy men to work with, you know, but what they have achieved is fantastic.'

Their first race together brought victory, in Rio. Alain is a man accustomed to winning, and usually he acknowledges the flag with a discreet wave of the right hand. This time both hands were raised in wild delight. It was, he maintains, his most pleasurable win.

'There was a bit of revenge involved, even if I don't care to admit it. After the split with Renault I got a very hard time from the French press. If Renault had won in Brazil, and I had not finished, some of them would have crucified me. But I won, and it was finished. The French public, too, changed their attitude towards me after this race. Suddenly they were for me — or more than they had been when I was in a French car . . . As I say, the French are strange in this way. Michel Platini plays for an Italian club now — and he's much more popular than when he was in France!'

Like every other French Formula 1 driver, Prost lives abroad, not surprisingly preferring to keep his money from the Mitterand government. As Jackie Stewart once said of his emigration: 'It suddenly occurred to

Happy days at Renault. Driver and mechanics celebrate after Alain's third victory for the team, at Monza in 1981.

Prost's win with the Renault RE40 at Silverstone in 1983 was his third of the year, and the title seemed to be beckoning.

me that, nine weekends out of ten, I was risking my life for the Chancellor of the Exchequer.' And Alain, too, is resident in Switzerland.

Stewart and Clark were his own idols, and it is on their example that he bases his own philosophy of racing. He shares with them that flowing style, immaculate of line. The hardest part, surely, is to make it look easy. Watch Prost in a McLaren, and you start to believe you could do it yourself. There lies the art of the thing.

'I know', he says, almost shamefaced, 'that I am not very exciting to watch — I don't think Clark was, either, and for me he was the best ever. I drive deliberately like that, very naturally, and I don't want to change. I don't decide to go quick, to make a big effort. I just go quick.

'Of course', he goes on, 'I like to slide a car, particularly in the rain. It's very satisfying, but not as much as the perfect lap. Always I am looking for that — and I mean a lap where you are not one centimetre

off line anywhere. I've *almost* done it a few times, I believe, but never completely.'

For Alain the perfect race is where he leads from first to last. That might seem obvious, but some drivers handle leading better than others. When Prost is in front I find it like watching a metronome. Victory is at the core, and he peels away the laps. A motor racing Bradman, races seem to surrender to him.

Still I find him distinctly underrated — as driver and man. For me Alain is now unquestionably among the great of all time, and the best of the mid-eighties moment, but there is in some quarters a reluctance to acknowledge his class. He has no apparent weaknesses, shines on all types of circuit, in every kind of weather. He qualifies brilliantly, wins more than anyone else.

Partly, I believe, this prejudice against him stems from Formula 1's puerile dislike of all things French — or, rather, all things *successful* and French. Certainly it is true that the Gallic contingent tends to

Prost and McLaren — the most effective racing partnership of the modern era. Alain's victory at Monza in 1985 was his twelfth for the team in two seasons, and gave him a firm grip at last on the elusive title.

be clannish, but at Kyalami in 1983 I seemed to be the only 'foreigner' in the place who actually wanted Prost to win the championship. On that occasion, in fairness, the overwhelming support for Piquet and Brabham probably had some of its roots in the fact that Alain was in a Renault. The faceless Régie was never popular within Formula 1, and the same is largely true of McLaren — or some of its personnel. Boundless admiration, yes, but little affection.

So perhaps this colours opinions of Alain himself. For some reason beyond me, those who don't know the man believe they wouldn't like him if they did. The truth is that Prost, like anyone worthwhile, takes a bit of getting to know. He does not instantly confide.

'I have found Formula 1 to be full of hypocrisy and deceit,' he says, 'and that disappointed me. When I was with Renault, I was on my guard all the time, always wondering if that hand slapping me on the back had a dagger in it . . . At Renault a defeat meant an

inquest afterwards. At McLaren they don't panic when there are problems. Racing is still for me a passion, but I see it differently now. I'm more relaxed.'

True enough, since the Renault days Alain's true personality has emerged. He still bites his nails — just as Clark did — and occasionally you catch sight of the old haunted expression. But usually he grins.

Jacques Laffite, he concedes, has played a considerable part in reshaping the way he goes about his life. More than any other driver of my experience, Jacques has Grand Prix racing in correct perspective. A bad practice session can be swept away by a good round of golf. And maybe tomorrow will be better. If not, the day after . . . Laffite introduced Prost to golf, now one of his passions, but more importantly helped him rationalize the business of being a Grand Prix driver.

'I used to stay at the circuit from eight in the morning until seven at night', Alain says, 'and feel that I had really done a lot of work. And if I hadn't done that, I would have felt guilty. But then I realized I could do the same from nine until three or four. Jacques showed me that. You leave the track, and there is plenty of time for golf or a swim. And that's good, makes you forget the car for a while. I used to think about it too much.'

Prost may win more than anyone else, but he also knows how to lose with grace. As memorable as any victory was his dignity after Estoril in 1984, his coming to terms with the fact that yet another win — his seventh of the year — had yet failed to land him the title. Lauda, with a lucky second place, was half a point ahead.

'Worse than that by far', Alain says, 'was losing the victory at Imola the following year because the car was a couple of kilos underweight. That was maybe my best drive — I went as fast as I could while calculating my fuel to get me to the finish line and no more. It

ran out a few hundred metres after I got the flag. I thought I had judged it perfectly, but the car was light because the tank was dry . . .'

At Zandvoort a few months later he was held off to the finish by a defiant Lauda. There was no whingeing that a slow tyre stop had robbed him of the race, no complaint that Niki — out of contention for the championship — refused to yield during the final laps. 'I knew', he says, 'where I stood. He had told me before the race he would win if he could, and that was fine. I would have been mad if, like Arnoux at Ricard, he had promised to help me, then not done it. He wanted to win a race in his final year, and I understand that.'

Prost's attitude to racing appeals to me. At one time, he admits, he was obsessive about the World Championship, believing it the only honour of consequence in the game. But eventually he found, as did Moss, that coming so close so often served in

Perhaps the most perfect drive of his life. At Jerez in 1988 Prost was faultless all afternoon, somehow making his 150 litres go the distance — and doing it from the front.

time to diminish, rather than increase, its importance.

'The record that is important to me is Stewart's 27 Grand Prix wins. That I really want. I think there have been some World Champions who were not so good — but those who have won many, many, races have all been great. Gilles Villeneuve once told me winning races meant more to him than titles, and at the time I didn't understand him. Now I do.

'Obviously I was glad to win the title eventually,' he says, 'because it was almost a relief — I felt it was out of the way, if you like. And I didn't enjoy *tactique* races, where I drove for points. That's not the way I like to drive.

'My second championship brought me much more pleasure, really, because it was unexpected. In '86 I drove much better than before, for sure, but the Williams-Honda was the fastest car, and I went to Adelaide with only a small chance to win. As it turned out, though, I won the race and the title . . .'

There was no championship hat-trick for Prost in 1987 — the Hondas were simply beyond reach — but three more victories took him beyond Jackie Stewart's longstanding record.

'I really wanted to do that. Sometimes I think records are more important to me than titles. You know, there have been some World Champions who were not so good — but those who have won many, many races have all been great. Gilles Villeneuve once told me winning races meant more to him than championships, and at the time I didn't understand him. Now I do.'

Amazing now to remember that Alain Prost won nine Grands Prix in a Renault! That, perhaps more than anything else, tells you of the man's worth. Most important of all, though, is that he is never off form, central to the action in every race. In 1988 — having done it all — he somewhere found the motivation to run new McLaren team mate Ayrton Senna close for the championship. Seven further victories brought his tally to a startling 35.

'I think maybe I am not so popular in France,' he says, with that gravelly chuckle, 'because in *everything* I want to win. As I said, the French like the man who is second with glory. I've always wanted to be first, and it's not vanity. It's because life is a game, and I want to be the best. Otherwise the game — life — is not interesting. Even playing cards, I want to win. If I begin to think otherwise, I don't play. That's me.'

The motivation never flags. In his ninth season Prost was often a match for Senna's desperate ambition, and at Ricard beat his team mate fair and square.

CLAY REGAZZONI
Bravest by far

'I think it's happening to me again', Clay Regazzoni ruefully smiled at Monza in 1979. 'I've got a good car in a team I really like — and they're going to replace me with Reutemann, like Ferrari did three years ago . . .' He was speaking about Williams, of course, with whom he had spent his Indian summer. Written off after two desultory seasons with Ensign and Shadow, he had been taken on as Alan Jones's number two, Frank believing he might do a reasonable job, not make waves.

A man with a brittle ego might have railed at the prospect. Had he not spent six years as a Ferrari works driver? Did he not lead Jones four to one on Grand Prix victories? Had not the Williams team — until very recently, anyway — always been considered something of a joke in Formula 1? Clay never thought like that, however, never had an ego problem. Pride he had in plenty, but that is something quite else. He went to work for Frank very happily, drove like a spring lamb all year long, gave Williams his first Grand Prix victory, finished fifth in the championship. Not too dusty for a has-been.

On the Wednesday night before Monza he celebrated his fortieth birthday with an elaborate, money-no-object, party at the legendary Moulin de Mougins near Cannes. It was a happy time in his life. Clay always loved a party.

At Monza he was brilliant. In years past he had been the darling of the *tifosi*, the best loved Ferrari driver. Now, as Scheckter and Villeneuve ran one-two, he and the Williams posed a lone threat to the red cars in the late laps. Storming along, he lapped almost a second faster than anyone else, and in the stands they went a little quiet. In the end, though, they got the perfect result. Jody and Gilles powered over the line, Clay a little under five seconds behind. Ferrari-Ferrari-Regazzoni — could life be better than that?

Regazzoni's previous race, at Zandvoort, had been

rather shorter. Within yards of the start, indeed, he had tangled with Arnoux's Renault, pulling off beyond Tarzan with the left front wheel gone. And it was a mark of the affection in which Clay was held that, at Monza, Renault presented him with a very special birthday present; a wheelchair with huge F1 wheels at the back, Williams front wings — and the left front missing. A few months later we recalled the ceremony with an ironic sadness.

That same day I suggested to him that now was surely the right time to stop. 'You've had a tremendous season,' I said, 'but now Reutemann is coming to Williams, and you're never going to lay hands on another car like that again. You're forty, so . . .'

Clay listened with tolerant amusement, then grinned. 'You must understand that, for me, it is not a matter of winning all the time. I am quite happy just to be a part of Formula 1 — I love it, and most of all I love to drive racing cars. So why should I stop when I feel this way?'

He spoke with such dignity and good humour that I felt embarrassed at having raised the subject. I suppose what I had meant was 'quit while you're ahead', but Regazzoni revelled in simply being a racing driver, and would never have entertained such a thought. 'I love it like Graham Hill did', he concluded. 'Everyone said he should have retired before he did — but why, if he was enjoying it still?'

Well, because there is a line of thought that if you go to the Gates often enough, eventually they open. But Clay shared Mario Andretti's opinion on that subject; every race is like a spin of the roulette wheel, a new beginning. You have as much chance of winning — or the other — every time the ball is flicked into play, no more than last week, and no less. This is a comfortable philosophy for a racing driver to hold.

There is a famous photograph of Regazzoni, taken at Monza in 1961 on the occasion of his first visit to

Monza 1970. Regazzoni's Ferrari 312B starts to go away from Stewart's March in the closing laps. It was Clay's first Grand Prix victory, and put him into Italian racing folklore.

a Grand Prix. He is standing in the old paddock, jacket slung over his shoulder, gazing at Baghetti's Ferrari. Just another young face in the crowd, dreaming. If only . . . Nine years later, on 6 September 1970, he was climbing aboard. Any mention of Clay Regazzoni — was ever there a more mellifluous name for a racing driver? — makes me remember that day in particular.

It was a day which dragged one through every emotion Grand Prix racing can muster. Down the road, towards Parabolica, the heat haze shimmered rhythmically. Once in a while the drone of conversation from the stands gave way to a bout of cheers as they recognized one of their heroes. The day before, a few hundred yards up the road, Jochen Rindt had crashed to his death, and thoughts of the accident kept bobbing to the surface of everyone's mind.

It was only the fifth Grand Prix of Regazzoni's career, and he won it after 68 laps of pure slipstreaming battle. There were no chicanes at Monza in those days. By half-distance Ickx and Giunti were out, leaving Clay as the only Ferrari representative. They willed him to

succeed, and with a few laps left he made a break, pulled out fifty yards over Stewart and the rest, weaving from side to side down the pit straight, breaking the tow. The wall of sound from the old stone grandstand was unforgettable as he emerged from Parabolica for the last time.

'Ah, yes, yes. To win at Monza with a Ferrari . . . for me, it was the maximum. Especially then. I won again there five years later, but it was very easy. In 1970 it was my first win, and I had to push very hard. Also, that car was my favourite. Was not an easy car, but very competitive. You had to concentrate very hard in the 312B.'

Regazzoni arrived in Formula 1 with a ragged reputation. In the lower formulae he had often been blindingly quick, but along with the pace went a certain tendency to live for the moment. He had survived accidents without number, in particular one in the Formula 3 race at Monte Carlo in 1968. There his Tecno had run wide at the exit of the chicane, passing *under* the single tier of guardrail! The roll-over bar was hard up against the barrier, yet Clay hopped from the cockpit — quite unhurt — on the harbour side. But he took to a Grand Prix Ferrari as if born to it. Brought into the team at mid-season, he drove in only seven races in 1970, yet was able to finish third in the World Championship.

In many ways, that first season stands as his best. True, he came within three points of the title four years later, but in 1970 he made no discernible mistakes. For the bulk of his Formula 1 career, you never quite knew what you were going to get from Clay. Sometimes his driving was sloppy and full of error; occasionally he would turn in a sublime performance, as at the Nurburgring in 1974, or Long Beach a couple of years later. Each of those 'precision' races he led all the way, without the hint of an error, and you wondered how this same man could pass another Sunday afternoon running over kerbs and clouting barriers.

He was longer at Maranello than any man in history,

although at no stage the official number one. It never ruffled him. Ferrari was his life and pride. Therefore it was doubly unfortunate that he should have been treated so shabbily at the end.

'I never understood why the Commendatore didn't speak clean with me at the end of 1976. Before Monza he told me there was no problem about 1977, but nothing would be finally decided until after the last race in Japan. At Monza I had offers from Brabham and McLaren, but I said I was staying with Ferrari.' Regazzoni was perhaps too ingenuous a man for modern Formula 1. After the Japanese Grand Prix he learned that Reutemann had signed with Ferrari many weeks previously. 'Carlos could have told me,' he said, 'but worse was that Ferrari was not correct with me, didn't speak clean. If he had said no, is finished for you, I say okay, I am happy to drive for you these six years.'

Now we come back to the subtleties of pride and ego. His Ferrari term done, Clay got in touch with

A desultory season with BRM in 1973. Regazzoni took the pole at the opening race, in Argentina, but thereafter everything went downhill, and he was relieved to quit at year's end.

At Long Beach in 1976 Clay was unstoppable in the Ferrari 312T, starting from pole position, leading all the way from team mate Lauda, setting fastest lap.

Bernie Ecclestone again. At Monza the Brabham boss had given him chapter and verse on a contract for 1977. Now, a couple of months on, they met at an hotel near Heathrow, Bernie now in more of a buyer's market.

'He asked me how much I wanted, and I mentioned what we had discussed at Monza. Now he offered me less than half. This was the end of the year, too late for me to join another big team, and for sure he thought I would agree. I told him it wasn't even worth talking about . . . It wasn't the money that was so important. I like to make race with nice people. I caught the next flight back to Switzerland.'

Thus it was that Regazzoni joined Ensign, moving at a step from one financial end of the Formula 1 spectrum to the other. It was a happy year, if not a particularly successful one, the glamorous ex-Ferrari star blending in very easily with Morris Nunn's little outfit, if less than totally familiar with the new lingo. 'You wanta cuppa tea?' he asked me one day in a dry

and dusty paddock. Then, calling Mo's wife: 'Sylvia, please put off the kettle . . .'

They all loved him, yet knew it was unlikely that he would stay for long. In 1978 he joined Shadow, and then came the offer from Williams. 'I remembered clearly that when he'd last driven a world-class car, back in 1976, he'd driven everyone into the ground at Long Beach, scored a lot of other points, and rarely crashed,' Frank said. 'Not by any means the greatest in the world, but a superb number two and a happy, uncomplicated man. It worked out very well. We did each other a favour. Clay is an absolute gentleman — very different from most racing drivers. A man who genuinely loves motor racing for its own sake. A totally adorable character.'

That he was, and is. And in 1979 he quickly reminded everyone he could still do it. At Monte Carlo he hustled Scheckter's Ferrari through the closing laps, finishing but a few yards behind. And at Silverstone he took over when Alan Jones retired, scoring the first

Williams victory. 'Bravo, Frank', he said quietly to his emotional boss. That was the essential modesty of the man. It was the team which had won.

When the Williams saga was over, he returned to Ensign, and was running fourth in the Long Beach Grand Prix at the time of the final accident, which happened at the end of Shoreline Drive, the fastest part of the circuit. Regazzoni's car approached at around 180 mph, as usual, but instead of slowing right down for the hairpin, disappeared, bullet-like, into the escape road. It could, in theory, have been an escape road without end for Shoreline Drive is a wide freeway, but a barrier had been erected, closing it off, and it was this the Ensign struck, still at colossal speed.

'At Long Beach for the first time we had titanium pedals on the Ensign, and when I pressed the brake pedal there was not the slightest resistance from it. Nothing. I tried to pump it. Still nothing. I had to lose speed, changed down from fifth to third, then cut the engine . . . Zunino's Brabham was parked in the escape road. I hit it, then bounced into the barrier. For about ten minutes I lost consciousness. Then I remember terrible pain in my hips . . .'

Clay soon knew he had to face the unimaginable. His spinal cord had been severely damaged and he was paralysed. Some similarly injured had recovered fully, notably the Swiss downhill skier Roland Collombin, but others had not. Over the next couple of years Regazzoni underwent operations without number, some in Basle, some — of a more radical kind — in Washington. Constantly, it seemed, his hopes of walking again were raised, then dashed. Similarly, his morale veered uncertainly between optimism and despair.

Finally, in 1985, he began coming to Grands Prix regularly again, working as a commentator for Italian television. 'I am quite tranquil now', he told me. 'At last I have accepted that the miracle will not happen. But life can still be worth something.'

I confess that, for a time, Clay's presence in the paddocks of the world made me feel uncomfortable. A selfish sentiment, perhaps, but none the less there. I suppose he represented the unacceptable face of motor racing, a very obvious casualty of a sport capable of untold callousness.

When a driver is killed there is great sadness among

Regazzoni's last Grand Prix victory came at Silverstone in 1979. When Williams team leader Alan Jones retired, Clay took over to win without a problem. Here Reutemann's Lotus follows him through the Woodcote chicane.

Silverstone 1979. Regazzoni, always immensely popular with British crowds, waves in triumph, flanked by second and third men Arnoux (left) and Jarier.

us, particularly if, against our better judgement, we have been close to him. A colleague once told me that time would harden me, that a particular friend would die and that no tragedy would hit so hard afterwards. He was right. In his case, it had been Bruce McLaren; in mine, Gilles Villeneuve. A death, though, means an absence, a wiping of the slate, if not the memory. Motor racing has killed a great many men, but always — for those of us outside his family — there is the convenient and consoling thought that 'he knew what he was doing — no one made him get in the car'. Accidents, therefore, tend to be all or nothing. The man dies or he recovers, even if scarred like Lauda. But Regazzoni, Niki's team mate those many years ago, has been crippled by motor racing, and that is less easy to accept.

During practice at Monaco in 1985, though, I saw him watching practice in Casino Square. And several minutes had gone by before it dawned on me; he was *standing*, leaning against the barrier, stopwatch in hand. Later I clumsily told him how moved I had been,

and that great bandit smile spread across his face. He was the same old Clay.

Over the years I saw him drive in so many races, saw him playing football and tennis and golf. An active man in every way, who adored every kind of sport. 'For a long time I felt very sorry for myself,' he said, 'but when something like this happens, you move into a different world — a world you never thought about. And you feel ashamed. I remember Gunnar Nilsson talking about the children in his cancer hospital, how he had had years of good life which they would never have. As for me, I can drive my Ferrari. I have my driving school for handicapped people. I can still go to races, enjoy them, be part of them. I don't want to be pitied, for people to feel sorry for me. I don't feel desperate any more.'

Clay was always a dignified man, as well as an abnormally brave one. And what he has faced since 1980 has put more call on his courage than the ten seasons of Formula 1 which went before.

Six years after his British Grand Prix victory, Clay comes back to Silverstone, working on the Italian television commentary team. He remains an intrinsic member of the Grand Prix fraternity.

CARLOS REUTEMANN

On a clear day . . .

If Reutemann had been a writer, I suspect he might have been a great one. A lot of stuff would have been thrown away, but what we actually saw would have been tinged with genius.

As it was, he chose to be a racing driver, where ability is on permanent show. Along with the dazzling manuscripts comes also the overflowing waste basket. Success and failure are nakedly exposed, public. And in no driver I have ever seen were they so clearly defined as in Carlos.

There were days, when the angels touched him, which reduced most of Reutemann's rivals to bit players. 'Today, nine points, no problem', he would murmur on race morning. But there were other times — too many for one of his talent — when his presence in a race went unnoticed. He wavered between sublime self-confidence and dithering uncertainty.

'I can honestly say', he told me once, 'that I have never been in a team which I felt was supporting *me* a hundred per cent.' And perhaps this was always the crux of Carlos's problem with Formula 1. He was never 'one of the boys', preferred his own little coterie. A quiet man, and shy, he was an easy target.

Somehow — and only Reutemann knows how — he contrived not to win the World Championship in 1981. With hindsight Frank Williams rightly ascribes some of the blame to his team: 'In terms of equipment, we gave Carlos exactly the same as Jones, but he needed psychological support more than most drivers. He needed to be aware that everyone in the team was wearing a Reutemann lapel badge and an Argentine scarf. Probably we didn't appreciate that sufficiently at the time.'

Reutemann's ability was therefore quixotic. He was unusually complex and sensitive for a racing driver, a man from whom great performances had to be coaxed. But if he felt all was right, he was next to unstoppable.

The whole of his career was encapsulated in that last season of 1981. He had joined Williams the year before as Jones's number two, a position he accepted readily. The team's priority had been for Alan to win the World Championship, and the mission had been accomplished.

That done, Frank should have thrown the whole thing open the following season. Instead he kept the 'Jones priority' clause in Carlos's contract, and this the Argentine showed early signs of ignoring.

Reutemann was hot at the beginning of the year, conclusively winning the non-championship race at Kyalami. At Long Beach he led Jones, but finished second to him after a silly mistake.

At Rio it rained, and there Carlos was in front throughout, Alan sitting a few seconds behind, awaiting a signal to pass which never came. Despite the pit signals, REUT-JONES was how they finished, and afterwards Alan, Frank — everyone in the team, it seemed — was livid.

True enough, under the terms of his contract Carlos had inescapably done wrong. It had been a mistake by Williams to impose such restrictions for a second season, a mistake by Reutemann to accept them. But such were the facts. Frank fined him for his action; Alan never forgot it. If Carlos were to win the championship, he could expect no support whatever from his team mate.

I never saw Reutemann as duplicitous, as Pironi was to be at Imola, but there again I liked the man and always believed him honourable. He did not, after all, steal a race from a trusting team mate on the last lap, and there was a curious innocence in the way he sought to justify himself.

'Jones had reason to be upset, I can't disagree with that. And it did affect our relationship afterwards. I saw the pit signal three laps from the end, and I knew the terms of the contract, but still I was in a dilemma.

As at Kyalami and Zeltweg in 1974, Reutemann and the Brabham BT44 were the class of the field at Watkins Glen. Hunt's third-place Hesketh follows.

'From the beginning of my career I always started every race with the intention of winning it, but now I was being asked to give it away, just like that. "If I give way", I thought to myself, "I stop the car here and now, in the middle of the track, and leave immediately for my farm in Argentina. Finish. Not a racing driver any more . . ."'

What, I asked, if the same situation were to occur again?

'Mmmm . . . very difficult. I don't think it will, but if it did I believe I would take the same decision I took in Brazil.'

Months later, Frank Williams had changed his opinion of the incident, perhaps a little jaundiced by Jones's late-in-the-day decision to retire: 'All I care about is the team, and the points we earn. I don't care who scores them — why should I? Drivers are only employees, after all.'

At the time, though, there was a distinct coolness towards Reutemann. He and Jones were no longer team mates, merely individuals who happened to operate out of the same pit. And through the season the abrasive Australian missed no opportunity to score, metaphorically and otherwise, off his introspective rival.

Still, it hardly showed in Carlos's driving. His legendary reputation for inconsistency seemed to have been shed. Zolder, where he won, was his fifteenth consecutive finish in the points, a record which will stand probably for ever.

The Belgian race, too, was significant from another standpoint. As Reutemann cruised out during the first afternoon of qualifying, an Osella mechanic fell from the pit wall into his path. There was nothing to be done, no opportunity in the narrow pit lane to swerve, and the young man later died.

Carlos, for all his poker face, is a compassionate man, less able than most to deal with this sort of tragedy. He was profoundly distressed, and later I wondered how his weekend might be affected, for this

Carlos (like most Brabham people!) never had much enthusiasm for Ecclestone's decision to go with Alfa Romeo engines. Here the Argentine's BT45 struggles to hold off Amon's Ensign at Jarama in 1976.

was a major test of his character. That he came through it superbly was no thanks to the driver and team manager of a rival outfit, who sank to previously unplumbed depths by mocking his misfortune, presumably hoping to add to his distress, psych him into temporary oblivion.

People like that belong in a place with rubber walls, and this cosy vignette was alone reason enough to root strongly for Carlos at Las Vegas — this, and the fact that he went to Italy to see the boy's parents.

After the British Grand Prix Reutemann led the World Championship by a daunting seventeen points. With but half a dozen races left, how could he lose? Astonishingly, he found a way.

At around that time I interviewed him for a magazine article, and began to detect the return of the flawed confidence. We are all overly familiar with the 'take it one game at a time' clichés of modern professional sport, but even in these terms Carlos was cautious.

'There is a long way to go', he grimaced characteristically. 'I have to think about the rest of the season. At present everything is going well for me — too well, in fact, and that worries me. To be honest, I feel a little bit alone . . .' That was Reutemann pure.

At the same time he bet a colleague of mine £50 that he would *not* win the title, presumably seeing it as some kind of superstitious insurance.

Thereafter Carlos's season disintegrated. The succeeding races brought only six more points; in the same period Piquet picked up another 24. Reutemann drove beautifully at Hockenheim, but retired with a blown engine. Elsewhere the failures were his own. Over-anxious in Holland, he drove into Laffite.

'Did you see Carlos's time? Unbelievable!' I can still recall the way Villeneuve rolled his eyes after practice at Monza, and indeed Reutemann had put in the lap of the season. At this, a power track, he qualified second and split the Renaults with a time well over a second faster than Jones and Piquet. But during the race there was rain, and he finished half a minute adrift of Alan's second place.

Canada — more rain. Carlos led away, was fifth

after one lap, nineteenth after six. Was this the man of the Rio monsoon? Yes, the Michelins had been good there, and now the Goodyears were not so, but Piquet also had the American tyres and was lapped only once. The winning Laffite went by Reutemann three times.

Still he went to the final race with a one point lead in the championship, and, shrugging off the dismay of Montreal, was again simply fantastic against the clock, taking the pole in the opening session. Through the days leading up to the race he was brimming with confidence and good humour. In the race he faded to nothing.

I watched that afternoon in total bemusement, embarrassed for him. He had this phenomenal talent — why did he squander it so often? Later he would mumble about cross-weighting and gearchange problems, but in truth he drove like a man who had suddenly realized he did not *want* the World Championship.

Perhaps there were problems with the car, but that did not explain his lack of aggression against a rival semi-comatose for the last quarter of the race — nor how a man on pole position, with the title beckoning, could have been down to fourth by the first corner.

To become World Champion, Carlos had only to keep a perilously unfit Piquet behind him, yet he allowed the Brabham past like one being lapped. His drive that day remains the most inexplicable I have seen. And Las Vegas, an appropriately pitiless place, was the scene of high tragedy in the life of a great racing driver. As Jones, the winner, and Piquet, the champion, took the plaudits, Reutemann slipped quietly away in his own private sorrow.

I have always liked Carlos, although, like most people, I can make no claim really to know him. His conversation mirrored his driving. Some days he was all monosyllables and facial contortions: 'Vairy deefficult here . . .' But there were also times when he was positively chatty, a little unsettling because it was so unexpected. You got used to the Ingmar Bergman depressions.

He was happiest, I believe, during his second year at Ferrari. People tend to remember of 1978 only that the Lotus 79s dominated, Andretti winning the championship and six of the races. Overlooked is that

At Brands Hatch in 1978 Reutemann and the Ferrari 312T3 qualified only eighth, but took a memorable victory, pressurising Lauda into an error of judgement late in the race.

Reutemann won four in the T3 — without the assistance of ground effect.

Also, he was on close terms with his team mate that season, and that was unusual. With Lauda the year before there had been problems all through, Niki resenting his presence at Ferrari in the first place. At Lotus he would not enjoy an easy relationship with Andretti, and the years with Jones we know about already. But with Villeneuve he got along fine.

Gilles, of course, was very much the Grand Prix novice at the start of 1978, with Carlos indisputably team leader. There was no battle of pride — and nor did one develop through the season, even though Villeneuve increasingly came on strong. With Gilles, Carlos said, there was an open sense of comradeship, no hint of polemics, and this he found refreshing.

'I would never say anything against Villeneuve — or against Ferrari. The atmosphere there was a little 'casino', but it was a very happy time for me. I would like to have stayed but . . . there was a very long-running romance between Ferrari and Scheckter.'

As early as August there had been confirmation from Maranello that Jody would be joining Gilles for 1979, and within a month Carlos had signed for Lotus. This would be a year of misery, the nadir of his Formula 1 career, and I think he suspected it even before he started work with Colin Chapman.

'What have I done?' he mumbled at Monza. 'Going to Lotus . . . I must be crazy . . .'

Events proved him right. Lotus tumbled in 1979, and from a great height. Chapman's forte — genius — had always lain in original thinking, in swinging a lamp over uncharted territory. He had conceived the theory of ground effect, briefly capitalized on it with the 79, then outsmarted himself with the 80.

In the early part of the year Mario ran the new car, Carlos the still obviously superior 79, and in time Andretti began to resent what he claimed to be Reutemann's reluctance to play his part in the development of the 80.

Reutemann signed a three-year contract with Lotus, but was so unhappy with the team that he left after only one season, 1979. Here at Monaco he qualified poorly, but finished a fine third.

Reutemann should have won the World Championship with Williams in 1981. Frank acknowledges that the team could — and should — have given their driver more moral support. Even so, Carlos's leisurely performance at Las Vegas remains a matter of mystery.

'I hated my year with Lotus right from the beginning — even more than my last year with Ecclestone, with the Brabham-Alfas. Chapman was a great engineer, but he was also a very . . . mmmm . . . special personality. I couldn't deal with him. He always had a different relationship with Mario — and yet he was prepared to get rid of Mario if I would stay for 1980! How long, I thought, before a similar thing happens to me?'

We were back to the same problem. Team owners, Carlos would claim, always had a better relationship with his team mate. Ecclestone was closer to Pace, Chapman to Andretti, Williams to Jones. And it seemed never to occur to him that perhaps this was more than coincidence, that maybe his own remoteness played some part, worked against him.

You can learn a lot about a racing driver from talking to his mechanics, particularly those who have been around a long time. For many there will never be another Jimmy, another Jochen or Ronnie. Some they remember with scorn, even dislike, others with professional respect if not personal affection. Carlos comes into this last category: 'On his day he was unreal, but I never really got to know him . . .'

He left Lotus as he had left Brabham, by buying himself out of a contract, and his final move was to Williams, which is where we came in.

After Vegas, where he allowed Piquet through to pinch his World Championship, there was not much compassion from his colleagues. One — in Reutemann's class as neither man nor driver — was astounded by his performance. 'What was he doing, letting Nelson past like that?' he incredulously asked afterwards, and that far down the line I travelled with him, but then — 'I mean, all he had to do was put Piquet in the wall and he'd won the championship . . .'

There we parted. For a man like Carlos, that would not have been *winning* anything. He had too much integrity, too much pride, even to contemplate a stunt like that.

I was not surprised when news of his retirement broke a few days after Vegas, but astonished when he later changed his mind. At the start of 1982 there he was at Williams again, back with the people who had frankly vilified him in the days after Vegas. And at Kyalami he was brilliant once more, second between the Renaults. In Rio he looked ordinary, crashing finally, and then came the final and irrevocable decision to stop.

Perhaps it had all changed too much for him. South Africa had witnessed the drivers' notorious strike, the 'dormitory' night at the Sunnyside Park Hotel in Johannesburg. For some of the younger men this was a bit of a jape, easily shrugged off, but to a man like Carlos — the haughty Latin champion, ten years a star — it was undignified and bewildering. He was approaching forty, and Grand Prix racing was into a period of turmoil and anarchy. Why did he need it any more?

A year or so later I broached the subject with him. He had shown up to spectate, as he quite often does. And he still looked like the racing driver from central casting, face tanned, electric-blue eyes hidden almost permanently behind Ray-Bans.

Some had extravagantly suggested that he had known where the Falklands dispute was heading, that he considered his position — an Argentine in an obsessively British team — untenable, that he had quit to save embarrassment both to Williams and himself.

'No, it wasn't that,' he insisted at once, 'although for sure it might have been difficult. If you want to know,' he said, 'I was suddenly very tired. The ambiance of racing changed so much. It was not fun for me like once it had been.

'I raced always because I liked to drive quick, to be precise with the car — and for that reason I hated ground effect cars, even though I had a very good one. There was pleasure in being quick still, in a good result, but none in the actual driving.

'As for losing the championship in '81 . . . well. I always said that if it happened, fine, it happened. If not, life would still be the same. The sun would still be in the same place. And it is . . .'

At Zolder in 1981 Reutemann showed tremendous resolution, managing to put the practice tragedy from his mind on race day. This was his last Grand Prix victory.

JOCHEN RINDT
Tragic title

One morning, in the autumn of 1969, I drove out along the M4 to Heathrow Airport. At that time I had a Lotus Elan, and I was driving it quickly because, as ever, I was late. There was little traffic around, and one of the cars I overtook was a yellow Elan Plus 2, dawdling in the middle lane. An instant later it had ceased to dawdle and was right behind me, lights flashing. For a while we continued like that, faster and faster, until eventually I moved over and let him by.

But the yellow Plus 2, instead of overtaking, drew alongside and held station. The driver, grinning broadly, was Jochen Rindt. I nearly went off the road.

'The thing about Jochen', Chris Amon reckoned, 'was this tremendous competitiveness in everything he did. Obviously it came out in his driving, but he was just the same playing table tennis or gin rummy.'

At the time of the M4 incident my only connection with motor racing was that of a complete fan. Rindt and I had never even met, so he wasn't fooling around with someone he knew. Simply, it seemed, he was overtaken by another Elan, and immediately all his competitive juices went to work. Perhaps that morning was a pointer to the man.

When the mood took him, Jochen Rindt was capable of anything in a racing car. And twice it took him at Silverstone in 1969. This was his first season with Lotus, yet by April the signs were that all was not well between Rindt and his new team. Jochen, in fact, was unequivocal in his criticism of the way Colin Chapman ran his team. When the first qualifying session began for the *Daily Express* Trophy, there was no sign of Gold Leaf Team Lotus. The celebrated transporter bearing the legend 'Racing for Britain' did not show up. Practising for Britain needed one day only, apparently. Saturday would be enough.

Friday was perfect, and while Stewart's Matra, Black Jack's Brabham and Amon's Ferrari hammered the lap record, Jochen watched and fumed. And

Saturday brought rain. Times were fifteen seconds slower, and Lotus were in trouble.

When the final session began the situation looked hopeless. Although the rain had stopped, the circuit was still very slippery. And then Rindt came out, grim-faced and determined, and we suddenly remembered why we had trekked great distances to stand, cold and wet, in a field in Northamptonshire. On the circuit, a virtuoso performance was under way.

At Woodcote I watched. A string of cars — Brabham, Siffert, Ickx — came through, slithering and twitching right out to the grass, and then Rindt arrived, the Lotus 49 travelling at a different sort of speed, and I knew, just knew, that this time he had overdone it, this time he wasn't going to make the corner. But always he did.

Every ninety seconds there was an audible gulp from the grandstands as Jochen pointed that car at the apex, then a roar of relief as it hurtled off towards the Motor bridge, having beaten Woodcote again.

The result of all this was a lap good enough for the inside of the third row. Race day was again cold and showery, and we all wondered if Jochen could reproduce the form of the day before. Ahead of him on the grid were seven cars, but his task was easier than Stewart's. The new Matra MS80 had been near undrivable in Saturday's conditions, and Jackie had opted to forgo his pole position and run the MS10 — a known quantity in the wet — from the back of the grid. Stewart and Rindt with lots of people to get past . . . it was something to relish.

As always happens on these occasions, however, travelling hopefully seemed to be the best of it. From the start it was obvious that two of the favourites, Amon and Rindt, had problems. Chris had missed the wet Saturday session, and was finding the Ferrari impossible in the wet. Jochen was on six or seven cylinders and dropping back, electrics soaked. In the early laps the only saving grace was Stewart, scything through the field and quickly gaining places.

And then the race came alive. Suddenly Rindt's Cosworth was on eight cylinders! After dropping to eleventh place, the Lotus picked up five places in five laps, Jochen also taking two seconds a lap from the leader, Brabham.

Conditions at this point were foul, with rain falling all the time and visibility terrible. But Rindt went past Stewart as if lapping him. That done, he was up into fourth, with Brabham, Ickx and Courage ahead. Piers and Jacky were into a private scrap, and as they headed for Stowe they came up to lap Graham Hill and Pedro Rodriguez who were disputing seventh place.

Already you had the ingredients for a perilous encounter at the end of the straight, but there was more to come. Behind the quartet, looming out of the spray, was Rindt. As the five cars approached the corner Jochen was at the back. When they came out of it he was at the front . . . Confusing for the others.

Brabham's lead, with twenty laps left, was almost half a minute, but Jochen refused to concede and the gap came down and down. Every time around the Lotus came through Woodcote at ludicrous angles, twitching this way and that, revs racing as the rear wheels scratched for grip. It seemed almost that the track was shifting to contain the car. It was a moving thing to watch, a man having one of those days.

Sometimes taking as many as four seconds a lap away from Brabham, Rindt continued to close, but simply ran out of laps. When Jack went into Copse for the last time his lead was nine seconds and it was all over — but then the green car began to run out of fuel! Coming through Abbey Rindt was swiftly closing, but it was just too late. Engine dead, Brabham coasted over the line, the Lotus only a couple of seconds behind. Those who were there will never forget.

Rindt caught the hearts of race fans across the world, and nowhere more than in England. He seemed to fit everyone's idea of what a racing driver should be. He had a good sense of humour, which came across in several languages. He was properly arrogant, never under any illusions about his ability. He knew precisely how good he was, and never troubled to hide it. 'I have only two rivals — Stewart and Amon,' he once said. But success was a long time coming in Formula 1.

Although he finished third in the 1966 World Championship there were no wins, and the next two years were disastrous. In 1967 Jochen was merely living out his three-year contract with Cooper, showing little enthusiasm for most of the year.

For 1968 he signed for Brabham and thoroughly enjoyed the season, despite the fact that the Repco four-cammers were horribly unreliable. Having decided to run Cosworth engines for 1969, Brabham was very keen to keep Rindt, and the Austrian thought long and hard about it, before regretfully opting for Lotus. His obsession was to win the World Championship, and he believed the Lotus was the car he needed. Through most of 1969 he regretted his decision.

Jochen's first drives for Chapman were in the Tasman Championship. He won some, he lost some, and finished second to Amon in the championship. But he came back from the Antipodes an unhappy man. An accident at Levin — no fault of his — had unsettled him. The Silverstone practice fiasco unsettled him, too. Barcelona did more than that.

Jochen got the pole at glorious Montjuich Park, and in the race he led from Amon's Ferrari before having a terrifying accident when the rear wing collapsed.

This was the era of the huge and high wings, mounted on flimsy struts which frequently failed. Hill's 49 had had an identical accident a few minutes earlier, and Jochen hit the wreckage. The car was completely wiped out, but the driver miraculously escaped with a broken jaw and concussion. The accident was completely to change Rindt's attitude to safety — and to motor racing in general.

In hospital he had time to think. The concussion was serious enough for him to miss Monaco, and while convalescing at home in Switzerland he wrote a letter to Chapman so strong as to be later omitted, on legal advice, from the English edition of Heinz Pruller's superb biography.

In the letter Jochen, as ever, was straight to the point: the cars were not strong enough; they were sufficiently competitive to stand the few extra kilos necessary to beef them up; he could only drive a car in which he had confidence — and, frankly, he was close to the point of losing all confidence where he was . . .

Like all the truly great, Rindt hated anything artificial which 'equalized' racing cars, made them easier to drive. Reasonable enough, this, for it works against the artist, to an extent cloaks his superiority. Thus Jochen loathed wings on racing cars, and was delighted when the stilt wings were banned.

Even so, throughout 1969 nothing would go right. Jochen was becoming desperate to win a Formula 1 race. Time after time he started from the pole, hurtled off into the far yonder — until the car broke. At Clermont Ferrand he had to retire because he felt sick, legacy of the concussion suffered at Barcelona. It was all going wrong.

Back at Silverstone for the British Grand Prix Rindt and Stewart staged an unforgettable battle from the fall of the flag, and Jochen seemed to have the upper hand. After fifty laps the Lotus headed the Matra by

Wet or dry, the style was the same. In 1969 Jochen had two memorable races at Silverstone, in the International Trophy (above) and the British Grand Prix (below), each time wringing everything possible from the Lotus 49. By the time of the Grand Prix the ludicrously flimsy — and unsightly — high wings had been banned on safety grounds.

three seconds, but suddenly Stewart was closer, much closer, right on Rindt's tail and into the lead.

The left hand wing sideplate had broken away and was fouling the tyre. Into the pits came the Lotus, its driver white with rage. Half a minute was lost while the sideplate was removed.

There was now no question of a win, but Jochen was still firmly in second place. A few laps later even that was denied him, for the Lotus ran out of fuel and had to stop once more. By the end he was a demoralized fourth — and those three points were his first of the season . . .

Rindt's race had, in fact, grossly flattered his team. Once again Lotus had failed to turn up for the beginning of practice — this time because all but one of the cars had been sold! Chapman was adamant that the four-wheel-drive Lotus 63 was the way to go, and Jochen was adamant that he wouldn't drive it. He said it wasn't safe. He wanted a 49 for the balance of the season, and then he was getting the hell out.

Certainly he had his choices for 1970. Brabham wanted him back, and Rindt was keen to return. Then there was March, in the process of being born. Jochen was in Robin Herd's mind from the start of the project, and at first was to be the team's only driver. When the new organization showed signs of becoming unwieldy, however, he lost interest. And at the same time relations with Lotus began, by and by, to pick up.

At the Nurburgring Chapman and Rindt had a heart-to-heart, their first, and Colin promised Jochen a new two-wheel-drive car for 1970. He would also be the unequivocal number one. Hill, Chapman said, could be farmed out to Rob Walker's private team.

It all sounded very attractive to Jochen, and on the track, too, things got better. At Monza he was second, at Mosport third and at Watkins Glen, finally, first. For years he had been dominant in Formula 2, and now he was a winner in Formula 1. That was a big hurdle cleared.

When the talk is of Jochen Rindt, most people think immediately of Monaco in 1970. Throughout practice he was despondent. The new Lotus 72 — Chapman's promised masterpiece — was so far a massive disappointment. He had driven it at Jarama and Silverstone, and it had pleased him at neither race. So for Monaco it was back to the 49, and he gave himself no chance at all. He was in Monaco because his contract required him to be there. That was the impression he gave, and it was borne out by a practice time which put him halfway down the grid.

For much of the race he drove efficiently, but without fire, in fifth place. Only when Stewart, Amon and others had fallen by the wayside did Rindt really start to move. There was only Brabham ahead: dispense with him, and Jochen would get to meet the Princess. But Jack was fifteen seconds up the road, and there

---

Rindt's first Grand Prix victory was a long time coming, but at Watkins Glen in 1969 everything hung together at last. Jochen's close friend Piers Courage was second in America with Frank Williams's Brabham.

Jochen, still faithful to his open-face Bell helmet, sits in the Lotus 72 during practice for the Dutch Grand Prix of 1970. The car took its first victory the following day.

The 72 was almost unbeatable through the mid-season of 1970, but this win, at Brands Hatch, was a fortunate one for Rindt, who inherited the lead during the final lap when Brabham ran out of fuel.

were few laps left.

If you were there — even watched on television — you will remember those closing minutes of Monaco 1970. You will recall Jochen hurling the 49 through Casino Square like a Formula 3 car, breaking the lap record, closing, closing . . .

As they went into their last lap Brabham still led by a couple of seconds, but Rindt was not flagging now. And Brabham, unbelievably, broke under the pressure of the moment and slid into the barriers at the last hairpin.

I was there, camera at the ready, knowing this was going to be close. Through the viewfinder I saw Jack, off-line and passing backmarkers, then slithering on the dust towards me. In total surprise I put down the camera, got it to my eye again in time to catch Jochen at the apex. He was staring to his left, watching the Brabham in disbelief. Monaco was his.

Amidst all the post-race pandemonium the commentator announced a new record for Rindt: 1:23.2. Set on the last lap, this was a second inside Stewart's pole time and nearly three seconds faster than Jochen himself had managed in practice!

Never have I seen so much emotion after a race.

There he was, up in the Royal Box, waving to the crowds as tears flowed down his cheeks. And there, in poignant contrast, was Jack in the pits, standing by his crumpled car.

Later that day — or rather, early the following morning — Jochen and his wife were outside the Casino, and I remember the exhilaration on his face as he held the cup aloft to yet more cheers. It was simple joy; there was no affectation. He was happy and he wanted everyone to share the moment with him.

The summer of 1970 was then one of almost complete triumph. In the revamped 72 he won at Zandvoort, at Clermont Ferrand, at Brands Hatch, at Hockenheim. But there was great sadness, too, for Bruce McLaren had died in a testing accident at Goodwood, and then Jochen's great friend Piers Courage was killed in the Dutch Grand Prix. Retirement — *survival* — was coming more and more into his thoughts.

I went to Monza in 1970, but only for the race. On the Saturday afternoon I was in my flat, packing a few things for the trip. In the lounge the radio was on and I heard something about Jochen Rindt and Monza.

Just one small step from his greatest ambition.

In death, ironically, he climbed it. When Jacky Ickx, the only man to threaten his title, broke a fuel pipe at Watkins Glen a month later, the great Austrian's posthumous World Championship was confirmed.

Everyone rejoiced. Although Jochen and Jacky never got along, the Belgian's position after Monza was invidious. Ferrari had come on strong during the second half of the year, and Ickx was of course obligated to race as always — to win.

At the same time he hardly wanted to steal away the title, and when he won at St Jovite the possibility was there. So he was not unhappy to finish only fourth at the Glen, and was able to go to Mexico in light frame of mind. There he also won.

Jochen never knew it, sadly, but he won his title at Hockenheim in early August, fighting all the way with Ickx. If Jacky had beaten him there he would have taken the World Championship — by a point. There's not much justice in the world, as they say. But there is some.

The British Grand Prix victory was Jochen's fourth of 1970, and already his rivals were acknowledging that the World Championship was as good as settled.

PEDRO RODRIGUEZ
No matter where you are

At the beginning of 1983 there was a touching little ceremony at Daytona Beach. In this cathedral of stock car racing, they were naming one of the infield road course turns for Pedro Rodriguez, twice winner of the 24 Hours when sports car racing was alive and well. Present at the ceremony was Pedro's mother. No, she said, she bore no grudge against the sport which had taken both her sons. They had loved racing, enjoyed their brief lives.

Daytona, often cold and bleak during the February Speed Weeks, was always good to Pedro. Towards the end of his life he had those two splendid victories in the Gulf Porsche 917, but it was an earlier win there, in 1963, which was perhaps the most crucial of his career.

In those days the annual sports car race was over 1,000 km, and Pedro came to it in a confused state of mind, still grieving at the recent loss of his brother and not certain that he wanted to continue. Ricardo, they all said, had been the more committed racing driver, the more gifted.

Winning at Daytona, in a Ferrari 250GTO with Phil Hill, swept away Pedro's doubts. He would not retire from racing, although several years would pass before it became his full-time occupation. For the moment he would take life as it came, accept drives as and when they appealed, live most of the time at home in Mexico.

Both Rodriguez brothers had enormous natural ability in a race car, and their father's huge wealth allowed them to show this precocious talent to the world. Don Pedro had made millions from judicious property speculation — buying chunks of Acapulco, things like that — and he wanted nothing more than to see his sons high in the racing firmament.

As a consequence, the boys were always several steps ahead, racing motorcycles at eleven, cars at fourteen. By 1957 the fifteen-year-old Ricardo had

his own Porsche RS, and the following year was bitterly disappointed to have his entry for Le Mans rejected. Sixteen, said the Automobile Club de l'Ouest, was too young.

In 1959 the two brothers shared an OSCA in the 24 Hours, and after that they frequently drove together, usually in Ferraris for Luigi Chinetti's North American Racing Team. At this time Ricardo was usually a little quicker than Pedro, but decidedly more wild and unrestrained. He worked his cars very hard, and had a lot of accidents. There was about him, said some contemporaries, a fearlessness of disturbing proportions.

Chinetti, though, believed that in time this side of Ricardo's racing personality would be calmed. And if patience could be blended with the explosive pace, he reasoned, a quite remarkable driver would emerge. He missed no opportunity to sing the praises of both Rodriguez brothers to Enzo Ferrari, and the wily Commendatore offered Don Pedro the opportunity to buy them into the factory team.

Ricardo, not surprisingly, lost no time in availing himself of the chance, but Pedro decided against it, not certain that he wanted to be a pro — amazing when one considers how compulsive was his attitude to the job a few years later.

For the moment, though, he opted to stay in the wings, build up his flourishing import business and partner his brother in the sports cars.

Ricardo went to Maranello at a bad time. Dominant the previous year, the Italian team found itself leapfrogged in 1962 by new V8 engines from BRM and Coventry-Climax. At the end of the year Ferrari refused to send any cars over for the inaugural Mexican Grand Prix at the end of the year. Ricardo could not bear to miss the race, and accepted a ride in Rob Walker's Lotus 24. At the end of the final practice session he went out once more, trying to steal away

At his beloved Spa-Francorchamps, Rodriguez managed to haul the heavy and under-powered Cooper-Maserati up to fourth in the 1967 Belgian Grand Prix, but retired four laps from the end.

pole position from Surtees. And on a banked, flat out corner the car went out of control. When officials reached him, Ricardo Rodriguez was past help.

Pedro, of course, was there that day to watch his brother, and a long time passed before he wanted even to think about racing cars again. But time at least cauterized his pain, and that Daytona win, three months later, resolved him to carry on. For two or three years he stuck to his policy of racing when it suited him, but by the end of 1966 felt he was ready to go for it seriously. When John Cooper offered him a one-off drive in the Maserati-engined car for the first Grand Prix of 1967, at Kyalami, Rodriguez took it up — and promptly won!

It was, in truth, a most fortunate victory. Although Pedro qualified fourth, considerably faster than team leader Jochen Rindt, he lost second gear early in the race and was not truly a front runner. The race looked like going to local man John Love, but six laps from the flag the Rhodesian had to pit for fuel, and Rodriguez had only to cruise in.

No matter. Cooper was sufficiently impressed to offer him a drive for the rest of the season. And the pattern was set. Pedro was now a full-time, professional racing driver, and would remain so for the rest of his life.

Moreover, his commitment to the business was complete. Not for Rodriguez, ever, the life of a Grand Prix specialist, racing only in Formula 1. Now that he was living in Europe, returning home only rarely, Pedro counted a weekend lost without a race of some kind.

Through 1967 he drove not only for Cooper, but also undertook a variety of sports car races and, whenever possible, Formula 2 in one of Frank Costin's Protos cars. It was in one of these, indeed, that he had a major accident in the late summer. At Enna the wooden-chassis device somersaulted, and Rodriguez was hurled away down the road, suffering a broken ankle and smashed heel.

Sicily was not the place to have an accident like that. With no anaesthetic available for him, Pedro went through the pains of hell while they set his ankle. And it seemed certain that he would not be able to race until the following season.

The Mexican Grand Prix, however, was the last race

In the appalling conditions at Rouen in 1968 Rodriguez and the BRM fought a long battle for second with Surtees's Honda, neither having any answer to the Ferrari of Ickx. Pedro's gearbox failed during the last few laps.

of the year. Against medical counsel Rodriguez drove — and finished sixth. Groggy and exhausted, he had to be lifted from the car afterwards.

For 1968 came the offer of a BRM drive, at that time a desirable proposition. And two memories of the year stand out. In the Race of Champions Pedro's engine died on the line, and the field was long gone by the time he was able to move off.

Brands Hatch was oily and treacherous that afternoon, but Rodriguez was a man who always excelled on a slippery surface, when delicacy and 'feel' came particularly into play. In the course of the forty laps he came through to second in the dark green car, which then ran out of fuel a mile after taking the flag.

Then there was Monaco, a circuit for which he never cared. Pedro's passion was for fast tracks, flat out sweepers; and Monte Carlo he considered something of a joke.

'You can play around there, slide the car and have fun, but I prefer somewhere like Spa. There you cannot make a mistake and be safe, you know. You have to race really precise . . .'

At Monaco in 1968 Pedro came down past the Tip-Top, put the brakes on for the tight right-hander at Mirabeau — and the pedal went to the floor. Putting the car sideways he somehow got it through most of the corner, but finally slid wide at the exit, climbed the kerb — no guardrail there in those days — and hit the wall very hard.

And then I remember that he climbed out and sauntered down to Station Hairpin, helmet swinging on his arm. I recall the jaunty walk, the absolute coolness, as if he had *meant* to park the BRM that way.

Rodriguez had no fear of death, but there was a rational explanation for this, he would say. He was a religious man, but also a devout fatalist. 'God is the only one that can tell you this is the end of the line, and it is no matter where you are. You can be racing, in the street, in church, you can be anywhere . . .'

This philosophy he held to very strongly. 'There was a man, an Indianapolis driver, who once raced in my country, in the Carrera Panamericana — Bill Vukovich. He won at Indianapolis two times. Was his only race in the year. And he was killed there, trying to win his third. But Nuvolari, he raced thirty years, every week — and he died of illness. Was God's way.

Was not his time to die in a car. My brother . . . was like the American . . .'

Perhaps because of memories of Ricardo, Pedro always had a particular ambition to win at Le Mans. And in 1968 he achieved it, sharing a JW Automotive Ford GT40 with Lucien Bianchi. To the end of his life he maintained that this victory overshadowed all others.

In Formula 1 there were several places but no wins for him that year. It was generally agreed, however, that he had done a fine job for BRM, holding the team together in the aftermath of Mike Spence's death at Indianapolis. And Rodriguez expected to stay for 1969, partnering John Surtees.

He had reckoned without the unpredictable hand of Louis Stanley. In a move of characteristic eccentricity the hefty BRM boss replaced him with Jack Oliver, leaving Pedro to face a thankless year in Tim Parnell's privately-run BRM. At the end of it 'Big Lou' was only too happy to rehire him . . .

Now began the Mexican's great period as a race driver, the sadness of it being that he had so little of life remaining to him. Not only was he back in a factory

BRM for 1970, but also in a Porsche 917.

Pedro and the 917. There have been, through the history of this sport, cars and drivers who belonged together, synonymous for all time, and this was one such partnership. No one ever drove this most daunting of sports racing cars like Rodriguez.

Unquestionably he was the star of the team. Once in a while Siffert was able to match him for sheer pace, but it was always a little frantic, lacking in his team mate's fluency and ease. And Seppi was very much harder on the cars.

'You always had the impression', said David Yorke, team manager of JW Automotive at that time, 'that Seppi did the job with arm muscles flexed, while Pedro sat there resting his thumbs on the wheel . . .'

Particularly unforgettable, of course, was the BOAC 1,000 km in 1970, run virtually throughout in torrential rain. How was it possible for a man — a Latin born to heat and dust — to excel his contemporaries with such ease? There was a magic about Rodriguez that cheerless April day. The race surrendered to him within minutes of the start. Although the result was never in doubt, the sodden spectators stayed because

A rare appearance for Maranello. Pedro was a man who might have been put on earth to drive Ferraris, but was seldom asked. This is the British Grand Prix of 1969, in the old and uncompetitive V12.

they wanted to pay their tribute to him at the end. They had witnessed an afternoon which would pass into motor racing legend.

In Formula 1, too, Pedro's star was rising. The BRM P153 was a competitive tool, if not an especially reliable one, and he was usually well on the pace. At Spa, his favourite circuit in all the world, he won, tailed throughout by Amon's March.

Jackie Stewart, of course, earnestly loathed Francorchamps, and considered Rodriguez 'irrational' in his enthusiasm for it. But Chris Amon — who followed him all day — disagreed. 'Pedro loved it,' he once told me, 'for the same reason that I loved it. Spa was Grand Prix racing as we always thought it should be. After a race there I felt high for hours, and Pedro was the same. Driving flat out at Spa — which we both did that day from start to finish — left you feeling you'd really *done* something. And Pedro's precision was fabulous. I knew that I would get past him only if he made a mistake somewhere — and he never did.'

There were no further Grand Prix wins for Rodriguez that year, but he was always a front runner, and in sports cars he was supreme. At the end of 1970

he renewed his contracts with BRM and JW Automotive.

Pedro, now, was entirely at peace with himself and the world. The days of selling cars in Mexico City, racing only as a hobby, were very far behind him. He had become, in fact, curiously Anglicized. Some time previously his marriage to Angelina had foundered, but he lived in great happiness with a girl at his house in Bray-on-Thames, drove around in an elderly Bentley which he adored, sought out the best restaurants and enjoyed them. *Never*, however, did he go anywhere without quantities of hot Tabasco sauce. And head waiters the world over were appalled to see him produce a bottle from his inside pocket, then spray its contents liberally over their local speciality . . .

His appearance, too, was hardly mainstream. The Bentley would glide into a paddock somewhere, and out would step this small cosmopolitan figure, black hair swept straight back, omnipresent sunglasses, Goodyear jacket. Then, very carefully, he would apply the finishing touch, the deerstalker from Bond Street! That done, there remained only the famous slow grin,

Spa 1970. Rodriguez, back with BRM now, had Amon's March in his mirrors for virtually the entire race, the two finishing a second apart after 245 miles. This was Pedro's most famous victory.

After his Belgian Grand Prix win Rodriguez acknowledges the crowd's applause. Amon is rueful, but exhilarated by a fine afternoon, and Beltoise, two minutes behind them, is well pleased with third.

and the picture was complete.

'Pedro was eccentric in many ways', David Yorke said. 'In fact, if you didn't know him you might have got the impression that he was a bit of a dilettante. But, my God, he was anything but a prima donna in a car. I don't think I ever knew a more totally committed racing driver. Absolutely nothing mattered to him but winning.

'One little incident to illustrate that has always stuck in my mind. At the Daytona 24 Hours in '71 he was sharing the 917 with Jackie Oliver, and during his stint Oliver was sick. The cockpit of that car was pretty cramped, you know, and awfully hot. When we opened the door to let Oliver out the whole scene in there was pretty frightful . . .

'Pedro was standing there, in fresh, clean overalls, but he didn't hesitate for a second. He just hurled himself into the cockpit, amid God knows what, and away he went!'

Rodriguez won that race, as he had the year before, and other victories followed. In the BRM, too, he looked set for his finest Formula 1 season. At Oulton Park, on Good Friday, he comfortably beat a small but select field, which included Stewart. And in the June rains of Zandvoort he and Ickx made their rivals look inept.

A week later it was back to the 917 for the Osterreichring 1,000 km, and this John Wyer has always considered Pedro's greatest race. After leading the early laps the Porsche lost nearly six minutes in the pits while the battery was changed.

'His stamina was extraordinary. He could drive absolutely flat out indefinitely, it seemed, and that day he had to. At half-distance he had to hand over to Attwood, who made up no further ground. In fact, Dickie was only out for ten laps before Pedro asked if he could take over again. Eventually he got himself back on to the same lap as the leading Ferrari, which Regazzoni then crashed. Mind you, we all believed that Pedro would have made up that lap, and won anyway . . . It was as great a drive as I have ever seen by anyone.'

The following week Rodriguez ran second to Stewart in the French Grand Prix before retiring, and he had the highest hopes for the BRM through the sweeping curves of Silverstone, next on the Formula

1 schedule. Ten days before the race he tested the car there, setting the fastest time.

Wyer went to watch that day, and afterwards invited Pedro down to his house for the weekend. He was astonished to be told, however, that the Mexican was committed to a minor league Interserie race at the Norisring, holding to his creed that any race was better than none. He would drive a Ferrari 512M for Herbert Muller.

Like Wyer, the BRM team was less than enthusiastic about Pedro's plan. 'We didn't want him to do that race at all', Raymond Mays said. 'But they wanted a "star" name for the weekend, and he was offered a reasonable Ferrari. Under the terms of the contract we could have stopped him going to the Norisring. And, of course, afterwards we wished to God we had...'

Rodriguez led the opening laps without problem. Then, a few minutes into the race, he came upon a slower car, which moved across as he went to lap it. The Ferrari went immediately out of control, hit the barriers with terrible force, somersaulted and exploded. It took a long time to release him from the wreckage, but Pedro was anyway beyond saving. At early evening he died.

'We thought the world of him at BRM,' Mays recalled. 'The mechanics worshipped him — and that is always a sure sign of a man's worth. The remarkable thing about Pedro was that he got better and better and better. In the latter part of his career I think he was, without any doubt, one of the three best in the world. And in the wet he was the greatest of his time.'

John Wyer, gruff and outwardly hard-bitten, was shattered by the news. 'Everyone in the team loved him. As a driver he was an absolute inspiration to us, as a man irreplaceable. We could not have wished for better. He always gave his absolute best, never complained about anything. Money was never very important to him. He simply loved to *race* . . .'

Afterwards there was much talk of the tragedy of it all, of the fact that so great a driver's life had been tossed away in so trivial an event. But Rodriguez himself would not have seen it that way. 'Once I had won *Le Mans,*' he said, 'all races were the same to me. Whatever they were, I wanted to win them.' And in the terms of his own fatalism, of course, he was quite right. God, he would have said, decided that 11 July 1971 was the end of the line for him — 'and it is no matter where you are . . .'

Pedro's last Formula 1 win came in the Rothmans Trophy, a curious one-off event run at Oulton Park on Good Friday in 1971. The Mexican's BRM P160 led throughout in highly spectacular style.

KEKE ROSBERG
Shooting from the hip

Each patch on his overalls, Keke would say, represented a house. He had a lot of patches. Once I mentioned another driver, a far lesser light in Formula 1, but a man of considerable height. Imagine, I said, if you were that tall, how many personal sponsors' names you could accommodate on a driving suit.

'You're right!' he responded at once. 'Maybe I should get myself stretched to his height. What's more,' he added, 'if I drove at his speed, you'd be able to read them . . .'

In that snatch of conversation, you have much of Rosberg's personality on display: the love of doing deals, the waspish sense of humour and the quick rejoinder, the feisty and confident little guy well aware of his own abilities. 'I'm a cocky bastard,' he grins, 'I know it.'

Right after the last race in the autumn of 1981 Keke rang one morning to say he was leaving the Fittipaldi team. 'I couldn't see any point in going on with them, so I've quit. No, I've nothing else to go to. I just want it to be known that I've left, and if anyone's interested I'm available.' Twelve months later I went to his house in Cookham Dean to interview the new World Champion.

This, by any standards, was a remarkable turnaround in a racing driver's career, but the man least surprised by it was Rosberg himself. All along, he said, he had been quite sure in his own mind that it was simply a matter of waiting for the right car to come along. If you didn't have that belief in yourself, how could you hope to persuade anyone else? At the same time, he admitted, his morale had been at a low point.

'That was a hellish season for me, 1981. I'd been around a long time, and *still* I wasn't qualifying sometimes. Everything was wrong, and I'll admit to you, in my last year with Fittipaldi, I became bloody terrified. I found that interesting because I didn't really know why. It wasn't that I thought the car was bad, although I had two or three suspension breakages. Perhaps it was because I wasn't achieving anything. The motivation wasn't there, that feeling that you're part of a gang in a competitive sense. I wasn't getting paid, so I had to fight for every penny, with a lawyer to help me.

'So everything was wrong, and the problem didn't disappear overnight — not even when I moved to Williams. It wasn't until the early part of the following year that I was able to enjoy driving racing cars again.'

By then, I said, you were the talk of the season, leading races, well up in the points. 'Right,' Keke agreed. 'I don't think it showed in my driving simply because the will was so much stronger than the fear. After all, I went to Williams only because Jones quit too late for them to find another top driver. This was the chance of my life, and I knew it. No other good drive had been on offer. There was a small hope of McLaren because I'd been a Marlboro driver for a long time. But realistically I knew Ron Dennis wouldn't take me because he needs a big star around him, and that I certainly wasn't at the time.'

Rosberg was always a realist, nicely aware of his worth at a given time. With pride he says he never paid for a drive in his life, that from the beginning he had to look upon motor racing as a business. It had to pay *him*, and he says it always did. To an extent, though, he had to put fiscal thoughts aside when the Williams offer came up.

'Frank was in a rush, just off to Saudi Arabia, when he called to say I could have the drive. We hadn't even talked about money, but I said "OK, I'll take it!" When he got back, he offered me peanuts, and I said at least he had to give me a living! Eventually he paid me exactly what I wanted, which was very fair. Knowing the position I was in, he could have said "Take it or leave it." And I probably would have taken it . . .'

Rosberg's first Formula 1 win was, to say the least, unexpected. While the hotshoes fell foul of the dreadful conditions at Silverstone in 1978, Keke kept the tank-like Theodore on the road to take the International Trophy.

The 1982 World Champion was probably the cheapest in recent history, but Keke never cried about it. Williams had thrown out a lifeline to him, and a deal was a deal. Prost had exactly similar thoughts when he returned to McLaren. Real market value could be established when it came time to renegotiate. For now having your name above the title would do.

Perhaps Rosberg has never quite received his dues for that championship. The 1982 season was the most cataclysmic that Grand Prix racing has known, a time of monstrous 'cars' with ground effect and no suspension, horrifying accidents, protests and acrimony, a FOCA strike. Formula 1 was cutting its own throat, and if it had bled to death that dreadful summer I, for one, would not have mourned it. By Vegas, where Keke clinched his title, I wanted only to get the last trip out of the way, take a holiday someplace where there weren't any racing cars — correction, any racing *people*.

I did leave Nevada with a sliver of optimism, however. Rosberg as World Champion was one positive aspect of 1982. True, he had won only one race, but no one had won more than two. More importantly, he was a man, like Andretti, who realized that the title brought with it responsibilities. We had had some pretty dour World Champions in the recent past. Keke was hardly that.

'Did you find the track different at all this year?' asked an intense Vegas commentator after the race.

'Yes, sure, I thought it was *much* better than last time.'

'Oh, really?' said the man, unable to believe his luck — and unaware of the trap before him. 'Why is that, Kay-Kay?'

'Well, since last year we've been to Detroit . . .'

So, as I say, the future of Formula 1 looked a little brighter as we flew out of McCarron. And it was more than a sense of euphoria at leaving Las Vegas. The World Championship was in good hands. And later, on holiday now, I bought *L'Equipe* one morning and read of FISA's overnight — if overdue — ban on ground effect. Perhaps the cancer had been caught in time.

Having left Rosberg in the sweaty Vegas press room, I next saw him at his house in Berkshire on a raw December morning. 'You know', he said, 'my clearest memory of that day has nothing to do with the race, but a little incident afterwards. Back in 1979 I signed a contract to do the CanAm for Carl Haas — who then calls me to say he's having Ickx instead.

I called my lawyer in Boston and told him to go for it.

'Well, I tell you, Haas was *shaking*! He kept calling me, saying he's one of Bernie Ecclestone's best mates and he can help me — so long as I don't burn my bridges. I said to him, "Listen, if I can't make it without you, I'll never make it . . ." Eventually I signed for Paul Newman's team, and that was the end of the lawsuit. But this hate from Haas — because I dared to start proceedings against him — was so strong that when he heard Frank was thinking of signing me he called several times to advise him against it.

'So there we are in Las Vegas, about two hours after the race.' At this point Keke paused to light a cigarette, savouring the story. 'I'm checking out, and there, at reception in Caesars Palace, is Haas. Big cigar in his mouth as usual. He comes over with a broad grin, and says, "Oh, I always knew you'd make it . . ."

'I said, "Carl, you are the same guy who took the trouble to call Williams, saying not to sign me. Is that correct?" Well, I tell you, he caught his cigar just before it hit the ground! Then I said, "Today I won the World Championship, but my biggest pleasure of the whole day has been to see your face." And then I left. Life doesn't give many opportunities like that.'

In fact, another such arose at the FISA prizegiving ceremony a week before Christmas. The new World Champion would have skipped it altogether, but the thoughts of the automatic $10,000 fine offended his keen regard for gelt. Rosberg held the governing body in some contempt, not least for its insistence upon conducting all its business in French. 'Everyone knows the language of the sport is English, but they won't have it. They gave me this great build-up in French — a language I don't speak — so I thought, fine, I'll let them known how it feels. I made my acceptance speech in Finnish, English, Swedish and German . . .'

You will see, then, that our Keke is not a man who suffers in silence. And the driver was the man. 'At Brands in '84 I was on my second set of qualifiers, on a quick lap — and there was de Cesaris in front of me. He knew I was there, so basically it was just an attitude of "who cares?" He just blocked me. But I got him back. Oh yes . . .

'You see, he was going slowly when I was on my quick lap. So when I finished my lap, he was just beginning his. And I simply forgot to look in my mirrors — just like he did. Fair enough, isn't it? I chose

During his Fittipaldi years Rosberg spared no effort, but the cars were neither reliable nor on the pace. Even driving like this failed to qualify him for the 1981 Monaco Grand Prix.

the middle of the road at Druids, but I did it with more *style*, you see. I waved at him as he went past. Apologising, you see, for getting in his way . . .'

Style. Rosberg indubitably has it. In some things he is unashamedly flash in a manner which would be hard to take in one who took himself too seriously. He has a certain arrogance, without a doubt, but tells jokes against himself with relish. He is wonderful company.

He was also wonderful to watch on a race track. Many a time I watched that remarkable single-mindedness and commitment bring in a stunning lap at the end of a troubled qualifying session. There was a classic example at Estoril in 1984, when his car blew up. Not yet qualified, he had the presence of mind to walk calmly back to the pits for the spare: 'No point in getting out of breath and knackered. I looked at my watch.' There was time for a single flier — what Lauda calls 'a chaotic lap', and Keke vaulted from 27th to fourth.

A few minutes later he was holding court at his table by the motorhome. Rosberg was not one to dash away from a race circuit. After the session he would speak to the engineers, then prepare to receive his guests. Unless the day was very dark, he would wear

sunglasses, perhaps don his favourite 'Hard Rock Cafe' jacket. Then he poured a cup of coffee, sat himself down. Got everything? Cigarettes? Right, what's the gossip?

To the despair of his teams, he had little use for euphemism. 'The car is shit, thank you,' he would beam, then go on to describe what it wasn't doing properly this weekend. Early in 1985 new efforts were made to persuade him towards diplomacy. They were not a success. 'The new engine? I can't tell you about that — it's on a list of things I'm not allowed to discuss. Of course, if I *were* allowed to, I'd say that the torque was much better, but that the power still came in with too much of a bang. But I'm not. Next question?'

For a journalist, then, Rosberg was a seam of gold, a maverick rather after the fashion of Villeneuve, one who spoke his mind. Where Gilles's irreverence, however, came from ingenuousness, Keke's is bullish: 'This must be the only team in the business with more PR men than championship points . . .' By the same token, when something in the car or team pleased him, he was generous with compliments.

Most of all, he loved to chat — about anything under the sun. Often I dropped in simply to ask about the turbo failure in the last session, or whatever, and

The reigning World Champion had a hard time of it in 1983, when the turbos really came of age. He won at Monaco, however, and was never better than here at Spa, the Williams-Cosworth at the limit throughout.

Rosberg, Williams and Head worked together for four seasons, during which Keke won five Grands Prix. Theirs was not always an easy relationship.

sat there an hour and more. Usually in attendance was his manager, Ortwin Podlech, a relaxed and friendly guy far removed from Svengali. He shared Rosberg's sense of fun.

'Over the winter, in Ibiza,' Keke started, 'we were in the office one evening. Ortwin had found a letter I wrote to him years ago — at the time I was going to drive that Kojima thing for Willi Kauhsen. In the letter I said that we'd really cracked it, from now on it was all going to be downhill. And after my signature I put, in brackets, "Formula 1 driver"!

'Anyway, that got us on to old times. We suddenly realized, you know, that through all these years we'd never celebrated anything — not even the World Championship. There was a bottle of brandy in the office, and we got started on it, reminiscing far into the night.

'Eventually it was time to go home, and I refused Ortwin's offer a lift. I'd ridden there on a big motorbike, and I fired it up, put it into gear — and fell off into the gutter . . . It was heavy, I'll tell you, and I had difficulty getting it upright again. Right, start engine, into gear, let out the clutch — and it happened again! "What's happening to me?" I thought. "Why won't it move?" Here I was, in the middle of the night, pitch black, no one else around. It was only some time later I realized the chain was still on the front wheel . . .'

Tales like that were welcome relief from a heavy diet of 'I can't get a balance', 'losing boost on the second run' or — the perennial all-purpose favourite — 'traffic'. Rosberg, like Prost or any other driver of real worth and confidence, never shirked blame for his own mistakes.

The lack of discipline prevalent in today's Formula 1 was one of Keke's hobby-horses. When he came into it in 1978, he would say, Grand Prix racing was regarded as the top of the tree, and the behaviour was to that standard. 'One thing I never forgot was South Africa that year, my first race. I felt a little bit out of place, you know, and I was wandering behind the pits somewhere. Mario (Andretti) came up to me and said, "Nice to see you in Formula 1, and I hope you'll do well", all that sort of thing. I appreciated that — he had no need to do it.

'Then, just as he was about to leave, he turned round. "By the way," he said, "you know we do things a bit differently in Formula 1? Take care of yourself," he said. "See that you learn the trade, do it like we all do it in Formula 1." That was all he said — all he *needed* to say. It was clear in my head. I remember when I started the primary thing was *not* to get in anyone else's way. What angers me today is the guy who makes a mistake, lets you get alongside, and then chops across straight at you, so you either lift off —

give way — or hit him. That's not Grand Prix racing. In many ways it's become a junior formula, but played with very dangerous weapons.'

As he thought quickly in conversation, so Keke was in a race, able to improvize like no one else. Only rarely did he have an out-and-out winning car, and his victories came primarily on 'wild card' days, when unusual circumstances put a premium on sheer driving virtuosity.

Consider: Monaco in 1983, where the track was wet at the start, but the rain had almost stopped. Rosberg was one of few to gamble on slicks. Fifth on the grid, second into Ste Devote, in the lead by lap two, never seen again.

Keke's most memorable win, though, was at Dallas in the dread Williams-Honda FW09, complete with unwieldy handling and all-or-nothing engine, the very last vehicle you needed on a tight track which was breaking up. I had a long talk with him that morning, and found a positive attitude virtually absent from the rest of pit lane. While Lauda, Prost and others scurried about the place, organizing meetings and speaking of boycotts, Rosberg relaxed in the Texas sun. 'I got here this morning at seven o'clock for the warm-up,' he said, 'took a look at the track and went back to the hotel. I've been watching TV.'

You don't seem to be as angry about the state of the track, Mr Rosberg, as the other drivers, a local reporter ventured. 'Oh, I'm angry all right,' Keke put him straight, 'I don't want to break bones any more

than the next guy. But let's be realistic. This is race morning. You've got 80,000 people in the stands, and 28 countries waiting for TV. Of *course* there'll be a race . . .

'This is no time to blame the Dallas organizers. It is the fault of Formula 1, the drivers included. There was a perfectly good rule about new circuits having to run a smaller meeting before staging a Grand Prix, and it's been waived, just as it was at Detroit and Las Vegas. Each time there was chaos. And where the hell is our wonderful FISA? Not here — it's too bloody hot for them.

'I think it's crazy to race on this surface, but we've got to bite the bullet. Let's face it, we're just whores, aren't we? We'll turn up and do our stuff for anyone, if the money's right.'

Rosberg kept himself well clear of the union meetings — he was not, in any case, a member of the Professional Racing Drivers Association — and was quite calm as he climbed aboard. In the appalling conditions his car was able to keep pace with the leaders, and he made no mistake at all on an afternoon which saw thirteen drivers — including Lauda and Prost — in the wall.

Keke's stamina was one of his strongest cards. Throughout 1983 he was weakened by a liver virus contracted in South America, but his driving never betrayed it. Heat appeared not to worry him. Even at Dallas he looked fresh enough, this on a weekend when journalists were spending half an hour outside,

---

Rosberg rarely had a good word for the Williams-Honda FW09, but always drove it to the limit. Here he holds off Warwick's Renault during a long battle at Kyalami in 1984.

There were no wins for Keke in his final season, with McLaren, but usually he was right in the picture. At Monaco he placed second to team mate Prost.

then diving back into the air-conditioned press room to dry out. And travel, too, seemed to leave him unaffected. 'In 1978,' he would recall, 'I did a total of 41 races in 36 weekends. That was doing F1, F2 and Atlantic. For a whole year I didn't get a proper meal. I *lived* on aeroplanes. So the travel now seems nothing at all.'

Usually he flew himself around, having progressed from a Piper Seneca via a turbo-prop Cheyenne to a Lear. When it came to biggish items — jets, villas, that sort of thing — he spent without qualm, but in day to day matters has a reputation, like Alan Jones, for being a close man with a dollar. For the North American races he went scheduled, and it always amazed me to find him at the back of the aeroplane, in 'steerage'.

'Keke,' I said to him, 'if I had your sort of money, I'd regard First Class as the bargain of the age.'

'Look,' he replied, 'what do I need to be able to do on a long flight? I need somewhere I can smoke, and somewhere I can sleep. Why should I pay three times more to sit upstairs?' On the flight back from Detroit in 1985, however, he did upgrade himself to Club Class. My, my, Mr Rosberg, I said . . .

'Well, I won the race! I'm treating myself. This is the problem with having your own aircraft. You tend to forget that flying isn't always fun, that it usually means eating plastic food and sitting next to a fat lady who's taking up half your seat . . .'

Rosberg, like Piquet and Lauda, needed a great deal of sleep. 'Have you been writing all night?' he asked me, as the flight neared London. I said I had.

'Well, there you are. That's a different sort of stamina. Jesus, I couldn't do that. I've been asleep for hours, and I *still* feel exhausted.

'For the first two hours of every day I make a point of not doing anything important. I'm not good at that time of the day, and I must allow for it. Once I got up early to go testing at Snetterton — and I wrote off a brand new Fittipaldi in the pit lane! I was going to take the last corner in fifth, and then suddenly decided to come down to the pit approach road . . . taught me a big lesson. Never drive when you're tired — which is why I would never do Le Mans. Mulsanne in the night, rain, 300 amateurs on the track . . . no thank you.'

This 'two hour' rule Keke applies also to the business side of his life which, he maintains, brings him as much pleasure as driving. For hour after happy hour he sits at his desk, ashtray at hand, rapping away on the 'phone about this deal and that.

Over the years Rosberg has built up a formidable array of business contacts, which have served him well since he retired at the end of 1986. His final season, with McLaren, he thoroughly enjoyed, although the results were a disappointment. The car, basically an understeerer, didn't suit his style, but in his last race — Adelaide — he really cut loose, leaving the title contenders behind until a tyre blew. There was no bitterness, though. He left the sport a relaxed man.

'Each of these patches,' he'd say, glancing at his overalls, 'has meant a lot of bloody hard work. Very important, patches . . .'

BERND ROSEMEYER
Freehand artist

Usually it is dusk as I drive from Frankfurt airport down to Heidelberg, the first part of the journey down the *autobahn* to Darmstadt. And every year I pause for a few minutes immediately beyond the Langen-Morfelden crossing. Here, set back among the trees a way, is a memorial to Bernd Rosemeyer.

In the still of a warm August evening, the circumstances of his accident seem scarcely believable. Can it truly be that Mercedes-Benz and Auto Union risked their greatest drivers in record attempts along this stretch of road? On a freezing morning in January 1938 all the genius of Rosemeyer was swept away by a cross wind of hurricane force, which caved in the Auto Union's frail aluminium bodywork. Suddenly shorn of streamlining at 280 mph, the car disintegrated in an accident of extraordinary violence.

A while ago I devoted one of my post-race columns to Rosemeyer. It was written, in truth, because a typically arid weekend at Hockenheim had failed to spark any topic worthy of expansion. Faced with virgin paper and a deadline I forgot about the German Grand Prix.

At seven or eight I laid hands on a copy of George Monkhouse's classic *Motor Racing with Mercedes-Benz,* and was captivated by this fellow who, almost alone, took on the might of the Three Pointed Star. Once in a racing generation there comes a man whose talent and personality mingle somehow to put him on a separate plateau in the public's affection. You cannot define this quality, far less manufacture it. Moss had it, and Villeneuve. And so did Rosemeyer.

Evidently I managed to convey something of this boyhood enthusiasm, for the brief tale prompted a remarkable correspondence, including a letter from his widow.

'Can it be', she said, 'that young people still want to read about our times? I was amazed to see your article . . .'

A year or so after her husband's death, Elly Rosemeyer published a book in tribute to him, *Mein Mann der Rennfahrer,* which makes poignant reading for anyone who knew Gilles Villeneuve, so uncannily similar do the two men seem to have been, in and out of a racing car.

Each, to begin, was the fastest of his time, and would fight for tenth as hard as first place, *never* accepting defeat. 'The service', Bernd would say, 'is not over until the Blessing has been said.'

It was not their pace, however, which so entranced as much as the style which came with it. Both men spent their racing lives in ill-handling cars, always forcing them harder than they cared to go. And no sight is more stirring than that of a great driver controlling a car beyond its limits.

More than that, they did it with a joy and passion which carried over to those who watched. Rosemeyer, like Villeneuve, simply adored driving a Grand Prix car. Each backed up sublime talent with abnormal fearlessness, a combination at once irresistible and, sadly, almost inevitably fatal.

'Bernd literally did not know fear,' Rudolf Caracciola said of his great rival, 'and sometimes that is not good. We actually feared for him in every race. Somehow I never thought a long life was on the cards for him. He was bound to get it sooner or later . . .'

Rosemeyer beat Caracciola memorably in the Swiss Grand Prix of 1936, but was afterwards furious with the Mercedes star for questionable tactics in trying to keep him back. 'Racing is quite dangerous enough', Bernd exclaimed, 'without the risks being increased unnecessarily,' and six months passed before they exchanged another word.

'That', said his wife, 'was absolutely typical of him. He would not — even if it were a matter of life and death — simply put up with what he thought was an injustice to him.

One of Rosemeyer's most celebrated victories was in the Vanderbilt Cup on Long Island, New York, in 1937. The Auto Union came in ahead of Dick Seaman's Mercedes. Here is Bernd before the start, a youthful Ferry Porsche (left) looking on.

'On another occasion Bernd believed that his Auto Union comrade Ernst von Delius had gone back on an agreement they had made before an event, and tried to cheat him. It was actually a genuine misunderstanding, but until that became clear Bernd was quite prepared to have nothing more to do with him. This man, straight as a die and the frankest of the frank, could stand anything but dishonesty . . .'

I heard that, and thought at once of Villeneuve's identical response to Pironi's duplicity at Imola in 1982.

Like every driver of real stamp down the ages, Rosemeyer was outstanding from the moment he first stepped into a racing car. Briefly and successfully he raced motorcycles as a means of making his name, and in early 1935 Auto Union tested him. At that time very much in the shadow of Mercedes-Benz, they had need of a true ace to supplement the reliability of Hans Stuck and the fading genius of Achille Varzi. Rosemeyer made his debut for the team at the Avus, and within weeks had become its mainstay.

He mastered an Auto Union as no one else — even Nuvolari — ever did. True, having no experience of racing a front-engined car, he had no technique to unlearn, but it needs to be remembered that his drive at the Avus was his first race in *any* car. And in his second, at the Nurburgring, he lost the lead to Caracciola only within a few hundred yards of the finish . . .

Rosemeyer ended his Grand Prix debut season with a victory, and the following year, 1936, was triumphant all the way. Seven victories brought him the European Championship, racing's highest honour.

Moreover, his battle with Mercedes was invariably a lone one, for Auto Union had no other driver of remotely his class. This became particularly wearisome in 1937, when Mercedes, fielding Caracciola, Lang, von Brauchitsch and Seaman, also enjoyed clear superiority from their W125. Four times that year Bernd contrived to beat them; *every* time he was their only threat.

The German Grand Prix was a typical Rosemeyer race. In practice he stunned Mercedes, taking pole position by six clear seconds, and by the end of the second lap led Lang, Caracciola and von Brauchitsch by nine seconds. He had beaten them earlier in the year at the Eifelrennen, and was set on winning again at his beloved Nurburgring. But on lap four he clipped a bank, which punctured his left rear tyre and, worse, broke off the ears of the knock-off hub cap. When he arrived at the pits finally, it took the mechanics nearly three minutes to hammer off what remained. Back into the race he went, tenth.

On lap eight, after a succession of record laps, the Auto Union was off again, on the descent to Adenau, Bernd persuading spectators to push him back on the road, whereupon the charge resumed.

In those days the *Grosser Preis von Deutschland* was a long race, 22 laps of the 'Ring taking close to four hours. By the end Rosemeyer had worked the Auto Union into third place, one minute behind the victorious Caracciola. In the hub-cap pit stop alone, he had lost more than three minutes . . .

Amid a rapturous ovation Bernd stepped from the car and walked up to the rostrum, where awaited Caracciola and von Brauchitsch — and Adolf Huhnlein, a Brownshirt appointed by Hitler as his man

in the field. The German Chancellor regarded Grand Prix racing as of immense importance to the country's propaganda machine.

All this was offensive to Bernd, for whom racing was a sport. As well as that, he had an instinctive dislike of pomposity, and rarely missed an opportunity to puncture Nazi authority. For his victory Caracciola was presented with a large bronze trophy depicting the Goddess of Speed, and as Huhnlein's back was momentarily turned, Rosemeyer stuck his cigarette between her lips! At the crowd's audible gale of laughter Huhnlein swung round to see Bernd the picture of innocence, cigarette back in his own mouth . . .

After the fun, though, came stark tragedy. No one had yet told Rosemeyer of the accident between Seaman and von Delius, whose cars had touched on the long straight at the end of the lap. The German's Auto Union had somersaulted clean out of the circuit

---

Bernd's last race was the Donington Grand Prix of 1937, and this grid picture sums up that era perfectly: Rosemeyer's Auto Union (5) against the Mercedes team. On this occasion his major opposition came from von Brauchitsch (3).

Is it any wonder that the people worshipped him? Bernd's brilliance and fearlessness in the immensely powerful but unwieldy Auto Union was in clear evidence at Donington, as everywhere else.

and on to the main road beyond. A few hours later he died.

The loss of his closest friend was the latest in a chapter of sorrows in Rosemeyer's life at this time. During the previous winter, while he was away racing in South Africa, his mother had died, and a few months later a road accident claimed his elder brother. Once, only once, his father asked him to retire from racing.

'Maybe I too will have to die', was Bernd's reply, 'but you must understand that without a racing car it is in any case the end of life for me . . .'

The 1937 season closed at Donington, where Rosemeyer scored one of his greatest victories after a memorable duel with a particularly on-form von Brauchitsch. And he looked to the future with renewed optimism. There was every hope that Nuvolari, to whom he was very close, would be joining Auto Union for 1938, and Bernd relished the prospect of a team mate capable of true support in the continuing battle with Mercedes. More immediately, he looked forward to a quiet winter with Elly, who expected their first child shortly before Christmas.

His work for the year, however, was not quite done, for the final week of October was given over to record attempts at Frankfurt. In previous years Rosemeyer had not been involved, Auto Union traditionally relying on Stuck, but Bernd begged Karl Feuereissen, the team manager, for the opportunity to take on Caracciola and Mercedes-Benz.

During 'Record Week' at Frankfurt, the *autobahn* to Darmstadt was, of course, closed, the drivers using one of the two-lane carriageways for their runs. Incredible as it may seem, though, when Rosemeyer first drove the Auto Union streamliner there, in June of 1937, the other side was left open! In fact, a contra-flow system was operated, with a substantial knee-high bar placed across the road to indicate to drivers coming from Darmstadt that they should cross to the opposite side. The bar also marked the spot by which, according to Auto Union calculations, Bernd should have been able to get the car stopped . . .

Officials at the spot were therefore appalled to see it approaching at great speed. Reacting swiftly, they removed the bar, and it was good they did because seconds later the Auto Union went by them at well over 180 mph, then continuing towards Darmstadt with normal traffic coming the other way!

'I was enjoying it so much', laughed Rosemeyer afterwards, 'that I forgot about the barrier. And when

Rosemeyer's wife, Elly Beinhorn, was very much a celebrity in her own right, 'the Amy Johnson of Germany'. After Bernd's death she wrote a fascinating book about him.

In October of 1937 Rosemeyer prepares for a record attempt on the Frankfurt-Darmstadt *autobahn* in the Auto Union streamliner. It was here, three months later, that he lost his life.

I saw it, there was no time to brake. As for the traffic, I thought, "I can see them and they can see me. I'll go on to Darmstadt and turn round at the crossroads . . ."' Which is what he did.

Within a couple of hours Bernd had set new records for the flying kilometre and mile, each at over 243 mph, after which the contra-flow was adjusted to allow for timed runs at up to ten miles — which he covered at 225 mph.

Keep in mind that we are talking about a two-lane road, by no means completely straight, with bridges at frequent intervals, and a clearer picture of the achievement begins to emerge. After the ten-mile run, Dr Feuereissen reported, Bernd did not immediately spring from the car but remained in the cockpit a while, even he a little overwhelmed by the intensity of the experience. A couple of times cross winds had blown the car on to the grass. No, he had not lifted, but . . .

'At about 240 mph', Rosemeyer said, 'the joints in the concrete road surface are felt like blows, setting up a corresponding resonance through the car, but this disappears at a greater speed. Passing under bridges the driver receives a terrific blow to the chest,

because the car is pushing air aside, which is trapped by the bridge.

'When you go under a bridge, for a split second the engine noise completely disappears and then returns like a thunderclap when you are through.

'The utmost concentration is needed to keep the car on the road — particularly near the bridges — because side winds are strong and erratic. It is necessary to make tiny, lightning, adjustments to the steering all the time, and after a few minutes the driver's nervous energy is completely exhausted.

'The strain of the ten-mile record attempts is actually greater than that of an entire Grand Prix, although the whole thing lasts less than three minutes . . .'

Later Rosemeyer and Auto Union had much the upper hand over Caracciola and Mercedes through the October record week. And Bernd went home for the winter, celebrating the arrival of his son a month later. Tazio Nuvolari, the boy's godfather, and his wife spent New Year with the Rosemeyers.

Days later, though, Bernd's holiday was interrupted. Mercedes, scalded by their defeat in the autumn, preferred not to wait another year before trying to redress the balance. Strings were pulled, and permission was granted to close the *autobahn* briefly in January. Auto Union immediately decided to respond, and Rosemeyer reluctantly left Berlin for Frankfurt.

January 28 dawned bitter, the road glistening with the jewellery of frost, but by eight o'clock it had cleared and Cararcciola took the Mercedes out. And by nine o'clock Auto Union had lost their mile and kilometre records. 'I was unnerved', Rudi said. 'The road seemed like a narrow white band, the bridges like tiny black holes ahead. It was a matter of threading the car through them . . .'

During his last couple of runs Caracciola noticed that a strong cross wind was starting to build, and was alarmed when he saw the Auto Union being unloaded. When Rosemeyer came over to offer congratulations, his rival advised him to forget about running that day.

Bernd, though, was anxious to take his record back

The Rosemeyer memorial stands where the Auto Union crashed in January of 1938, beyond the Langen-Morfelden crossing on the Frankfurt-Darmstadt *autobahn*.

as soon as possible. He wanted to get it over with, go home. So he stubbed out a last cigarette, put on his linen helmet and climbed aboard for a test run. Not running flat out, he nevertheless recorded 268 mph, only a couple shy of Caracciola's new mark. But he looked a little shaken, and admitted that there *was* quite a cross wind at the Morfelden clearing.

Now his own mechanics implored him to postpone the run, but he said no, let's do it. And shortly before midday the sinister device, its high-sided aerodynamics new and untried, accelerated away.

They found the wreckage strewn over an area of six hundred yards. It was like an aeroplane accident, a scene of utter devastation. And in the forest they found Rosemeyer. His eyes were open, and there was not a trace of blood. But there had been no miracle. It is here that the memorial statue stands.

'I was deeply moved', Elly Rosemeyer read, 'by the news of the tragic fate of your husband. I offer you my sincerest condolences. May the thought that he fell in his devotion to the honour of his country mitigate your profound grief.'

The words were Hitler's, and along with his letter were many others, from names history would come to despise, each laden with the ferocious zeal of Third Reich nationalism. Soft words of sympathy were followed by the thought — presumably intended to comfort — that Bernd Rosemeyer died, as Goering put it, 'in service to the fight for Germany's world prestige.'

Rosemeyer, even in death, was of propaganda value to Hitler. The personification of a fair-haired Aryan dream, the glorious warrior fallen. For others, though, he was simply a hero they would see no more, a man who had flashingly enriched their lives.

'There was but one Rosemeyer', Dr Feuereissen said in tribute. 'He combined an art of driving, cultivated to the highest point of perfection, with a sense of absolute fairness, absolute enthusiasm. For him there were no half measures.

'As an individual he was ever the same boyish, good-natured fellow. He was entirely without guile, and said exactly what he thought of all men, heedless of whether it might profit or injure him. He will remain for ever in our memory as the good friend, the fair sportsman. And the great, triumphant, fighter . . .'

The anecdote which tells most about the man, though, came from Ludwig Sebastian, Bernd's devoted mechanic. During one of the record days in 1937, he was awaiting his return after a run and saw the Auto Union approaching. Suddenly it flicked sideways at 125 mph, first one way, then the other. Eight or nine times this happened, Sebastian watching in horror, but finally the car was brought to a stop.

'There!' cried its driver, as he stopped from the car. 'I'd like to see anyone else do that . . .'

AYRTON SENNA
One track mind

'Even when he's supposed to be relaxing,' says a close friend of Ayrton Senna, 'his mind is on racing. He'll be watching TV, say, sitting there in an armchair, and you notice that his right hand is constantly changing gear . . . 'I'm quite sure that he has no idea he's doing it. But that's him. I don't know what he'll do in later life, but for now there's only racing — only winning the World Championship.'

When first he went to Europe he was 'Ayrton da Silva', and it seemed like the perfect handle for a Latin American race driver. Then he raced a while as 'Ayrton Senna da Silva', bringing his mother's maiden name into play, but it was a clumsy mouthful for commentators, and finally he settled for plain 'Ayrton Senna'.

It was a bit unfortunate, I said to another driver one day, that in English-speaking countries the revised surname had laxative connotations. 'It's just right for him,' the reply snapped back. 'That's the effect he has on me . . .'

Many of his colleagues in Formula 1 have their enthusiasm for Ayrton Senna well under control, and in part — admitted or not — this stems from envy of his sublime talent. In all circumstances Senna excels. But if they grudgingly admire what he can do with a race car, they do not care for the ruthlessness he has sometimes shown when another driver has the presumption to try a passing manoeuvre on him.

There was classic example of this in the Portuguese Grand Prix of 1988. All season long Ayrton had been into a battle for the World Championship with McLaren team mate, Alain Prost.

On the track Prost is honourable, occasionally hard, always scrupulously fair. When Senna passed him for the lead in Montreal earlier in the season, he could have blocked the move, and afterwards some suggested he should have done. 'What would that have proved?' he answered with some contempt.

'Anyone can block, but that's not racing — not my way to race, anyway. That day he was quicker than I was, and he won the corner.'

So to Estoril, three months on, and this time the roles were reversed; this time it was Prost passing Senna for the lead. Right in front of the pits he drew alongside his team mate — who swerved right, pushing Alain towards the pit wall. At one stage Prost was in a gap with the wall a couple of feet to his right, Senna considerably closer than that on his left. And all of this in open-wheeled cars at more than 180mph.

Prost didn't lift, took the lead, won the race. But afterwards he was soberly livid. 'If we have to take risks like that,' he murmured, 'to win the World Championship, then I don't want to know about it . . .' Was he going to speak to Senna about it? Yes, he said, he was going to speak to Senna about it.

The pity of it is, as Keke Rosberg has observed, that Senna is too good to have need of resorting to junior league hooliganism. 'What you have to remember about Ayrton,' says Peter Warr, team manager for Lotus (for whom the Brazilian drove for three years), 'is that he genuinely believes he can do things with a car that are beyond anyone else. This is fact. His self-belief is such that it's never occurred to him that someone — even Prost — might beat him, in equal cars, in a straight fight.'

At the very least, Senna is devastatingly sure of himself, you can say that. In 1981 he dominated the Formula Ford scene in Britain, yet passed up the most important meeting of all, the Festival at Brands Hatch. 'I thought I'd done enough,' he said, 'to progress, to get a Formula 3 drive for the following season, but nothing was offered. I had no intention of spending the winter begging for sponsorship, so I thought, OK, I'll quit, go home and work in Brazil.' Apparently a retired racing driver at 21, he then flew off to Sao Paulo with his wife.

Monaco 1984. Senna slithers the Toleman through Casino Square. This was only the sixth Grand Prix of his career, and he very nearly won it.

Over that winter, however, he thought things through, concluding finally that he wanted to carry on. And when he arrived in Europe this time he was alone: 'If I was going to establish myself, make it into Formula 1, I knew I had to give it all my time and attention. I couldn't do that if I was married, so we parted.

'You have to understand,' he said, 'that what I really care about is my career. I've given up a lot of important things for it, including my marriage, including living in Brazil with my family and friends.'

It sounds chillingly detached, and perhaps it is. At first Senna's frankness is stark and disturbing. You get the impression that he speaks as he does chiefly for reasons of economy, that sugaring an unpalatable pill would waste time which could be put to better use.

Some years ago, in his Lotus days, Ayrton vetoed a move by the team to have Derek Warwick as his team mate. Lotus, he flatly said, had shown themselves incapable of preparing two cars to the same standard; Warwick was too good to be a number two driver, and therefore the team would devote too much time and effort to his car — which would inevitably detract from the preparation of his own. So find a rabbit for the second car.

In the midst of all this Warwick, then consequently out of work, received a Christmas card, offering best wishes for the New Year. It was from Senna. And you may be sure he never saw the irony as he signed it. Nothing personal. Just business.

Patrick Tambay was another man then under consideration for the second Lotus-Renault drive. He remembers the saga well, even laughs about it. 'One day I asked Ayrton how he would feel about me as a team mate. "You!" he said, "But you're *French*! That means Renault would give you the best engines!"

'That was his instant response. He was thinking, "How could it hurt me?" I thought it was amazing — not that he was thinking only of himself, but that he didn't trouble to hide it . . .'

Most drivers recognize that in Senna they are dealing with a special force, although the majority would dance on glass before admitting it. Tambay never made any bones about it: 'He is a phenomenon. While I was racing, I saw three drivers with something extra, something which put them on a plateau above the rest: Villeneuve, Prost and Senna. I don't know what the special quality is — only that it exists.'

In Ayrton's case, single-mindedness and a ferocious degree of ambition are high on the list. He is one of those few drivers who can truly motivate a team, make everyone get behind him. Prost has the same gift. As a mechanic, you feel a whole lot better about working an all-nighter if your man then goes out and gets pole position. Make the car just a little better, and it shows at once in his lap times. Ayrton has that kind of talent and commitment. For his crew, it is instant reward for effort.

He seemed like a shy fellow when first he arrived in Formula 1 with the Toleman team in 1984. At the track he wasn't desperately communicative because clearly all his thoughts were directed at the race car, at how to improve it, how to drive it better. He had arrived from the junior formulae with an awesome reputation, but in the past plenty of those had foundered at Formula 1 level. Not so with Ayrton. His sixth Grand Prix — Monte Carlo — he would have won, but appalling weather halted the race just as he was about to take the lead.

On the rostrum afterwards there was no newcomer's delight at finishing second. No, Senna's expression was angry. He should have *won*!

He left Toleman for Lotus at the end of that year, and perhaps, in 1985, we saw him at his most approachable. Now in an absolutely competitive car, he brilliantly won his first Grand Prix, a class above the rest in a Portuguese downpour.

Senna seemed consciously to enjoy racing at that time, relished offending the Establishment. If he drove

Senna was on the point of taking the lead from Prost when the 1984 Monaco Grand Prix was stopped. On the rostrum his feelings about that decision are clearly evident.

the whole race in Estoril with the calm and precision of a Jackie Stewart, he acknowledged victory as a true Latin. Within seconds of taking the chequered flag he had the seat belts unbuckled, and was half out of the cockpit in his joy, waving both arms like a kid at an airport. It was the same when he won his first ever Formula 3 race, at Thruxton little more than two years earlier.

He doesn't do that now. Three years with Lotus produced only half a dozen wins, but since moving to McLaren in 1988 he has come almost to expect victory. At one stage, in midsummer, he took four on the trot, but there were no signs of obvious exhilaration afterwards. Each win, clearly, represented another nine points towards the World Championship, nothing more or less.

Similarly, Senna's manner with the press has changed. Time was when he would gabble excitedly — win or lose — after a race, graphically describe his battle with Rosberg or whomever.

Not any more. Quite often in 1988 he and Prost scored a 1–2 for the McLaren-Honda team, and at the post-race press conference you might readily have believed, from their expressions and manner, that Alain had won, Ayrton been beaten. Prost, in other words, is more gracious in defeat than is Senna in victory.

Ayrton is wary and offhand with the press now, the more so since the widespread criticism of his refusal to allow Warwick into Lotus.

He is a loner, and very much an exile in Europe. Home is an apartment in Monte Carlo, tax lair of many Grand Prix drivers, but whereas compatriot Nelson Piquet — who lives close by — has willingly embraced the European way of life, and spends little time in Brazil, Senna's affections remain with Sao Paulo, to which he returns as often as possible. You have the impression he is away from it solely because the job demands it.

'I don't have many friends in Europe,' he says, 'and at a track I have no time for anything but work. When I'm working, I don't care about anything but my own

Ayrton's first Grand Prix victory came in only his second drive for Lotus. In the monsoon rains of Estoril in 1985 the Brazilian was a class above the rest.

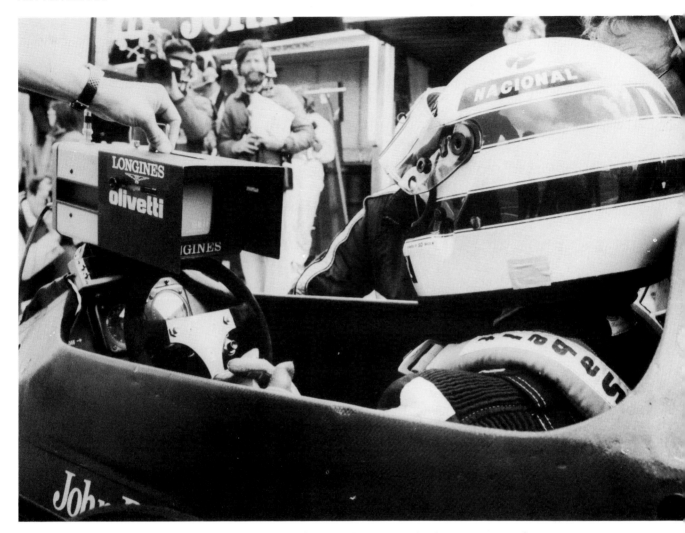

Drivers dream of this. During final qualifying at Brands Hatch in October 1985 Aytron studies the monitor, waiting for someone to beat his time. Piquet managed it — and Senna immediately set a new mark.

team and mechanics . . .'

'I don't care' is a phrase he uses frequently, sometimes, perhaps, when he can't be bothered to argue a point. 'So-and-so says you blocked him' — 'I don't care . . .' Often the words come wearily, the voice bored. 'That's his problem' is an alternative, and sometimes he will shrug, 'Hey, come on. I was in front — I stick to my own line.'

Away from a circuit Ayrton is often different again, courteous and affable, revealing a cynical humour which rarely surfaces in the paddock. And I suspect that, behind the outward indifference, he does care what people think of him. At present, though, his ambition holds away.

The fact that Prost and Senna are working together says much for their self-esteem. For so long the Frenchman has been rightly hailed as the best, but there was always a voice of opinion suggesting that the Brazilian would usurp his place in the scheme of things if only he had the car to do it.

Prost had the confidence to raise no objection when McLaren boss Ron Dennis suggested Senna as his team mate; and neither did Ayrton have any fear of joining what was seen as 'Alain's team'.

At first there were problems, albeit not particularly serious ones. Senna's natural autocracy was in no way subdued by his new surroundings, and Prost wasn't impressed by that — any more than he enjoyed the interminable end-of-the-day team debriefings which are intrinsic to Senna's tunnel-vision approach to the job.

Gradually, though, their relationship improved. As human beings they are too disparate ever to become close friends, but their respect for each other has

After early pace-setter Mansell had gone out, Senna and the 'active' Lotus-Honda 99T were unstoppable at Monaco in 1987. On other than street circuits, though, the car was a disappointment.

grown. Each has several times beaten the other in a straight fight. McLaren won all but one of 16 Grands Prix in 1988, Senna leading Prost eight to seven.

Two of Ayrton's victories, in England and Germany, provided further evidence that he is without question the best wet weather driver in the world, a fact freely acknowledged by Prost. And before the start of the season Alain predicted, too, that Senna would be quicker than himself in qualifying, putting together that single almighty lap for pole position in the race. As for the races themselves, well, Prost saw his team mate as potentially superior 'in traffic', which is Formula 1 parlance for threading through backmarkers as you lap them.

'It's obvious he'll be quicker in these ways,' Alain said. "He is where I was four or five years ago, with everything to prove. His ambition and motivation *must*

be greater than mine and in these circumstances you take bigger risks . . .'

Certainly Ayrton takes huge chances sometimes, the raw racer subjugating the glacially calm and methodical thinker. And Alain's words have proved uncannily accurate: in the wet, in qualifying, in traffic, Senna pulls out time on him; on a clear track, by contrast, Prost tends to claw it back.

There has been another indisputable difference between them, as well, which is that Senna has made more mistakes, the most unaccountable being his throwing away of the '88 Monaco Grand Prix, which he dominated absolutely until, having reduced his pace in the late stages, he simply lost concentration and hit a barrier — leaving victory to Prost . . .

'At the moment,' said a watching Keke Rosberg, 'Ayrton is putting a hundred per cent of himself into being quicker than anyone, but that's not how you beat Prost. Alain puts his hundred per cent into winning races . . .'

Senna's car was written off, and it was his second of the season. In five years with McLaren, Prost had never badly damaged a car, let alone destroyed one.

At dusk on the eve of the Spanish Grand Prix a Mercedes set out on a slow lap of the Jerez circuit. It was away a long time, its driver stopping at each corner, studying intently the run-off areas, rumble-strips and kerbs. This is Senna's way of doing things, and years ago it used to be Prost's.

Now, though, Alain was playing cards with his friends, having left the circuit much earlier for a few holes of golf. Showered and changed, he was enjoying himself before dinner. The next day he won the race going away, leaving Ayrton a little bewildered.

The odds, though, were still with the Brazilian, who needed only a victory in Japan or Australia to make sure of the World Championship. 'If Ayrton wins the title this year,' Prost had suggested earlier in the year, 'he will be *more* dangerous as a rival in 1989, not less. I'm sure of that, because that's what happened to me. Once I'd become World Champion, I relaxed a lot, lightened up, stopped being so intense about racing.' Senna did take the championship, but there has been no return of the ready smile of the mid-eighties.

His earnings are put at US$10,000,000 a year, and he has his place in Monaco and his Learjet, the essential accoutrements of the contemporary Formula 1 superstar. But his only relaxation from racing is playing with radio-controlled aeroplanes, and one always fears for anyone with a genuine obsession. Watch him on the limit through the tight confines of a street circuit, inch-perfect as his McLaren shaves the barriers, and you know that here is an artist. A genius, if not without flaws. A brilliant drive at Suzuka brought him victory and the World Championship. It remains to be seen whether or not the title will eventually bring Ayrton Senna any peace.

The combination of Senna and McLaren was all everyone expected, and in 1988 Ayrton was never better than at Silverstone, completely dominant in the wet.

JACKIE STEWART
No free lunches

'I'm running in the fast lane just now', JYS is fond of saying. 'Could you call me back tomorrow at 2.30? I'm clear then for 40 minutes . . .' Such is the pace of his life. Telephone calls of any length must be arranged in advance, put in the appointments book.

A friend of mine had once to 'phone him in London. Jackie was staying at Grosvenor House, the call booked for 10 am. On the stroke of it my colleague was put through to his suite. No reply. Not like Stewart, he thought, putting the receiver down. Instantly it rang: 'Hello, it's Jackie. Listen, I'm calling just to say I'm stuck in traffic on Park Lane. Can you give it ten minutes and then call my room?'

In 1971 Stewart came out with a book based on his diaries from the previous Grand Prix season. Its published title was *Faster!* Jackie had wanted to call it *Where Am I Going Today?* Should he ever choose to write a further volume of autobiography, that title would hold good. His travel schedule remains ferocious. Quite why remains a mystery to some of us. There are times now when it seems to me that Stewart is chasing his own tail. He has, on the face of it, every material thing a man could want. His house by Lac Léman, in Switzerland, is glorious, and one can only wonder that he spends comparatively little time in it, why he needs to pass so many hours in aeroplanes, so many days in unpleasant places. Part of it must be ego; Jackie's is well developed and healthily maintained. It is not a matter of overt conceit. He is, of course, well aware of how great a driver he was, but he speaks of it as a matter of fact. You don't easily win three World Championships and more Grands Prix than anyone else in history.

What many found unacceptable was that he retired at 34, at the summit of his driving career. He's made his money, they said, and now he's getting out. What was the matter with him? All this talk of safety . . . didn't he *want* to die in a racing car? Not like the old days . . . why, the chap couldn't even get his hair cut . . .

Thankfully, it *wasn't* like the old days. Mario Andretti says of Stewart, and others who followed him down the early path to retirement, that they cannot have loved racing enough. Their talent still alive and vibrant, how could they allow it to fall into disuse? 'For me it's like a fix', Mario says. 'The sheer animal pleasure of it, I mean. And until you start to lose the habit — to *know* you're not as quick any more — I don't know how you kick it. I couldn't stand to be watching and thinking I could still beat those guys.'

Andretti, though, is more emotionally tied to racing than most. Stewart says he was burned out when he retired, that he needed to change his life, and suffered no withdrawal symptoms. 'It was a simple decision for me to make', he says. 'I'd been driving myself too hard for too long.' Moreover, the decision was planned well in advance. In April of 1973 I asked him how long he intended going on. It was true, he answered, that he was thinking of retirement.

'Logically, that must be the goal of everyone in the sport. I enjoy enormously what I'm doing — the driving and the life of being a racing driver — and it's not an easy thing to give up. But I want to retire, not only for my own sake, but also for my family.

'I do see there are other things in life, and however much pleasure you get out of something you can't always have what you want. There are some sacrifices you have to make, and the time will come when I'll have to make mine. And it will be irrevocable. The time will be right, and I'll do it. No comebacks. It has to be clean and final.'

We were talking at a Silverstone test session, and it was during that very week, he later told me, that he made up his mind. Within days he had confided to Ken Tyrrell and Ford's Walter Hayes that he would be stopping at the end of the year. And the three of

Jackie and his favourite car. During the opening laps of the 1969 Monaco Grand Prix only Amon's Ferrari could keep in touch with Stewart and the Matra MS80. This was JYS's first World Championship year.

them sat on that secret until 14 October, when Jackie confirmed his retirement at a function in London.

'I did feel a bit light-headed that day', he remembers. 'There was a sense of relief, but also regret. If things had ended a little more happily, in fact, the regret might have been more in my mind. We'd intended to do the announcement a week after my last race. The way it worked out, though, it was a week after Francois's accident, three days after his funeral . . .'

Watkins Glen should have been the perfect finale for Stewart's career: fine autumn weather in upstate New York for a great driver's 100th Grand Prix. But Cevert, who had won there two years earlier, died in an accident of extreme violence during practice, and the Tyrrell team withdrew from the race.

From the very early days Jackie took a close interest in safety, and there is no doubt that his accident at Spa in 1966 nurtured it. It took a long time to get him out of the wreckage, and fuel was leaking. Thereafter his BRM had a spanner taped to the steering wheel to facilitate its speedy removal. And Stewart was the first Grand Prix driver to use a seat belt. He became the drivers' natural spokesman on all safety matters, and in many quarters was castigated for it.

'In fact', Chris Amon once told me, 'we were all beginning to think about it, particularly after Jimmy Clark was killed. It angered us that the greatest driver's life was tossed away because he had a tyre failure and then plunged into trees. It wasn't really 'done' in those days to speak about safety. I admired Stewart tremendously as a driver — but much more for his courage in saying things which he knew would make him unpopular in some quarters. He was speaking for all of us — but he was the only one with the balls to do it.'

Jackie himself put it this way: 'A lot of people criticized me personally, saying I was trying to wrap everyone in cotton wool. Dreamers, all of them. Christ Almighty, when did *they* ever hit an Armco barrier at 150 mph? They talked about barriers as if they were candy floss! Motor racing will never be safe. There will always be accidents, and there will always be fatalities. But at least people now accept there's no room for *unnecessary* hazards. People with half a brain, anyway . . .'

He saw the ground effect era in the same terms. Although long retired, he considered the sport was putting itself under serious threat with the suspensionless trucks of the early eighties. There were accidents every weekend. The cars looked horrible. The drivers hated them. All the artistry was fading away.

'A lot of people criticized me for *that*, too — mainly those who had ground effect cars which were working well. My answer to them was that Gilles Villeneuve, as pure a racing driver as you will ever see, was obsessive about getting rid of skirts and ground effect. He thought the cars were unnecessarily dangerous, and they gave him no pleasure.

'The big problem, you see, is that the people in authority have vested interests. If Formula 1 were a normal business, based in America, the Federal Trade Commission would stop it, because of the conflict of interests.

Stewart hated Spa, but it never showed in his driving there. Despite having to hold the gear lever in place for much of the way, Jackie took the difficult BRM H16 to second place in 1967.

'The irony is that Gilles — the bravest of the brave — thought more constructively about safety than any driver since. No one else is going to take care of them. FISA will always see new talent coming and going. The teams themselves can always replace drivers. The period of mourning is short . . .'

So Jackie has never been afraid to voice the unpalatable. 'When I was a driver it would have been far easier to have kept quiet about safety. I'd have been a much more popular World Champion if I'd said what people wanted to hear me say. I might not have been alive, mind you, but more popular . . .'

His greatest drive, he says, was almost the last of his career, at Monza in 1973. I was surprised at that, assuming he would cite the Nurburgring five years earlier, when he won by four minutes. 'No, no,' he dismisses the suggestion. 'That was in the wet, and it was a seat-of-the-pants thing. At a place like the 'Ring flair and talent can always play their part. Also, I think I maybe had a tyre advantage that day.

'Monza, though, was different. I'd had an early pit stop, lost a lap, and then got my head down. The thing about that place is that it's so easy — I mean, *anyone* can go quickly at Monza. So therefore it was much more difficult to gain ground there. You had to be technically perfect, clinical and clean, because otherwise you scrubbed off speed. That drive was dictated entirely by my head, and it was as good as ever I did, I believe. Don't fight the car, let *it* do the work — that's the secret.'

It has been my good fortune to be driven by many Grand Prix drivers over the years, occasionally at a circuit, usually on the road. And none has so far impressed me as much as Stewart. It is all a matter of ease. You have the impression that the car is driving itself, that Jackie is there merely to take care of odd wayward moments.

Towards the end of 1981 there were strong, if scurrilous, rumours that he, like Niki Lauda, was contemplating a comeback. Although the Austrian did return with conspicuous success, the sport's insiders never took seriously the Stewart stories. He was now 42, retired for eight years.

'If he had come back', Frank Williams remarked at the time, 'I've no doubts he would have been competitive. He is immensely skilled, and he has even more application than Niki. He's still very fit. I think undoubtedly he was the best all-round driver of the last decade.'

The two men have much in common, including what amounts to an obsession with fitness. Cannibals would give neither a second glance. Each has that hollow, gaunt, look which is traditional in jockeys like Piggott, but Lester's traditional menu for 'making weight' — coffee and cigars — would horrify Williams and Stewart. Even Frank, though, has moments of weakness. Alcohol and tobacco he may have eschewed all his life, but I have observed him working through an entire cheesecake while discussing the character of Jean-Marie Balestre. Stewart's hair shirt is even coarser. For many years he carried quantities of All-Bran in his luggage, and these days the world's great hotels are required to produce each morning porridge made to his own specification — 'Absolutely no salt!' Lunch is a light salad, and occasionally he permits himself a 'spritzer', a blend of white wine and soda . . .

It is, however, easy to poke fun at such an ascetic way of life. And one of Jackie's great strengths is that he is easily capable of laughing at himself. He plainly enjoys holding court in the paddock, sitting around, discussing the latest gossip. On one occasion I was sitting with a couple of friends outside the Elf motorhome. It was a wet practice session at Zolder, and there was little incentive to venture beyond the awning. We heard a familiar voice hailing us:

'I hate to intrude on your conversation, but there's 26 guys out here. And they're perspiring! They're competing for your attention . . .'

We turned round to see a small figure from a Burberry advert, collar buttoned up, check cap, wide grin.

'No, no, on second thoughts you stay there. Don't overstress yourselves. Stay put — I'll bring the times to you when it's finished . . .'

Often, though, I have watched at a corner with Jackie, and his unofficial commentary is fascinating: 'See that? He *still* turns in too early — he's been doing that since he started . . .' And when he takes you round a circuit, he demonstrates what he means, assuming different drivers' styles: 'Right, now this time we'll go in as so-and-so would. Can you feel that? Can you feel how the car's trying to run wide?'

Retired these many years he may have been, but the memories of his great days remain. I watched him at Monaco in 1971, and it seemed like one of those flag-to-flag wins which were a matter of routine that summer. Years later Ken Tyrrell put it into fresh perspective. 'After the warm-up lap', he said, 'Jackie thought there was something amiss with the brakes, and the mechanics found the brake balance bar was actually *broken!* No time to do anything about it, of course, so he had to do the whole race — at Monaco, of all places — with front brakes only. Afterwards we took out the rear pads, and they were like new, untouched . . .'

Stewart was as good as irresistible through that season, without a serious rival. Rindt was gone, Peterson and Fittipaldi just arriving. Ickx's Ferrari was occasionally a minor irritation, nothing more. By Zeltweg, in mid-August, the second World Championship was secure. As with Jimmy Clark in 1965,

Stewart and 003. One of the most successful cars ever built, this particular Tyrrell chassis took Jackie to eight of his Grand Prix victories, including the six in 1971 which gave him his second title.

it was a matter of one man completely demoralizing his fellows. I was in the Tyrrell pit at Ricard when Ickx beat his time during the closing minutes of qualifying.

'Christ,' Jackie said, 'that means I'll have to go out again . . .' With apparently minimal effort he went a second quicker, took back the pole. 'Is that it now?' he enquired, unbuckling his helmet. Surely he was not to be inconvenienced again? It was confidence sublime, a careless arrogance, and you rarely see it in Formula 1.

The fact is, Stewart is brilliant in front of an audience, be they spectators in a grandstand, a hard-bitten group in a board room or a small cluster of friends in the paddock or pits. Like Mario Andretti, he is a born performer and loves — needs — to be the centre of attraction. Jody Scheckter retired into total obscurity; Jackie, I suspect, would find that unbearable. He relishes the tangible signs of success, likes to be recognized. Most people like that are insufferable, but when JYS turns up at a race he is greeted with genuine affection.

He is, on the face of it, frighteningly organized, but he says that for him that is the easy way. When he buys clothes he orders several of each, and these are stationed conveniently around the world. In London he stays at Grosvenor House, and there resides a Louis Vuitton cabin trunk containing everything he is likely to need. In New York he keeps a large apartment.

'It's only common sense', he says. 'In the long run it saves you time and trouble. I used to look at Chris Amon's way of life, which I'm sure got in the way of success for him. A lovely guy with enormous natural talent in a race car, but he'd turn up late at the airport without a ticket! Then he'd get to the other end and not know where he was staying . . . All these things are unsettling, and that's the last thing a driver needs.

'I like my life to be ordered, because that's how I function best — that's the only way I can function. It was just the same when I was driving. To get the best out of myself I had to be in the right frame of mind. It's terribly bad to be up or down. You must be neutral. If I was good at anything, it was eliminating emotions. That's why I was always pretty sharp and together in the first few laps of a race.'

So, too, he was. My abiding memory of Stewart in a racing car is bound up not in a famous victory day, but in a single instant of magic at Silverstone in 1973. It was the opening lap of the British Grand Prix, and into Becketts Peterson's leading Lotus 72 braked late, Stewart's Tyrrell later. Jackie was past, through and away, and Ronnie could only shake his head in disbelieving admiration. Thirty seconds into a race the Scot was already at that pitch of confidence.

That last season was his best, I think. There was not the out-and-out domination of his two previous World Championships, but nor was there the superiority of the Matra MS80 (the car he best liked) or Tyrrell 003. In 1973 the short-wheelbase 006 was twitchy and difficult to drive, if competitive in the hands of a Stewart. It was not the equal of a Lotus 72, and Peterson and Fittipaldi were by now very good indeed.

Jackie's last win was at the Nurburgring, and that pleases him. 'Had I not won a Grand Prix there, there would have been something sadly missing from my career — but, really, wasn't it a ridiculous place? Leaping from one bump to another, 187 corners or whatever it was! The number of times I thanked God when I finished a lap there . . . I can't remember doing one more balls out lap at the 'Ring than I needed to. It gave you amazing satisfaction, no doubt about it, but anyone who says he loved it is either a liar or he wasn't going fast enough . . . Me, I like that place best

By 1973 Stewart had decided on retirement at the close of the season. To the end of his driving career, though, the brilliance and ambition remained.

For much of 1973 the Tyrrells ran like this, Stewart a few yards ahead of Cevert. Here at Monaco Jackie won for the third time. At the Nurburgring and Zandvoort they finished 1-2.

when I'm sitting by a log fire on a winter's night', he smiles. 'Clearly in my mind are all the braking distances and gearchanges, and that's surely the only way I've ever lapped it without a mistake! Each apex clipped, each exit clean . . . lovely.'

I have frequently spoken to him about his life now. Why, with all his wealth, does he not sit back more, take a little time to enjoy it? Why the ceaseless travel, tedious public relations functions, interminable business dinners?

'Look,' he patiently explains, 'when I retired from driving I was sufficiently well off to anticipate living the rest of my life without too many financial worries. But times change. Inflation appears, currencies fluctuate. I was 34 when I stopped, and hopefully I'll live until three score years and ten. I didn't have to be a master mathematician to know that I couldn't go on living in the same style without supplementing capital earnings. People don't believe me when I say this, but my business life stimulates me every bit as much as my driving did. And I still earn as much as most of the top drivers . . .

'I admit that in the last ten or fifteen years there have been many times when I would have preferred to be somewhere else, not be in front of a great audience, uttering the same words I'd heard from my own mouth on countless previous occasions. But it was what the company needed, or what the audience wanted to hear. If I made them laugh, made them feel some emotion, made them have more respect for motor racing, then I was doing what I was paid for — and at the same time performing a service. It's a much bigger responsibility being World Champion than most people realize — certainly most of those racing today, anyway.

'You know,' he says, 'there's one American catchphrase I really like; 'there are no free lunches'. You drive and you earn good money. You have your yacht and your Learjet and your place in Monte Carlo, and when you stop driving you don't want to give them up. You also want something to keep you from getting bored. It's a lot of years now since I drove a Grand Prix car in anger, and I have neither missed it nor yearned for it. I have no desire to climb into the cockpit at three o'clock on a Sunday afternoon. I love my life as it is. I still adore the sport, but it's so much easier talking about it . . .'

Last time around. Four years after his retirement, in the winter of 1977, JYS drove most of the Grand Prix cars at Paul Ricard for a series of magazine articles. This is the Tyrrell 008.

ACHILLE VARZI
Latin tragedy

Not long ago I talked to a driver just out of hospital after a major accident. He was recuperating well, and considered himself fortunate to be living. For a while his agony had been so intense that they had given him morphine, these days something of a last resort. 'But if there's a next time,' he insisted, 'I'll get through without it. The pain was nothing compared to going "cold turkey" when they stopped the morphine.

'And all the time you know', he added, 'that another shot would make you feel fine — for a while . . .'

The conversation set me thinking of Achille Varzi, whose personality and career were lost in this same tide.

'The outstanding man', Enzo Ferrari said of the early thirties, 'was Nuvolari, but he found a worthy adversary in Varzi, who surpassed him in his cool, perfect, style.' The words have bite, for the Commendatore put Nuvolari with the gods.

The enigma of Achille Varzi has always intrigued me. Where Nuvolari was an uncomplicated hero of the people, his rival was a creature of mystery, uncommunicative and aloof. Of one nationality and vocation, they incited in their countrymen such passion that Italian motor racing splintered into *Nuvolariani* and *Varziani*.

On the track they shared only speed. Nuvolari was the great improviser, surviving on intuition and reflex, an emotional man often seen to beat the side of the cockpit of his frequently uncompetitive cars. Varzi was of ice and stone, impeccable of line, the classical artist. Like the Lauda of today, he was at his deadliest in pursuit, inducing mistakes in others, making none himself.

'His style,' according to Ferrari, 'reflected his personality: intelligent, calculated, ferocious in making the most of his opponent's weakness, mistake or accident. I'd say he was ruthless.' And the great Rudolf Caracciola remembered chiefly this: 'When you saw Varzi behind, you shivered . . .'

Born into a wealthy family in Galliate, near Milan, Varzi's arrival in Grand Prix racing was painless. After a successful motorcycling career, he simply bought himself an Alfa Romeo P2 in 1928, which led to a factory drive — and many Grand Prix victories — for the next couple of seasons.

For 1931, while Nuvolari remained with Alfa, Varzi moved to Bugatti, a decision considered traitorous by many Italians. Their response left him profoundly unmoved. His only requirement of a car was its competitiveness, and at this point he considered the French one better. After three successful seasons he returned to Alfa Romeo, again a purely pragmatic move.

These were the great years of rivalry with Nuvolari, a blessed time for sports writer and gossip columnist alike. In an obvious way, Tazio was the embodiment of extrovert heroism, the true Italian who talked with his hands and loved children, a jovial man. Achille, by contrast, was dry of wit, remote and arrogant, apparently irresistible to women. He dressed elegantly, stayed only in the finest hotels, did not kiss babies. Like most racing drivers, he lived for himself. What many found unforgivable was that he did not trouble to hide it.

For all their differences in character, though, and despite a pitiless professional hostility, the two men got along well. So long as Nuvolari was not around to hear it, Varzi would invariably refer to him as

Right A watching Hitler was not amused when Varzi took this Type 54 Bugatti to victory at the Avus Grand Prix of 1933. In the background Nazi officials look on.

Tunis 1935. Varzi has joined Auto Union for the new season, and here prepares for his first race in the unpredictable rear-engined car. Not yet in the grip of morphine, he won without problem.

'Maestro', and their respect for each other was absolute.

Once a match race was proposed, an attempt to settle the question once and for all. 'If I lose', Nuvolari said, 'I shall never again find peace. And if you lose, I shall feel sorry for you. Whatever happens, our friendship will be tainted. If you like, we'll do it, but I don't think it's worth it.' They shook hands, and the matter was never raised again.

In the 1930 Mille Miglia — at that time a race of more than sixteen hours, finishing in darkness — they fought the expected battle, no other car within half an hour of their Alfas. In the closing stages Varzi began to suspect that the game was lost. Ahead on the road, he recognized in his mirrors the headlight pattern of Nuvolari's car — and Tazio led on time by ten minutes.

'It's him', Achille mouthed to his co-driver.

After a while, though, Varzi began to hope again. The lights behind were gone. Was Nuvolari out?

He was not. Within thirty miles of the finish, Varzi was jolted from thoughts of victory by the flash of lights and the blast of a horn. For miles Nuvolari had been sitting there on his tail, lights off . . .

There can be no sweetness in defeat, but perhaps Varzi was consoled in part by the implicit compliment he had been paid. It takes faith, oh yes, to rely on another to guide you through the mountains at night.

In 1934, both in Alfas again, it was Varzi first, Nuvolari second, but Grand Prix successes were coming hard by this time. Each man knew in his heart that an era of German domination was coming, but while Tazio eventually committed himself to the Scuderia Ferrari team of Alfa Romeos for 1935, Achille, head in command, accepted an offer from Auto Union. And it was this decision, apparently so logical and dispassionate, which led ultimately to chaos in his life.

At first the new liaison worked well. With talent as natural as his, Varzi adapted without particular problem to the immense power and wayward handling of the rear-engined cars, winning at Tunis and Pescara. He was, by common consent, at the height of his powers.

Early in 1935, however, during tests at Monza, the saturnine Milanese had met Ilse, the wife of Paul Pietsch, Auto Union's young reserve driver. Their affair began almost immediately, discreet only for a while, and soon they were together everywhere.

Varzi stayed with Auto Union for 1936, his partners Hans Stuck and the meteoric Bernd Rosemeyer, whose great year this would be. And all was well until Tripoli.

This was Achille's favourite circuit, fast and demanding, a track where precision was all. Already he had won the Grand Prix twice, and now came a third victory — by a couple of lengths from Stuck, whom he overtook on the run up to the line. On the last lap he averaged more than 141 mph, and was afterwards a well contented man — until the banquet that evening, at which the Governor of Tripoli asked for silence, lifted his glass and proposed a toast to the winner . . . Hans Stuck!

There was an excruciating silence. Varzi, someone murmured, had won the race, not Stuck. But the Governor would have none of it; Varzi may have finished first, but Stuck was the winner . . .

And gradually the truth of the matter emerged. These were the days of the Rome-Berlin Axis, and von Ribbentrop had directed that, whenever possible, Italian drivers should win Italian races — so long as they were in German cars, of course. In the closing stages Stuck had been slowed by his pit, allowing Varzi to pass. The race had been, in short, a political demonstration. A fix.

Like Stuck, Varzi had been ignorant of this, and believed he had won on merit. Now, his honour publicly impugned, he hurled his glass to the floor and stalked out, raging. In his room he found sleep impossible, his mind in turmoil.

'Try this', said Ilse. 'I often use it when I can't sleep. It helps a lot . . .'

Her fingers held a syringe. They had been together a year, but this was the first he knew of her addiction. It had started, she said, in hospital after a minor operation. What more, Achille wondered, could go

In the pits — with ever-present cigarette — at San Sebastian in 1935.

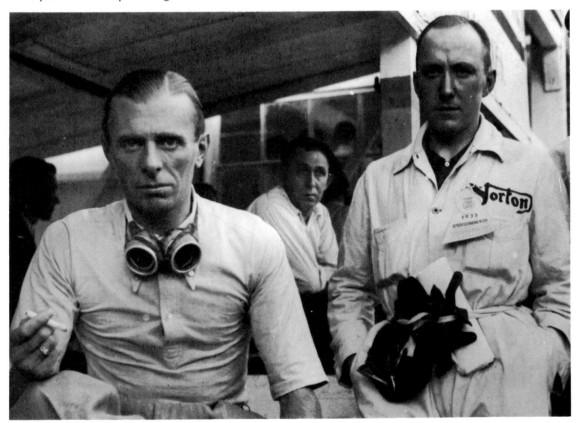

wrong this night? Hours later, still sleepless, he held out his arm for the needle.

Had he been an unkempt man, garrulous and undisciplined, the change in Varzi might have been imperceptible for a while. But in one such as he the transformation was startling. Morphine is not kind.

What had happened? His colleagues wondered and worried about that. In Tunis, only a couple of weeks later, he was unshaven, dishevelled and shaky. Much of the time he chattered, often without making a lot of sense, then lapsed into bouts of desperate silence.

More, his driving was awful, stripped suddenly of its glitter and precision. That weekend he had the first major accident of his career, the Auto Union somersaulting at close to 180 mph. Somehow he came out of it without injury, too shocked even to hold a cigarette.

After another couple of undistinguished races, Varzi disappeared. Not even his parents knew where he was, but the Auto Union management finally traced him to a villa in Rome, surrounded by simpering dilettantes. He was existing, the team's doctor discovered, on champagne, coffee and cigarettes. By now morphine's hook had complete hold, and he was slipping away from reality, face ravaged, speech slurred. He was 32, and old.

The medical man reported back. Not surprisingly, Auto Union decided against a renewal of the contract for 1937.

There was no sign of Varzi through most of the season. By now he had moved to an hotel in Milan,

By now an ill man, Varzi nevertheless took third place and fastest lap with the Auto Union at Pescara in 1936. Here he protects his head from flying pieces of tyre tread, while pressing on to the pits.

Cured of his addiction, Varzi returned to racing after the war, rejoining Alfa Romeo. Here is the famous easy style in evidence at Buenos Aires in early 1948, the year in which he died at Berne.

friendless and quite without cares. Only his mistress remained, but the relationship was all but over, and Achille eventually walked out.

In his saner moments he thought again of the career he had tossed away. At the San Remo Grand Prix he drove his own Maserati — and won against indifferent opposition. Enthusiasm reawakened, he then turned up for the Italian Grand Prix at Leghorn, pleading with Auto Union for one last chance. He had been treated, he assured them, and was cured. Rosemeyer supported him, and Varzi was tentatively booked for the last three races of the season.

During practice at Leghorn it was as if he had never been away. He was sensational in the Auto Union, beaten only by Caracciola's Mercedes. But the race was a different matter. If his genius remained, his stamina did not, and before half-distance he was into the pits, exhausted, drenched in sweat.

'I understand', he muttered when they told him not to bother turning up at Donington.

Early the following year Rosemeyer was killed in a record attempt, and Auto Union had desperate need of a top-class driver. Again they briefly thought of Varzi, but there was no way. He was back with Ilse, still in the snare of drugs. It was Nuvolari, ironically, to whom they turned.

Varzi was not seen at the circuits through 1938-39, but when racing resumed after the war he was back as a member of the Alfa Romeo team once more. And he was himself again, free of addiction after months in a home and now married to Norma, whom he had known before the years of tribulation. On the track, and off, he had regained all his former grace. With the great Jean-Pierre Wimille as Achille's team mate, Alfa dominated the early post-war years.

The first Grand Prix of 1948 was the Swiss at

Bremgarten, and early evening was settling in as Varzi went out on the opening day of practice. It was damp and murky, and the track was slick. As Louis Chiron followed, the Alfa went into a slide through the fast Jordenrampe S-bend, then clipped a wooden barrier and somersaulted, throwing Varzi out on to the road.

Chiron immediately stopped, but there was nothing to be done. Varzi, as ever wearing only a linen helmet, had been killed instantly, and it was left to the Frenchman to bear the sorrowful news back to the pits.

Signora Varzi, already evident as a woman of fortitude and dignity, responded with amazing courage. No, she said, she did not wish Alfa Romeo to withdraw from the race: rather, the team should honour the name of Varzi by winning the race for Italy. And on Sunday Felice Trossi's car duly triumphed.

No one grieved more deeply than Fangio, at that time unknown outside South America. He had met Varzi in Argentina, where Achille had won, and they had become firm friends. The country had so captivated Varzi that he spoke of retiring there to open a racing school. And when Juan Manuel came to Europe a year later, his team raced under the name of Squadra Achille Varzi, based at Galliate.

'Varzi was, to me, a god', Fangio has said. 'He spoke with great simplicity, and gave me precious advice. He is probably the driver I have most admired in my life, a man who cared only for his art . . .'

GILLES VILLENEUVE
The people's champion

A friend of mine in America sent me a cassette a while ago. On it is the sound of a lone racing car, unmistakably a Ferrari flat-12, and it is clearly audible all the way round the lap. There is a lot of wheelspin — you can hear the revs abruptly scream out of every turn — and then the volume builds until the car swishes by in a welter of spray.

He taped it during the first afternoon of practice at Watkins Glen in 1979, when conditions were as bad as I have ever seen at a race circuit. In places the track was flooded, and only eight drivers ventured out. One of those who did was Scheckter, who was second fastest behind team mate Villeneuve. Eleven seconds behind . . .

The tape, of course, is of Gilles, and it revived memories of a day when we forgot the wintry rain until he came in, the Ferrari breathless and steaming. In the pits other drivers, aghast, had giggled nervously every time the car skittered by at 160 mph. 'He's different from the rest of us', Jacques Laffite said. 'On a separate level . . .'

'I scared myself rigid that day', Jody remembered. 'I thought I had to be quickest. Then I saw Gilles's time — and I still don't really understand how it was possible. Eleven seconds!

'Motor racing was a romantic thing for him, you see', Scheckter went on. 'We were close friends, doing the same job for the same team, but we had completely opposite attitudes to it. My preoccupation was keeping myself alive, but Gilles had to be quickest on every lap — even in testing. He was the fastest racing driver the world has ever seen. If he could come back and live his life again, I think he would do exactly the same — and with the same love.'

By lunchtime on that fateful Saturday at Zolder I thought nothing more could increase the disenchantment I then felt for Grand Prix racing. The atmosphere in the paddock was poisonous from end to end. A fortnight before there had been FOCA's foot stamping boycott at Imola, and earlier in the year there had been the drivers' strike at Kyalami. The sport was in ugly turmoil, split down the middle. Between the Saturday practice sessions a talk with Teddy Mayer led to his accusation that I, and other British journalists, had been 'bought' by Renault. Only that, he said, could explain our aversion to what FOCA had done. I was still in a rage when the last session started.

Three-quarters of an hour later, though, under that grey and morose sky, Gilles crashed, and this immediately reduced to trivia anything else which might have been wrong. A colleague and I went to the scene of the accident. There was no official word, but I think we knew at once we were in the presence of death.

A chat with Gilles that morning had been the only cheery thing about the day. As we walked in silence back to the paddock now there seemed no good reason for ever going to another Grand Prix — save that any day at a race circuit had to be better than this.

For me, and countless others, the problem was that Gilles had become the sport's redeemer, the antidote to all the disillusionment we felt. The cars of the time made a parody of 'Grand Prix racing', and the cancer of vested interests had eaten through a hundred friendships. But while Gilles was around, there remained a focal point to a race weekend, a reminder that not all was rancid. The driver was the man, uninhibited and natural, positive in all ways, absolutely without guile. And the thought of Villeneuve on a qualifying lap made you leave the pits, seek out a 'good' corner, knowing you were going to be stirred.

Some images stay with you for ever. During practice at Dijon in 1981 Gilles crashed at the Courbe de Pouas, an undulating, flat-in-fourth, right-hander, with no run-off worth mentioning. During the lunch break I found him dabbing a cut on his jaw: 'Bloody catch fence pole cracked my helmet and broke the visor . . .'

'You overdid it?' I asked. 'Just ran out of road?' 'No, no,' he grinned. 'I ran out of lock! The car is really bad through there — an adventure every time. Go and have a look this afternoon, and you'll see what I mean.' I did. I watched the Cosworth-engined Williams and Brabhams drone through on their rails, and waited.

At its clipping point, at the top of a rise, the Ferrari was already sideways, its driver winding on opposite lock. As it came past me, plunging downhill now, the tail stayed out of line, further and further, and still Gilles had his foot hard down. As it reached the bottom of the dip, I knew the position was hopeless, for now it was virtually broadside, full lock on, Villeneuve's head pointing up the road — out of the side of the cockpit.

Somehow, though, the Ferrari did not spin, finally snapping back into line as it grazed the catch fencing, then rocketing away up the hill. For more than a hundred yards, I swear it, the car was sideways at 130 mph. 'That's genius', said David Hobbs, watching with me. 'Are you seriously telling me he's won two Grands Prix in *that*?'

At that time a couple of French doctors were engaged on research into the strains imposed on a man by driving a Formula 1 car, and throughout that particular day Gilles was 'wired up', his heartbeat monitored. Through the morning session, prior to his accident, his rate never exceeded 127, and when he hit the guardrail there was a flash reading of 168. These were unbelievably low figures, the report concluded — particularly when compared with those of Pironi, whose heart thumped away at 170-207 throughout the Monaco Grand Prix!

As I read it, I remembered a 'phone call from Amon in the summer of 1977, during which Gilles drove Chris's CanAm Wolf. 'Have you seen this guy Villeneuve? Well, I tell you, in fifteen years of racing I've never seen anyone behave like he does after a shunt. He just doesn't react at all . . .' 'Is he quick?' I asked. '*Quick?*' Amon retorted. 'He's got more potential than anyone I've ever seen . . .'

Perhaps, if the doctors' report were anything to go by, there were sound medical reasons for Villeneuve's apparent fearlessness. 'No doubt about it,' Keke Rosberg says, 'Gilles was abnormally brave. To race against, he was the hardest bastard I ever knew, but absolutely fair. He was an honourable man, and he raced the same way. Although he would always be the last man to lift off, if he considered you'd beaten him fair and square into a corner, he would never

In early 1979 the World Championship looked briefly like Villeneuve's for the taking. In the new Ferrari 312T4 Gilles scored back-to-back victories here at Kyalami and at Long Beach.

The Canadian Grand Prix of 1979 was another Jones-Villeneuve *tour de force*, Gilles holding off Alan's undeniably superior Williams for most of the way.

move over on you, never change his line to block you. For that reason, you always felt completely safe in a battle with him. He was a giant of a driver.'

Villeneuve himself never saw his courage as anything out of the ordinary. 'But', he said, in the next breath, 'I don't have any fear of a crash. No fear of that. Of course, on a fifth gear corner with a fence outside, I don't want to crash. I'm not crazy. But if it's near the end of practice, and you're trying for pole position maybe, then I guess you can squeeze the fear . . .'

He was always sure that this attitude came from his snowmobiling days. 'Every winter, you would reckon on three or four big spills — and I'm talking about being thrown on to ice at 100 mph. Those things used to slide a lot, which taught me a great deal about control. And the visibility was *terrible*! Unless you were leading, you could see nothing, with all the snow blowing about. Good for the reactions — and it stopped me having any worries about racing in the rain.'

The first real interview we did, at Zolder in 1978, startled me. Everything about this fellow was fresh and different. As Scheckter says, his attitude to racing was unashamedly romantic. He was embarking on his

Formula 1 career, and he saw it as a great adventure, the culmination of his dreams: 'If someone had said to me "Villeneuve, you can have three wishes", my first would have been to get into racing, my second to be in Formula 1, my third to drive for Ferrari . . .'

How can you say, I wondered, that you have no fear of a crash? 'Look,' he answered, 'the first meeting I ever went to was at St Jovite, with TransAm, Formula Ford, and so on. And I thought most of the drivers were really Mickey Mouse, people with a lot of money, going slowly. Spectators always think they can do better, and I was no different.

'I never think I can hurt myself — not seriously. If you believe it can happen to you, how can you do this job? If you're never over eight-tenths, or whatever, because you're thinking about a shunt, you're not going as quick as you can. And if you're not doing that, you're not a racing driver. Some of the guys in Formula 1 . . . well, to me, they're not racing drivers. They drive racing cars, that's all. They're doing half a job. And, in that case, I can't figure why they do it at all . . .'

Gilles presented this almost as a thesis, a straightforward and logical case. And, as I came to

Monaco 1981. The cumbersome Ferrari 126C hurtles down to Mirabeau on the way to a famous victory. Two weeks later Gilles won again, in Spain.

know well over the years, he was like that in everything. The longer he was in Europe, around Formula 1, the more confident and salty he became, but always his opinions were positive and reasoned, argued with passion.

'Everything in his life was done at 200 mph,' says Patrick Tambay, perhaps his closest friend. 'Everything! Skiing, driving the speedboat, playing backgammon . . . And his spending was the same, whether it was buying Christmas presents for his kids or playing blackjack at the casino. "Gilles, you're crazy!" I used to say to him, but that's the way he was.

'Some evenings in the winter we all used to play Monopoly, and even in that he handled himself as if he was driving his Formula 1 car, very decisive, never hesitating, taking risks, going forward, forward, all the time. Once his mind was made up, he would go for it — as he did in his driving. There was panache in

everything, but it wasn't forced. That was him.' The kind of man, in sum, who would do crosswords in ink.

He also had a wonderful sense of humour, and could have you falling about with his impressions of certain Formula 1 people for whom he did not care. At Zandvoort one year he related a story about his brother, then dominating Formula Atlantic in Canada, when he was on the road. What was this, I said, about Jacques jumping the start last weekend?

'You heard about that? I was right there on the starting line, and for the first feet he moved I said, "Jesus, he has a good start!" Nobody else had moved yet. Then he had done fifty metres — and *still* nobody had moved yet! I thought, "Whoaaa, something wrong there." He just went on the red light!

'So. He jumped the start by eight seconds . . . what do you do? So he reversed — and they gave the signal to start. They were going one way, and he was going the other. I think', Gilles said thoughtfully, 'there should be some way of stopping everything when that happens, you know, because it's bloody dangerous if you get the green light and someone's backing up towards you . . .'

Yes, I said, I could see that.

Motor racing people differed widely in their opinions of Villeneuve the racing driver. Niki Lauda, paying tribute at Zolder, said this: 'Gilles was a perfect racing driver, I think, with the best talent of all of us. He didn't race for points, but to win races. He was the best — and the fastest — driver in the world.'

Nelson Piquet, though, did not agree. 'I never understood why people admired him so much. He could have won the championship in 1979, but threw it away. He was spectacular, sure, but anyone can slide a car around — then your tyres are finished, and so is your chance in the race.' Easily said from the cockpit

of a Gordon Murray car.

In this judgement, Piquet assumes that Villeneuve's motives for going Grand Prix racing were the same as his own (and, it must be said, those of most drivers), but such was emphatically not the case. Once Prost was out, at Kyalami in 1983, Nelson was quite happy to drop back from a commanding lead to be sure of just enough points to clinch the World Championship. The idea of giving up a race win, whatever the incentive, was anathema to Gilles. 'I would always prefer to go for a possible win rather than a certain third place', he would say. 'I am a racing driver, and to me that means winning races, not putting points in the bank.'

The theatre of motor racing was very important to Villeneuve. He did like to please spectators, but would never slide a car — in a race — for the sake of it. The fact was that, throughout his four-and-a-bit years in

'It had about a quarter of the downforce of a Williams or Brabham', said Postlethwaite of the 1981 Ferrari. On this evidence, at Zandvoort, Harvey's estimate may have been generous.

'More than anyone I've ever known,' Mauro Forghieri said, 'Gilles had a *rage* to win . . .'

Formula 1 he never had a chassis remotely comparable with the best, never had a car which would work with him. Consequently he was obliged to force his Ferrari along faster than they cared to go. And the crowd loved him for it. He, of all the men out there, was so clearly working without a net.

'When you have a really bad car', he would say, 'you have two choices. Either you can drive easier and slower, run at the back, finish tenth, or you go balls out, enjoy yourself, keep sharp for when the good car comes along. Very easy to keep your tyres together when that happens . . .' He preferred to charge, change tyres, then spit on his hands and start all over again. Which is why, of course, he was worshipped like no one else by the people who paid to watch.

Villeneuve's most celebrated victories were those at Monaco and Jarama in 1981. 'That car, the original

126C turbo,' says Harvey Postlethwaite, 'had literally about one quarter of the downforce that, say, Williams or Brabham had. It had a power advantage over the Cosworths, sure, but it also had massive throttle lag at that time. In terms of sheer ability I think Gilles was on a different plane from the other drivers. To win those races — on tight circuits — was quite out of this world. I *know* how bad that car was.'

You could not be indifferent to Villeneuve, in other words. Either you thought him irresponsible, a rock ape, or you saw in him a sublime talent. Certainly he brought to motor racing more drama than anyone I have ever seen. He had, in Mauro Forghieri's words, 'a rage to win'.

He had also a fine contempt for Formula 1 protocol. When the huge camper with Quebec plates first began appearing in the paddocks of Europe, the high rollers looked askance — who was this gypsy racing driver? Gilles didn't give a damn. For him, Joann and the kids, this was home for most of the season. He hated sitting in traffic every morning and evening, slept better in his own bed, had no taste for *haute cuisine*.

Willy Dungl must have shuddered at the sight of Villeneuve at the table. 'Milk shakes I love, and steaks, hamburgers and, most of all, French fries . . .' 'You're on the Foyt diet', I said one day, and it delighted him: 'Yeah, you're right — well, he's done quite well on it. . .'

He made a lot of money, of course, but it never changed him. Living in Monte Carlo was relatively convenient for testing at Fiorano. 'For normal people', Scheckter commented, 'that was a five-hour drive. If you were really quick, you could do it in three and a half. Gilles — two and three-quarters!' At one stage, indeed, beating his 308GTB record to the Ferrari test track was almost as important as setting a new lap

record when he got there . . .

Then helicopters came into his life. For a while he hired them, but in early 1982 he bought an Agusta 109 — 'It's the fastest in its class, cruises at 175, I love it.' He was speaking at Imola, where the red and orange machine made its first appearance. This was the weekend when the FOCA gentlemen stayed home, and Villeneuve also spoke of his worries for Formula 1. In Rio he had said that if something were not done to change the cars, he would quit for a while. I asked him if he still felt the same way.

'I don't know how serious I am about that — depends on the mood I'm in! But, seriously, you have to go in one of these cars to see how bumpy they are. It's ridiculous having skirts and no suspension. It's not driving, just a matter of aiming for the corner, flooring it and hoping you're on the right line — because you can't see it, and you can't correct it.'

Final lap. Villeneuve comes out of the *Bianchibocht*, a few seconds before encountering Mass's cruising March in the middle of the road.

'There's no satisfaction in these bloody things. You have to drive them on rails, and I like it when a car's cornering speed has something to do with the ability of the driver, not how well the skirts are working . . .'

Surely, I said, you haven't lost all pleasure in driving? He thought for a few seconds. 'Look,' he said, 'let me put it this way. I get a headache every time I drive the car now. If you make love to a woman, and at the same time someone sticks a knife in your back, eventually you won't like so much making love, right? So, if you like driving, but if you feel your head's being punched every time you come into a corner, eventually you don't like that so much. But . . . if you take away the knife, I still like making love!'

It was a supreme irony that Gilles, always known as the bravest of the brave, constantly sought to rid the sport of dangers he considered unnecessary. Particularly, he felt strongly about the qualifying procedure in Formula 1.

'You have only two sets of qualifiers. You sit in the pits for half an hour, you come out cold, you go slow and then you go banzai for one lap to set a bloody time. Jesus Christ, it's dangerous! Then you find someone in your way. You can't lift if you're on a quick lap. No way. All you can do is hope he's looking in his mirrors . . .'

The following day Villeneuve took the fight to the Renaults, did all the work and was then duped by 'team mate' Pironi on the final lap when he thought they were cruising home. After the slowing down lap he brought the Ferrari very swiftly into the scrutineering bay, braked to a violent halt, flung off his belts and stalked away. For the sake of the fans, he made a token appearance on the rostrum, then left.

A couple of days later I called him. 'No,' he said, 'I haven't said a word to Pironi, and I'm not going to

again — ever. I have declared war. I'll do my own thing in future. It's war. Absolutely war . . .

'Imola was going to be my race, because I was in front at the time we inherited the lead. Those have always been the team orders at Ferrari, ever since I've been there. I was almost cruising that last lap, because we were very marginal on fuel, and because I trusted him. People seemed to think we had the battle of our lives! I'd been ahead of him most of the race, qualified a second and a half quicker than him. Where was my problem? I think I've proved that, in equal cars, if I want someone to stay behind . . . well, I think he stays behind. Second is one thing, but second because the bastard steals it, that's something else.'

'I flew home from Imola with Gilles,' Jackie Stewart said, 'and he was livid at what had happened. The World Championship was incidental to him. He told me that evening that his one goal was to beat my record, win more races than I had. He was stunned by that race. I think he was a very clean, almost innocent, man, with no maliciousness in him. It was very sad that the last two weeks of his life were so tormented and disillusioned.'

A lot of people thought Gilles over-reacted to the Imola affair, but that took no account of the man's character. He was absolute in all things, and that included his trust of others. But you crossed him only once. The furies were still inside him when he arrived at Zolder. In his own mind, he had to reassert himself in the team. He was on his final qualifying run when the accident came, in precisely the circumstances he had feared.

How good was he? For me, Laffite put it best: 'No human being can do a miracle, you know, but Gilles made you wonder . . .'